MAL

THE MINI ROUGH GUIDE

D0196468

Rough Guides online

www.roughguides.com

Rough Guide Credits

Text editor: Ruth Blackmore
Series editor: Mark Ellingham
Typesetting: Helen Ostick
Cartography: Ed Wright

Publishing Information

This second edition published May 2000 by
Rough Guides Ltd, 62–70 Shorts Gardens, London WC2H 9AH
Reprinted June 2001 and May 2002

Distributed by the Penguin Group:

Penguin Books Ltd, 80 Strand, London WC2R ORL
Penguin Putnam Inc., 375 Hudson Street, New York 10014, USA
Penguin Books Australia Ltd, 487 Maroondah Highway,
PO Box 257, Ringwood, Victoria 3134, Australia
Penguin Books Canada Ltd, 10 Alcorn Avenue,
Toronto, Ontario, Canada M4V 1E4
Penguin Books (NZ) Ltd, 182–190 Wairau Road,
Auckland 10, New Zealand

Typeset in Bembo and Helvetica to an original design by Henry Iles.
Printed in Spain by Graphy Cems.

© Simon Baskett 2000, 336pp includes index
A catalogue record for this book is available from the British Library.
ISBN 1-85828-535-6

MADRID

THE MINI ROUGH GUIDE

by Simon Baskett

We set out to do something different when the first Rough Guide was published in 1982. Mark Ellingham, just out of university, was travelling in Greece. He brought along the popular guides of the day, but found they were all lacking in some way. They were either strong on ruins and museums but went on for pages without mentioning a beach or taverna. Or they were so conscious of the need to save money that they lost sight of Greece's cultural and historical significance. Also, none of the books told him anything about Greece's contemporary life – its politics, its culture, its people, and how they lived.

So with no job in prospect, Mark decided to write his own guidebook, one which aimed to provide practical information that was second to none, detailing the best beaches and the hottest clubs and restaurants, while also giving hard-hitting accounts of every sight, both famous and obscure, and providing up-to-the-minute information on contemporary culture. It was a guide that encouraged independent travellers to find the best of Greece, and was a great success, getting shortlisted for the Thomas Cook travel guide award, and encouraging Mark, along with three friends, to expand the series.

The Rough Guide list grew rapidly and the letters flooded in, indicating a much broader readership than had been anticipated, but one which uniformly appreciated the Rough Guide mix of practical detail and humour, irreverence and enthusiasm. Things haven't changed. The same four friends who began the series are still the caretakers of the Rough Guide mission today: to provide the most reliable, up-to-date and entertaining information to independent-minded travellers of all ages, on all budgets.

We now publish more than 150 titles and have offices in London and New York. The travel guides are written and researched by a dedicated team of more than 100 authors, based in Britain, Europe, the USA and Australia. We have also created a unique series of phrasebooks to accompany the travel series, along with an acclaimed series of music guides, and a best-selling pocket guide to the Internet and World Wide Web. We also publish comprehensive travel information on our Web site: www.roughguides.com

Help Us Update

We've gone to a lot of effort to ensure that this second edition of *The Rough Guide to Madrid* is as up-to-date and accurate as possible. However, if you feel there are places we've underrated or over-praised, or find we've missed something good or covered something which has now gone, then please write: suggestions, comments or corrections are much appreciated.

We'll credit all contributions, and send a copy of the next edition (or any other Rough Guide if you prefer) for the best letters. Please mark letters: "Rough Guide Madrid Update" and send to: Rough Guides, 62–70 Shorts Gardens, London WC2H 9AH, or Rough Guides, 345 Hudson St, 4th Floor, New York, NY 10014.

Or send email to: mail@roughguides.co.uk

Online updates about this book can be found on Rough Guides' Web site (see opposite)

The Author

Simon Baskett lives and works in Madrid with his wife, Trini, and their young son, Patrick. He is a long-suffering Atlético Madrid fan, and has not yet given up hope that he might live long enough to see them do "the double" once more. His ambition is to win El Gordo (the huge Christmas lottery) and retire to a local bar.

Acknowledgements

Special thanks to Trini once again for all her hard work and patience. Thanks, too, go to James, Penny, Santiago, Rocio, Ruth and all those who gave recommendations or advice for this edition.

Readers' Letters

Many thanks to the following who wrote in with useful comments and contributions to the previous edition: Bill and Carolyn Thomas, Dr P. Blackwell–Smyth, Christopher Turner, B. Walmsley, Ryan Prout, Clive Scott, D. Warfield, Mrs. M. Perrins, Felix Riesenhuber, Lynn Anderson, Anne Hall, Mrs. Jan Murphy, Marianne Kalsbeek, Lynn Hellmuth, Graham Douglas, Babs Gisborne–Land, Johanne Scott, Geoff Worrall, Frank Farmer, T. Ellacott, J. L. Reid, Julia Speht, Angela Ager, Bill Boynton and Sandra Davies, Peter Wilkes, Angela Barker, Anita Joy Weston, Linda Fowler.

CONTENTS

Out of the City

Contexts

Introduction

Madrid became Spain's capital city at the whim of one man, **Felipe II**. Its site possesses few natural advantages – a fierce climate, no harbour and a pretty poor excuse for a river – but it lies exactly in the centre of Spain. In 1561, Felipe decided to base the formerly itinerant court here to avoid giving too much power and status to any one region in the recently unified Spain. In Madrid he created a symbol of the unification and centralization of the country, and a capital from which he could receive the fastest post and communications from each corner of the nation. However, it was only the determination of successive rulers to promote a strong central capital that ensured the city's survival and development.

Today, Madrid is a large, predominantly modern city, with a population of some four million and a highly schizophrenic character. There are, in effect, two cities: "Madrid by day" and "Madrid by night"; the capital is freezing in winter, burning in summer; outwardly flamboyant, yet inwardly conservative; seemingly affluent, yet concealing serious levels of poverty. The highest, sunniest and greenest capital city in Europe – despite being choked with traffic and people – its inhabitants, the **Madrileños** modestly declare, "*Desde Madrid al Cielo*": that after Madrid there is only one destination left – Heaven.

Largely a city of immigrants, it is difficult to find a person whose real roots are in Madrid, apart from the *castizos* who proudly exhibit their *Madrileño* heritage during the *San Isidro* festival and the summer *verbenas* (street fairs). As a consequence, the city is a mosaic of traditions, cultures and cuisines. As you get to grips with the place you soon realize that it is the *Madrileños* themselves that are the capital's key attraction: hanging out in the cafés or the summer *terrazas*, packing the lanes of the Rastro flea market, or playing hard and very, very late in a thousand bars, clubs and discos.

Madrileños consider the **nightlife** of other European cities positively dull by comparison; for them enjoying themselves is a right not a luxury. Much of their everyday life is acted out in the streets of Madrid outside their rather small houses or apartments. They dress up whenever possible, never wanting to be seen at anything but their best. They are noisy – horns blare, TVs are set at full blast and conversations are conducted at top volume. Whatever Barcelona might claim, the Madrid scene, immortalized in the movies of Pedro Almodóvar, remains the most vibrant in the country.

Despite its recent rapid growth, Madrid still seems small for a capital city. It is strikingly compact, yet each *barrio* still manages to retain its own individual identity. However, the city can no longer be accused of provincialism, for it has changed immeasurably in the two and a half decades since Franco died, guided by a poet-mayor, the late and much-lamented **Tierno Galván**. His efforts, including the creation of parks and the renovation of public spaces and public life, have left an enduring legacy, and were a vital ingredient of the **movida Madrileña**, the "happening Madrid", with which the city made its mark in the 1980s. The *movida* may have gone but Madrid has survived as a stylish city, highly conscious of its image and in better shape than for many years, after an $800m refurbishment for its role as 1992 European Capital of Culture and the continuing urban regeneration programmes by the active local authority.

As a tourist destination, Madrid has been greatly underrated. By comparison with the historic cities of Spain – Toledo, Salamanca, Sevilla, Granada – there may be few sites of outstanding architectural interest, but the monarchs did acquire superlative picture collections, which form the basis of the **Prado** museum. This has long ensured Madrid a place on the European art-tour, and even more so since the 1990s arrival – literally down the road – of the **Reina Sofía** and **Thyssen–Bornemisza** galleries, state-of-the-art homes to fabulous arrays of modern Spanish painting (including Picasso's *Guernica*) and European and American masters.

When to visit

Traditionally, Madrid has experienced a typical continental climate, cold and dry in winter and hot and dry in summer. There are usually two rainy periods, in October/November and March/April. With soaring temperatures in July and August, the best times to visit are often spring and autumn, when the city is pleasantly warm. In recent years, however, the weather has become more unpredictable and there have been hot periods in spring and autumn, while summer temperatures have dropped.

Madrid virtually shuts down in the **summer**; from around July 20 you'll suddenly find half the bars, restaurants and offices closed, and their inhabitants gone to the coast and countryside. Not until September does the city properly open for business again.

Luckily for visitors, and those *Madrileños* who choose to remain, sights and museums stay open and summer nightlife takes on a momentum of its own. In addition, the city council has initiated a major programme of summer entertainment. All in all, it's not a bad time to be in town, as long as you're not trying to get anything done.

Madrid's climate

	°F Average daily		°C Average daily		Rainfall Average monthly	
	MAX	MIN	MAX	MIN	IN	MM
Jan	47	35	9	2	1.5	39
Feb	52	36	11	2	1.3	34
March	59	41	15	5	1.7	43
April	65	45	18	7	1.9	48
May	70	50	21	10	1.9	47
June	80	58	27	15	1.0	27
July	87	63	31	17	0.4	11
Aug	85	63	30	17	0.6	15
Sept	77	57	25	14	1.3	32
Oct	65	49	19	10	2.1	53
Nov	55	42	13	5	1.9	47
Dec	48	36	9	2	1.9	48

THE GUIDE

Introducing the city

The city's layout is pretty straightforward. At the heart of Madrid is the **Puerta del Sol** and around it lie the oldest parts of Madrid, neatly bordered to the west by the **Río Manzanares**, to the east by the park of **El Retiro**, and to the north by the city's great thoroughfare, the **Gran Vía**.

Throughout the guide we have abbreviated all street names, using c/ for *calle* ("street") and omitting the articles "de", "de la", etc. We've shown Calle de Toledo, for example, as c/Toledo and Calle de la Libertad as c/Libertad. Although on Madrid street signs the full form is used, Spaniards hardly ever say the partitive article, pronouncing, for example, Calle de la Libertad as Calle Libertad.

It's within this very compact area that you're likely to spend most of your time. The city's three big museums – the **Prado**, **Thyssen-Bornemisza** and **Reina Sofía** – lie in a "golden triangle" just west of El Retiro along the **Paseo del Prado**, while over towards the river are the oldest, Habsburg, parts of town, centred on the beautiful arcaded **Plaza Mayor**. After Gran Vía, the most important streets are **c/Alcalá** and its continuation, **c/Mayor** – which cut right through the centre from the main post office at **Plaza de la Cibeles** to the Bourbon **Palacio Real** – and the long south–north boulevard beginning as the elegant Paseo del Prado and finishing up as the multi-lane **Paseo de la Castellana**. Although there is plenty of nightlife in the city centre, especially around **Plaza de Santa Ana** and **Huertas**, you may well find yourself venturing further north to the *barrios* of **Chueca** and **Malasaña** for the hippest bars and clubs.

Beyond the city centre, within a radius of 100km – and no more than an hour's travel by train or bus – are some of the greatest cities of Spain. Above all there is **Toledo**, immortalized by El Greco, which preceded Madrid as the Spanish capital, but other excellent day-trips include **Segovia**, with its stunning Roman aqueduct; Felipe II's vast palace-mausoleum of **El Escorial**; **Aranjuez**, an oasis in the parched Castilian plain, famed for its strawberries and lavish Baroque palace; and the beautiful walled city of **Ávila**, birthplace of Santa Teresa.

Calling Madrid from abroad, dial your international access code, then 34, followed by the subscriber's number, which will nearly always start with 91.

Arrival

International **air**, **train** and **bus** arrival points are all some way from the centre. Transport into the city, however, is relatively easy and efficient. If you are **driving**, be prepared for a long trawl around the streets to find parking, or – a lot safer – put your car in one of the many signposted *parkings*. If you're staying more than a couple of weeks, you can get long-term parking rates at neighbourhood garages.

BY AIR

The **Aeropuerto de Barajas** is 16km east of the city, at the end of Avenida de América. It has three terminals: T1 for *vuelos internacionales* (excluding some Iberia flights to Schengen Treaty countries); T2 for *nacionales* (domestic services, including some Iberia flights to Schengen Treaty countries); and T3 for Iberia regional flights.

The airport has recently been connected to the **metro** system (line 8) and takes you into the centre in about thirty minutes, with a change at Mar de Cristal (line 4). There is also a shuttle **bus** that leaves from outside the arrivals terminal every ten to fifteen minutes (daily 5.15am–2am; 385ptas) and drops you at an underground terminal in the central Plaza de Colón (Metro Serrano; pedestrian entrance from the c/Goya). If your plane arrives outside these times, there should be additional connecting bus services. **Taxis** are always available and cost around 2000ptas into the centre, assuming you don't get stuck in traffic. Supplements are charged for baggage, for going outside the city limits (which includes the airport) and for night-trips (11pm–6am). The journey time by bus or taxi into central Madrid is highly variable, depending on rush-hour traffic and can take anything from twenty minutes to an hour.

Half a dozen or so **car rental** companies have stands at the airport, and there's also a 24-hour currency exchange, a post office, a RENFE office for booking train tickets (daily 8am–9pm), a tourist office and hotel reservations desk.

BY TRAIN

Trains from France and north/northeast Spain arrive at the **Estación de Chamartín**, a modern terminal isolated in the north of the city. A metro line connects Chamartín with the centre, and there are regular connections on the commuter train line (*cercanías*) with the much more central Estación de Atocha.

The **Estación de Atocha**, recently expanded and imaginatively remodelled, has two separate terminals: one for Toledo and other local services, the other for all points in southern and eastern Spain, including the high-speed AVE trains.

If you're coming from local towns around Madrid you may arrive at the **Príncipe Pío** (aka **Estación del Norte**), fairly close to the centre, near the Palacio Real.

BY BUS

Bus terminals are scattered throughout the city, but the largest – used by all of the international bus services – is the **Estación Sur de Autobuses**, recently relocated on c/Méndez Álvaro at the corner of c/Retama (Metro Méndez Álvaro), south of Estacíon de Atocha. For details of others, see the "Directory" (p.250).

BY CAR

All the main roads into Madrid bring you right into the city centre, although eccentric signposting and even more eccentric driving can be very unnerving. The inner ring road, the M30, and the Castellana are notorious bottlenecks, although virtually the whole city centre can be close to gridlock during the peak rush-hour periods (Mon–Fri 7.30–9.30am and 6–8.30pm).

It's advisable to find a hotel with a **car park** and keep it there during your stay in the city. Your own transport is really only of use for out-of-town excursions.

ARRIVAL

Information and maps

There are year-round **Turismo** offices at the following locations: Barajas International Airport (Mon–Fri 8am–8pm, Sat 9am–1pm; ℂ91 305 86 56); Estación de Chamartín (Mon–Fri 8am–8pm, Sat 9am–1pm; ℂ91 315 99 76); Plaza Mayor 3 (Mon–Fri 10am–8pm, Sat 10am–2pm; ℂ91 588 16 36); Mercado Puerta de Toledo, Ronda de Toledo 1 (Mon–Fri 9am–7pm, Sat 9.30am–1.30pm; ℂ91 364 18 76); and c/Duque de Medinaceli 2 (Mon–Fri 9am–7pm, Sat 9am–1pm; ℂ91 429 49 51 or 91 429 31 77).

In summer, Turismo posts also operate at popular tourist spots such as the Puerta del Sol and the Prado, and there are **guides** (in blue-and-yellow uniforms) on call outside the Palacio Real, Plaza de la Villa and the Prado, and in the Plaza Mayor and Puerta del Sol. Estacíon de Atocha also has an information kiosk with a hotel reservations service. You can **phone for information** in English on ℂ902 202 202 within Madrid and ℂ010 91 366 66 04 from outside Madrid.

Listings information is in plentiful supply in Madrid. The newspapers *El País* and *El Mundo* have excellent daily listings, and on Friday both publish sections devoted to events, bars and restaurants in the capital. If your time in Madrid doesn't coincide with the Friday supplements, or you want a full rundown, pick up the weekly listings magazine *La Guía del Ocio* (125ptas) at any kiosk. The Ayuntamiento (city council) also publishes a monthly "What's On" pamphlet, *En Madrid*, free from any of the tourist offices. Finally, *In Madrid* is a free monthly magazine available in many bars, which bills itself as "Madrid's English monthly for the Hip, Cool and Transient", and features useful reviews of clubs and bars.

Madrid on the Internet

The Useful Guide to Madrid *malika.iem.csic.es/~grant/madi.htm*
The best index of Madrid-related sites from museums, tourist
attractions and fiestas to sport and education.

Ole ! *www.ole.es*
Popular search engine, giving access to most Spanish sites.

Spanish Tourist Office *www.spaintour.com/madrid/htm*
Straightforward tourist information on the city.

The Madrid City Council *www.munimadrid.es*
The city council's official site is available in English, with a variety of tourist-related information, including forthcoming events
in the city.

The British Council *www.britcoun.org/spain/index.htm*
Useful information if you're thinking of teaching English, and
for more on the Council's activities in Madrid.

The Pink 'Un *ourworld.compuserve.com/homepages/robraabe*
Homepage for the English five-a-side league in Madrid and a
good introduction to the British pub scene.

Atlético Madrid *www.at-madrid.es*
Spanish-language official site for *Los Colchoneros*. Everything
from history and fixtures to the club song and videos.

The Prado *www.museoprado.mcu.es*
English version available, including sections on news, activities, and the history of the Prado, together with in-depth analy-
sis of a number of the museum's most famous paintings.

One word that might perplex first-timers in Madrid – and which crops up in all the listings magazines – is **madrugada**. This refers to the hours between midnight and dawn and, in this supremely late-night/early-morning city, is a necessary adjunct to announcements of important events. "*Tres de la madrugada*" means an event is due to start at 3am.

Free **maps** of Madrid are available from any of the Turismos detailed on p.7. However, if you intend to do more than just a day's sightseeing, you would be well advised to invest in the *Almax Madrid Centro* map (350ptas), available from just about any kiosk in the city. This is very clear, 1:10,000 in scale, fully street-indexed, with a colour plan of the metro on the reverse, and covers just about everywhere of interest. Almax also produces a 1:12,000-scale *Madrid Ciudad* map (750ptas), which is rather less clear, but goes right out into the suburbs. Again, it's widely available.

Safety and crime

As far as **safety** goes, Madrid gives little cause for concern. Central Madrid is so populated – and so busy at just about every hour of the day and night – that it never seems to carry any "big city" threat. Which is not to say that **crime** is not a problem, nor that there aren't sleazy pockets to be avoided. Madrid has a big drug problem, all too evident around the Plaza de España and some of the streets just north of Gran Vía. Drugs, it is reckoned, account for ninety percent of crimes in Madrid, and if you are unlucky enough to be threatened for money, it's unwise to resist.

Tourists in Madrid, as everywhere, are prime targets for **pickpockets** and petty thieves. The main shopping areas, parks, the metro and anywhere with crowds are their favourite haunts; burger bars and the Rastro market seem especially popular. Be aware that they often work in groups, and associates will try to distract your attention while your pocket is being picked. Cars are particularly vulnerable, and drivers may find their vehicles broken into and the radio stolen. The **police** are usually sympathetic and will give you a report form for insurance claims. In an emergency, dial ⓒ112; English is usually spoken on this number.

City transport

Madrid is a pretty easy city to **get around**. The central areas are walkable, the metro is modern and efficient, buses serve out-of-the-way districts, and taxis are always available.

If you're using public transport extensively and staying long-term, monthly **passes** or *abonos* (which cover metro, train and bus) are worthwhile. They must be ordered before the calendar month in question and put into service before the tenth of that month. If you have an InterRail or Eurail pass, you can use the RENFE urban and suburban trains (*cercanías*) free of charge – they're an alternative to the metro for some longer city journeys.

THE METRO

The **metro** is by far the quickest way of getting around Madrid, and the system serves most places you're likely to want to get to. It runs daily from 6am until 1.30am and the flat fare is 130ptas for any journey, or 680ptas for a ten-trip ticket (*bono de diez viajes*), which is valid for buses as well. Lines are colour-coded and the direction of travel is indicated

Sightseeing tours

Several companies offer daily **bus tours** of the main sights in Madrid, which are worthwhile if your time is limited. Full details from the Municipal Tourist Board, c/Mayor 69 (©91 588 29 00).

Madrid Vision, c/San Bernardo 23 (Metro Noviciado; ©91 767 17 43 or 91 302 45 26). Bus tours of all the major city sights, with pick-up points including Puerta del Sol and the Prado. Tickets cost 2000ptas and you can get on and off as many times as you like.

Juliá Tours, Gran Vía 68 (Metro Santo Domingo; ©91 559 96 05). Day-trips to the cities surrounding Madrid. Prices start from 3000ptas.

Pullmantur, Plaza de Oriente 8 (Metro Ópera; ©91 541 18 05). Guided tours of Toledo, Segovia and Aranjuez.

Walking tours of old Madrid are organized by the Municipal Tourist Office, Plaza Mayor 3 (©91 588 16 36 or 91 588 29 00). Tours in English are on Saturdays at 10am. Cost is 500ptas (meet outside the office thirty minutes before departure).

by the name of the terminus station. The metro is clean and efficient, and the network has recently been extended and modernized. Note that if you wish to venture to the end of Line 9 in the south you will have to pay a small supplement.

See colour map 10 for a plan of the metro.

BUSES

The urban **bus network** is comprehensive, but you'll need to get hold of a map (see overleaf) to work out your route.

CITY TRANSPORT

Bus stops show the numbers of the buses that stop there, along with details of the other stops on the route. There are information booths in the Plaza de la Cibeles, Plaza de Callao and Puerta del Sol, which dispense a huge route **map** (*plano de los transportes de Madrid*) and, along with other outlets, sell bus passes. Fares and tickets are the same as for the metro, at 130ptas a journey, payable on the bus, or 680ptas for a ten-trip ticket. When you get on the bus, you punch your ticket in the machine by the driver.

Buses run daily from 6am to midnight. In addition, *Búho* (owl) **night buses** operate on twenty routes around the central area and out to the suburbs, departing from Plaza de la Cibeles and Puerta del Sol: from Sunday to Thursday departures are half-hourly 12.30am–2am, hourly 2–6am and more frequent on Fridays and Saturdays.

TAXIS

One of the good things about Madrid is that there are thousands of **taxis** – white cars with a diagonal red stripe on the side – and they're reasonably cheap; 700ptas will get you to most places within the centre and, although it's common to round up the fare, you're not expected to tip. Supplements are charged on trips from the airport, bus and train stations, for luggage, journeys between 11pm-7am and on holidays. In any area in the centre, day and night, you should be able to wave down a taxi (available ones have a green light on top of the cab) in a couple of minutes. To phone for a taxi, call ©91 547 82 00, 91 447 51 80, 91 405 12 13 or 91 445 90 08.

LOCAL TRAINS

The **local train** network or *cercanías* is the most efficient way of connecting between the main railway stations and

Useful bus routes

#2 From west to east across town: Argüelles metro station along c/Princesa, past Plaza de España, along Gran Vía, past Cibeles and out past the Retiro.

#3 From south to north: Puerta de Toledo, through Sol, up towards Gran Vía and then Alonso Martínez and northwards.

#5 From Sol via Cibeles, Colón and the Paseo de la Castellana to Chamartín.

#27 From Embajadores, via Atocha, up the length of the Castellana to Plaza de Castilla.

#33 From Príncipe Pío out via the Puente de Segovia to the Parque de Atracciones and Zoo in Casa de Campo.

#C The Circular bus route takes a broad circuit round the city from Atocha, via Puerta de Toledo, Plaza de España, Moncloa, Cuatro Caminos, Avenida de América and Goya.

provides the best route out to many of the suburbs and to nearby towns such as Alcalá de Henares. Most trains are air-conditioned, fares are cheap and there are good connections with the metro. Trains generally run every fifteen to thirty minutes from 6am to midnight/1am.

CITY TRANSPORT

Plaza Mayor and La Latina

Madrid under the Habsburgs was a mix of formal planning – at its most impressive in the expansive and theatrical **Plaza Mayor** – and areas of shanty-town development, knocked up in the sixteenth century as the new capital gained an urban population. The central area of old Madrid still reflects both characteristics, with its Flemish-inspired architecture of red brick and grey stone, slate-tiled towers and Renaissance doorways set in a twisting grid of streets, alleyways and steps. In fact, the layout of this area has changed little since the Middle Ages, and although there are few traces of the original buildings, you can still spend an enjoyable day exploring the remains of the old city. Most tourists head straight for the Plaza Mayor and leave it at that, but there are other appealing sights scattered throughout the area, especially in the characterful *barrio* of **La Latina** which stretches south of the square. The delight-ful **Plaza de la Villa**, with its amalgam of architectural styles, the Baroque excesses of the **Basílica de San Miguel** and the **Capilla de San Isidro**, as well as the decaying splendour of **San Francisco el Grande** are all worth seeking out, as are the culinary delights of the *mesones* (taverns) and tapas bars in and around **c/Cava Baja**.

....

**The area covered by this chapter is shown
in detail on colour map 4.**

....

PLAZA MAYOR AND AROUND

Map 4, G2. Metro Sol.

The grand Plaza Mayor was originally the brainchild of Felipe II, who wanted to construct a more prestigious focus for his new capital of Madrid. The Casa de la Panadería, on the north side of the square, is the oldest building, begun in 1590. Once housing the city bakers and bakers' guild, it later became a palace. The original building has been almost completely rebuilt, as it and much of the rest of the square was damaged by the many fires that occurred in the plaza in the seventeenth and eighteenth centuries. Its main facade features a balcony from which the royals could watch proceedings below and is decorated with recently repainted frescoes. The real work on the plaza did not get off the ground until the reign of Felipe III, but the city architect, Juan Gómez de Mora, worked quickly and finished it in just two years in 1619. Capable of holding up to fifty thousand people, the square was used for state occasions, autos-da-fé, executions, jousts, plays and bullfights. The Italian-designed bronze equestrian statue in the middle of the plaza is of Felipe III. Dated 1616, it was originally sited in the Casa de Campo (see p.120) and was only moved to its present position in 1847.

Today, Plaza Mayor is primarily a tourist haunt, full of outdoor cafés and restaurants that advertise themselves as "typical Spanish" – best stick to a drink here. However, an air of grandeur clings to the place, and the plaza still performs public functions. In the summer months, it becomes an outdoor theatre and music stage; in the autumn, there's a book fair; and in the winter, around Christmas, it becomes a bazaar for festive decorations, site of one of the largest *belenes* (cribs) and home to stalls selling all kinds of practical-joke material for Spain's equivalent of April Fool's Day, *El Día de Los Santos Inocentes*, on December 28. Every Sunday, too, stamp and coin collectors convene here to talk philately and rummage through boxes of rare coins in the open-air market. On the whole, though, unless you're a fan of tacky souvenir shops and caricature artists, you'll find more of real interest in the areas surrounding the square.

Around Plaza Mayor

Just to the east, on **Plaza de la Provincia**, the design of the **Palacio de Santa Cruz** echoes that of the Plaza Mayor and may also be the work of Juan Gómez de Mora. It was built between 1629 and 1639, was once the city prison and now houses the Ministry of Foreign Affairs.

Calle Postas, a fascinating street linking the northeastern corner of Plaza Mayor with Puerta del Sol, has a selection of good-value bars and shops selling all manner of religious articles, from models of the baby Jesus, rosary beads and icons to dog collars and habits.

Over on the west side of the square, **c/Cava San Miguel** used to be the ditch of the twelfth-century city wall and still retains an ancient feel, lined by towering seventeenth-century houses, whose facades have recently been restored. To the southwest of Plaza Mayor, down the steps by the bar *El Pulpito*, you'll find one of Madrid's more famous institutions, **Botín** at c/Cuchilleros 17, serving classic Castilian fare in traditional surroundings. Mentioned in Galdós' novel, *Fortunata y Jacinta*, and in the *Guinness Book of Records* as the oldest restaurant in Europe, its other claim to fame is that the 19-year-old Goya worked here washing dishes. In typically understated fashion Hemingway merely described it as the "best restaurant in the world".

For more on Botín see p.153.

In this and the other *mesones* you'll no doubt be serenaded by passing **tunas** – musicians and singers dressed in knickerbockers and waistcoats who wander around town playing and passing the hat. These men-only troupes are attached to various faculties of the university and are a means for students of supplementing their grants.

Finally, leading south from the square down to San Isidro (see p.24), **c/Toledo** has a host of idiosyncratic little shops, specializing in fortress-like corsetry and hairpins. Casa Hernanz, at no. 81, is a must if you're a fan of espadrilles. The king reputedly buys his here and you can purchase models of every description, with prices ranging from 900 to 3000ptas.

CALLE MAYOR

North of Plaza Mayor, **c/Mayor** is one of the most ancient thoroughfares in the city, along which religious processions from the Palacio Real to the Monasterio de Los Jerónimos have passed for centuries. The street is home to a whole host of intriguing little shops and bars and is flanked by the facades of some of the most characterful and evocative buildings in the city, their grimy exteriors concealing an array of treasures. Heading west from the entrance to Plaza Mayor, you'll soon pass the decorative ironwork of the **Mercado de San Miguel**, built in 1916. Magnificent early twentieth-century apartment blocks are swathed in wrought-iron balconies, their brooding facades lightened by splashes of colour from flowering geraniums. Further along, it's worth pausing at the gloriously antiquated **Farmacia de La Reina Madre**, at no. 59, where, according to legend, Isabel de Farnese, second wife of Felipe V, preferred to purchase her medicines rather than in the royal pharmacy in the palace, because she feared being poisoned by her stepson Fernando VI. The decoration dates from 1914 and inside are over three hundred sixteenth- and seventeenth-century ceramic and glass jars. The highlight of this section of the street is **Plaza de la Villa**, but it's worth stopping off at no. 84, the **Casa Ciriaco**, for a wine or a coffee. A favourite meeting place for the intelligentsia, politicians and bullfighters, this traditional *taberna* is full of memorabilia, detailing the colourful history of the building, in particular the notorious attack on the royal wedding procession of Alfonso XIII and his English bride, Victoria Eugenie, in 1906. A bomb secreted in a bunch of flowers was thrown from one of the second-floor balconies, killing 23 onlookers, but leaving the royal couple unscathed. The assassin, Mateo Morral, was executed a few days later and a bronze angel commemorating the victims can be seen on the opposite side of the street in front of the Iglesia Arzobispal Castrense. To the north, up c/San Nicolás, stands the oldest surviving church in Madrid, **San Nicolás de los Servitas** (Tues–Sat 6.30–9pm, Sun & Mon 8.30am–1.30pm & 5.30–9pm), with its twelfth-century Mudéjar tower featuring Arabic horseshoe arches (currently being restored). The rest of the church was rebuilt between the fifteenth and seventeenth centuries and houses a very small, but interesting, display on the history of Muslim Madrid. Continuing on along c/Mayor you'll pass the **Italian Institute of Culture** on the right. It stands on the site of the house of the Princess of Eboli where Juan de Escobedo, Don Juan de Austria's Secretary, was murdered by three assassins in March 1578, a murder in which King Felipe II himself was implicated. Opposite is the grand **Palacio de Uceda**, originally built by one of the favourites

of Felipe III in the early seventeenth century and now home
to the Capitanía General (Military Headquarters), while on
the corner of the busy c/Bailén, the wonderful music shop
crammed full of ancient musical instruments and accessories
merits more than a cursory look.

PLAZA DE LA VILLA AND AROUND

Map 4, E2. Metro Sol.

Plaza de la Villa is the oldest square in the city and
reflects three centuries of Spanish architectural development. It was originally the old market square of Muslim
and medieval Madrid, and today the centre is marked by a
statue of the Marquis of Santa Cruz, an admiral under
Felipe II and hero of the great naval battle of Lepanto in
1571. The battle involved over 100,000 men – including
Cervantes, who lost an arm in the engagement – with the
Spanish navy vanquishing the Turks off the coast of Greece
much to the relief and joy of Christendom. Ironically, it
only served to spur the Turks into building an even
mightier fleet soon afterwards.

The oldest ensemble of surviving buildings is the simple
but eye-catching fifteenth-century **Torre y Casa de Los
Lujanes**, where Francis I is said to have been imprisoned in
1525 after his capture at the Battle of Pavia. The fine
Mudéjar tower has been substantially restored, and the
characteristic arched doorway bears the original coat of
arms of its owners, the powerful Lujanes family. On the
southern side of the square is the **Casa de Cisneros**, constructed for the nephew of the celebrated Cardinal
(Inquisitor-General 1507–1517 and Regent of Spain after
Fernando's death in 1516) in the sixteenth-century
Plateresque style, a style of architecture and sculpture that
incorporated the intricate techniques of silversmiths or
plateros. The building was acquired by the Ayuntamiento of

PLAZA DE LA VILLA AND AROUND

Madrid in 1909, and was extensively remodelled by Luis Bellido. It now houses the Mayor of Madrid's offices.

The Casa de la Villa

The west side of the square is taken up by the **Casa de la Villa** (tours normally only in Spanish at 5pm every Mon), one of the most important, emblematic buildings of Habsburg Madrid. It was constructed in fits and starts from the mid-seventeenth century in order to house the offices and records of the council which had outgrown its previous home in the church of San Salvador. The initial design was by **Juan Gómez de Mora**, but the construction wasn't completed until 1693, 45 years after his death, and was mellowed by the addition of Baroque details in the late eighteenth century.

The weekly tour is well worth it if you're here during one of the quieter periods, but if there are more than fifty people in the group, you'll see very little as you're herded through the lavish municipal interior. The **Salón de Goya** contains a copy of Goya's *Allegory of Madrid* – the original being in the Museo Municipal (see p.103) – a testament to the turbulent political history Madrid experienced in the nineteenth century. The painting underwent no less than seven alterations in order to satisfy the sensibilities of the various rulers of Madrid during this period, and the final version shows the story of "*Dos de Mayo*", commemorating the heroic resistance of the city against the French in 1808 (see "Contexts", p.296). Also here is the monumental canvas by Palmorli, *The Morning of May 3rd*, in which you can see the dawn panorama of Madrid featuring the Palacio Real and the dome of San Francisco El Grande. The **Patio de Los Cristales** contains a stunning stained-glass roof depicting some of the most celebrated city sights and houses busts of famous *Madrileño* writers, painters and playwrights, including Tirso de Molina, Lope de Vega, Claudio Coello and Quevedo. The highlight of the tour is the **Salón de Plenos** or Assembly Room, where meetings of the council still take place. The chamber is dripping with gold leaf and lavishly decorated with burgundy velvet curtains, red leather benches and frescoes by Antonio Palomino.

The Convento de Las Carboneras and the Basílica de San Miguel

Next to the Torre de los Lujanes, a small alleyway, c/Codo (Elbow Street), leads out of the square down to c/Sacramento. On the right as you walk down, an unassuming wooden door hides the **Convento de Las Carboneras**. The convent was founded in the early seventeenth century and belongs to the closed Hieronymite Order. The name itself originates from a painting of the virgin found in a coal bunker and donated to the convent. The convent also makes and sells its own cakes – a tradition that has existed in Spanish convents since the time of St Teresa of Avila, who gave out sweetened egg yolks to the poor of her city. The cakes can be purchased every day 9.30am–1pm and 4–6.30pm. Ring the bell and you will be let in; the business takes place by means of a revolving drum so that the closed nature of the order is not violated.

At the end of the alleyway you reach the **Basílica de San Miguel** (daily 10am–2pm & 5.30–9pm) on **c/Sacramento**, a beautiful, well-preserved and quiet street, crowded with municipal buildings. The church itself was designed at the end of the seventeenth century for Don Luis, the precocious five-year-old Archbishop of Toledo and youngest son of Felipe V. It's one of the few examples of a fully-blown Baroque church in Madrid, showing the unbridled imagination of Italian architect, Santiago Bonaviá. It features an unconventional convex facade with four recesses each containing a statue, variously representing Charity, Strength, Faith and Hope.

LA LATINA

Immediately to the south of c/Sacramento is the **Plaza de la Cruz Verde**, one of the sites of the notorious autos-da-fé and executions organized by the Inquisition. From here the Costanilla de San Andrés leads up into the old Muslim quarter, **La Morería**. Keep an eye out on your left for the Mudéjar tower of the second oldest church in Madrid, **San Pedro El Viejo** (daily 6–8pm), said to have been founded in the fourteenth century by Alfonso XI on the site occupied by the old mosque, although the rest of the church was largely rebuilt in the seventeenth century. At the end of the Costanilla you'll reach one of the real gems of old Madrid, the **Plaza de La Paja**. This sloping, acacia-shaded plaza was the commercial and civil hub of the city before the construction of the Plaza Mayor and has recently been superbly remodelled, with the newly restored frontages of the houses beaming down on the former market square. There's a fine selection of bars and restaurants in and around the square, and in the summer you'll usually find a *terraza* here. This is one of the few areas in the city where you can get a break from the interminable Madrid traffic.

La Iglesia de San Andrés, Capilla del Obispo and Capilla de San Isidro

On the southern side of Plaza de la Paja stands the **Iglesia de San Andrés**. The church was badly damaged by an anarchist attack in 1936, and, together with the adjoining **Capilla del Obispo**, has been closed for restoration since 1991, although the brick cupola has now been repaired and restored to its former glory. Another of the adjoining chapels, the Baroque **Capilla de San Isidro** (Mon–Sat 8.30–11.30am & 6–8pm, Sun 9am–2pm), is, however, open to visitors and can be reached by walking round the building into the courtyard. Note, though, that it's particularly strict about not letting people in with short sleeves or shorts. The chapel was built in the mid-seventeenth century to house the remains of the saint which were later transferred to the Catedral de San Isidro in c/Toledo (see overleaf). The *capilla*'s interior is richly decorated, with a beautifully sculpted dome in greens and yellows, depicting angels laden with fruit. The lower level, inspired by the pantheon in El Escorial, features a red-marble backdrop, fronted by black columns embroidered with gold leaf and sculptures of saints.

La Morería

To the west of Plaza de la Paja you can explore the narrow, labyrinthine streets of **La Morería**, still clearly laid out on the old Moorish lines; it is said that c/Morería 3 is the oldest house in Madrid. On **Plaza Gabriel Miró** *El Ventorrillo* is a good place to stop for refreshment. This *terraza* is also known as *Las Vistillas* (Little Views) and here you can sample a reasonably priced menu and assorted tapas accompanied by unrivalled views of the Almudena Cathedral, Casa de Campo and the Sierra Guadarrama. North, towards the cathedral, you'll reach the **Cuesta de la Vega**, the former site of one of the main entrances to Muslim Madrid. In the adjoining Parque Emir Mohammed I, a rather scruffy patch of sandy open land, are some of the few remaining fragments of the **city walls** dating back to the ninth and twelfth centuries.

Calles Cava Baja and Cava Alta

Map 4, E5. Metro La Latina.
Continuing south from the San Andrés complex you'll

LA LATINA

23

come to a series of plazas, variously named Plaza San Andrés, Plaza Puerta de Moros, Plaza de Los Carros and Plaza Humilladero, which now effectively merge into one. They form an excellent site for summer *terrazas* and tapas bars which are always crowded with locals at the weekends. The web of streets running northeast out of the square back towards Plaza Mayor – c/Almendro, **c/Cava Baja** and **c/Cava Alta** – are also well worth investigating. Here you'll find some of the best places to eat and drink in all of Madrid. C/Cava Baja used to be full of workshops, but is now famous for its *mesones,* serving traditional Castilian and *Madrileño* fare, and its wide selection of bars (see the "Eating" and "Drinking" chapters for more details).

San Isidro

Map 4, G4. Mon–Sat 8am–12.30pm & 6–8.30pm; Sun & public holidays 9am–2pm & 6–8.30pm. Metro La Latina.

North of La Latina metro station on c/Toledo stands the massive church of **San Isidro**, built in 1622–33 as part of the Colegio Imperial – the centre of the Jesuit Order in Spain – according to the express wishes of Felipe IV's wife, Mariana de Austria, who left a very large legacy to the Jesuits. Its illustrious alumni include the writers Lope de Vega, Calderón de la Barca, Quevedo and Góngora. After Carlos III fell out with the Jesuits in 1767, the church was dedicated to San Isidro, the patron saint of Madrid. His remains and those of his wife were brought here in 1769 from the Capilla de San Isidro just down the road. The church became the city's provisional cathedral from 1886, when Madrid was given its own diocese, until 1993 when the new Catedral de la Almudena was finally completed. It contains a single nave with large, ornate lateral chapels and an impressive altarpiece.

San Francisco El Grande

Map 4, B7. Tues–Sat: June–Sept 11am–1pm & 5–8pm; Oct–May 11am–1pm & 5–7pm; 50ptas with guided tour. Metro Puerta de Toledo/La Latina.

From Plaza Puerta de Moros there's a splendid view of the Neoclassical exterior of the huge domed church of **San Francisco El Grande**. Tradition has it that St Francis of Assisi came to Spain in 1214, on a pilgrimage to the tomb of St James in Santiago and built a humble home next to a monastery on this site. The monastery was enlarged and enriched over the years, but was demolished in 1760 in order to build a still more beautiful one. Plans were ambitious and included a great dome with radial chapels crowned by a cupola, modelled on the Pantheon in Rome. The building was finally completed in 1784, its magnificent dome exceeding that of St Paul's in London by a metre in diameter. In 1837, the church was converted into a national mausoleum reverting to the control of the Franciscan friars in 1926. Inside, it's difficult to appreciate the size of the church, as it's filled with a forest of yellow scaffolding, in place for a painfully slow restoration scheduled to be completed in 2012. The paintings are the church's greatest treasures and include an early Goya, *The Sermon of San Bernadino of Siena*, as well as works by José de Ribera and Contreras.

The Palacio Real and Ópera

T he compact area around Ópera metro station, bounded by c/Mayor and c/Segovia to the south, Cuesta de San Vicente to the north, Paseo Virgen del Puerto to the west and Puerta del Sol to the east, contains a rich array of architectural and artistic treasures. The main sites date from the sixteenth to the eighteenth centuries, although the area itself only became really fashionable from the mid-nineteenth century onwards. The imposing **Palacio Real** dominates the area, bordered by the somewhat disappointing **Catedral de la Almudena** to the south and the tranquil gardens of the **Campo del Moro** to the west. The recently renovated **Teatro Real** and **Plaza de Oriente** are restoring some of the original nineteenth-century sophistication to the area, while the two monastery complexes, **La Encarnación** and **Las Descalzas Reales**, conceal an astounding selection of artistic delights behind their modest exteriors. You will have to plan your itinerary carefully to dovetail the opening times of the sights, as the hours of the monasteries are restricted.

The bulk of the area covered by this chapter is shown
in detail on colour map 3.

THE PALACIO REAL

Map 3, B3. April–Sept Mon–Sat 9am–6pm, Sun & holidays
9am–3pm; Oct–March Mon–Sat 9.30am–5pm, Sun 9am–2pm;
closed occasionally for state visits; guided tours 950ptas,
unguided 850ptas, concessions 350ptas; Wed free for EU citizens.
Metro Ópera.

The **Palacio Real** (Royal Palace) scores high on statistics. It
claims more rooms than any other European palace; a library
with one of the biggest collections of books, manuscripts,
maps and musical scores in the world; and an armoury with
an unrivalled collection of weapons dating back to the fifteenth century. Guided tours are no longer compulsory,
which means you don't have to whizz round the rooms at
high speed listening to the guide rattle off figures. Much
better to wander through the rooms on the fixed route
yourself, although bear in mind that the rooms are poorly
labelled and the visitors' guide books, while beautifully illustrated, are badly translated. Not all the rooms are open to
the public – some are closed for restoration, while unfortunately, others, such as the King's Library, can only be visited
by prior arrangement for research purposes.

The palace stands on the site of the old Alcázar, erected by
the Arabs in the ninth century to defend the route to Toledo.
This became the royal residence of Felipe II when he moved
his court to Madrid in 1561. However, on Christmas Eve
1734, the Alcázar burned down after some curtains caught
fire, destroying, in the process, some of the great works of
Velázquez and Rubens. Felipe V, a Bourbon who had been
brought up in the considerably more luxurious surroundings

of Versailles, took the opportunity to order the construction of an altogether grander palace. However, he did not live to see the completion of his project; the palace only became habitable in 1764 during the reign of Carlos III.

Inside the palace

To enter the palace, you first cross the vast shadeless **Plaza de la Armería**, used for state parades and the changing of the guard (noon, first Wed of each month, except July & Aug). From the plaza there are superb views of the vast colonnaded southern facade, the Cathedral, Casa de Campo and the Sierra. As you enter the building you are directed up the magnificent main staircase; light pours in from the port-holes in the vaulted ceiling, reflecting off the golden stucco work and illuminating the epic frescoes of Corrado Giaquinto. In the **Salón de los Alabarderos** (Halbardiers' Room), Tiepolo's masterpiece fresco, *Venus commanding Vulcan to forge arms for Aeneas*, features billowing clouds, heroic military figures and majestic gods, while the **Salón de las Columnas** (Hall of Columns) contains several excellent Flemish tapestries woven with wool, gold, silver and silk. One of the highlights is the **Salón del Trono** (Throne Room), with its magnificent celestial fresco by Tiepolo, *The Grandeur and Power of the Spanish Monarchy*. The walls are decorated in red velvet, with ornamental framed mirrors exaggerating the size of the room, while gold drips from the furniture, the stucco work and the bronze lions guarding the thrones – an ostentatious display of wealth and power rather at odds with Spain's declining status at the time. There is also a selection of splendid clocks, two rock crystal and silver chandeliers and assorted candelabras. The **Antécamara de Gasparini** (Carlos III's Conversation Room) contains two pairs of Goya masterpieces: one pair portraying Carlos IV and his wife Queen María Luisa of Parma in formal style, with the king wearing the uniform of a Royal Guard colonel and the queen dressed in court clothes; the other, more casual, with the king in hunting attire and the queen dressed as a *maja* in a black skirt and mantilla. The exotic fancy of the **Salón de Gasparini** (the Gasparini Room), decorated in an incredible oriental style by Carlos III's court painter, features a swirling marble floor, gold and silver embroidered wall hangings and beautiful stucco plants, animals and fruits. There are yet more fantastic frescoes, ornate furniture and lavish decoration in the **Salón de Carlos III** (Carlos III's bedroom).

One of the palace's real treats is the marvellous **Sala de Porcelana** (Porcelain Room), decorated with one thousand gold, green, and white pieces, made in the Buen Retiro porcelain factory in the eighteenth century and depicting cherubs, garlands and urns. The **Comedor de Gala** (State Dining Room) is a truly massive affair, again blessed with a selection of superb frescoes, this time by Antonio González Velázquez and Francisco Bayeu, and adorned with golden French candelabras and sixteenth-century tapestries. The table seats 145 and is still used for official banquets. Other rooms display royal silverware from the nineteenth century (Joseph Bonaparte ordered the original silver dinner service to be melted down to meet war needs), crockery and a very impressive collection of musical instruments, including a number of Stradivarius's creations and a fantastic jewelled guitar by José Frias. The tour of the main building is completed with the **Capilla Real** (Royal Chapel) and Queen María Cristina's official apartments (currently closed for refurbishment), which are more modest in scale.

The Armería Real, Farmacia and Jardines de Sabatini

The palace outbuildings and annexes include the **Armería**

Real (Royal Armoury), a huge room full of guns, swords and armour, with such curiosities as El Cid's sword and the suit of armour worn by Carlos V in his equestrian portrait by Titian in the Prado. Especially fascinating are the complete sets of armour, with all the original spare parts and gadgets for making adjustments, and the suits designed for children, horses and dogs. Also open to visitors is the eighteenth-century **Farmacia**, which served the Royal Family and employees at the palace; it's a curious mixture of alchemist's den and laboratory, and the walls are lined with jars labelled for various remedies. Immediately north of the palace, the disappointing **Jardines de Sabatini** contain some well-manicured trees and bushes and give a pleasant view of the northeast facade of the palace, but the ornamental lake is often dry and many of the benches have been spoiled by graffiti.

THE CATHEDRAL

Map 3, B6. Mon–Sat 10am–1.30pm & 6–8.30pm, Sun 10am–2.30pm & 6–8.30pm. Metro Ópera.

Facing the Palacio Real to the south is Madrid's cathedral, **Nuestra Señora de la Almudena**, its bulky Neoclassical facade designed to match the palace. Planned centuries ago, the building was plagued by lack of funds, bombed out in the Civil War and eventually opened for business in 1993 by Pope John Paul II. Its cold Gothic pastel-coloured interior is uninspiring, though the boutique-like Capilla Opus Dei is worth a look amid an array of largely unfilled chapel alcoves.

Outside, nestling on the south wall behind the cathedral, facing the Parque Emir Mohammed I, is a figure of the **Virgin of the Almudena**, marking the site of the first recorded miracle in Madrid. The figure was said to have

Madrid's Freebies

Free entrance can be gained to many of Madrid's premier attractions at certain times of the week. Sites classed as *Patrimonio Nacional* such as the Palacio Real, the Convento de la Encarnación, El Pardo (see p.121) and the Monasterio de las Descalzas are free to EU citizens on Wednesdays (bring your passport). Most museums are free for under 18s and the retired, and give substantial discounts to students (bring ID in all cases). In addition, many museums and sights that normally charge entry set aside certain times when entrance is free. These include the following:

Centro de Arte Reina Sofía: Sat 2.30–9pm & Sun 10am–2.30pm.
Ermita de San Antonio de la Florida: Wed 10am–2pm & 4–8pm, Sun 10am–2pm.
Museo de América: Sat 2–3pm & Sun 10am–2.30pm.
Museo Arqueológico: Sat 2.30–8.30pm & Sun 9.30am–2.30pm.
Museo de Artes Decorativas: Sun 10am–2pm.
Museo Cerralbo: Sun 10am–2pm & Wed 9.30am–2.30pm.
Museo del Ejército: Sat 10am–2pm.
Museo Lázaro Galdiano: Sat 10am–2pm.
Museo Municipal: Sun 10am–2pm & Wed 9.30am–8pm.
Museo del Prado: Sat 2.30–7pm & Sun 9am–2pm.
Museo Romántico: Sun 10am–2pm.
Real Academia de Bellas Artes: Sat & Sun 9am–2.30pm.

been brought to Spain by Saint James and was concealed in the wall of the old castle here by early Christians to protect it during the conquest of the city by the Muslims. When the city was reconquered by Alfonso VI at the end of the eleventh century, he was anxious to unearth the virgin to re-establish the city's Christian credentials. He organized a

MADRID'S FREEBIES

huge procession appealing for divine help, and when the faithful arrived at the appointed spot a woman offered her life in return for the statue's reappearance. The wall crumbled away to reveal the virgin in all her splendour and the woman dropped dead immediately.

EL CAMPO DEL MORO AND THE PUENTE DE SEGOVIA

Map 2, A5. Metro Príncipe Pío.

North of the Jardines de Sabatini, the Cuesta San Vicente leads past the partly restored **Estación del Norte** and the modern replica of the eighteenth-century Puerta de San Vicente to the **Campo del Moro** (9am–8pm; occasionally closed for state visits; entrance on Paseo de la Virgen del Puerto). One of the most underused and most beautiful of Madrid's parks, it was the site of the Moors' encampment, from where, in 1109, they mounted their unsuccessful attempt to reconquer Madrid and the Alcázar. It later became a venue for medieval tournaments and celebrations. After the building of the Palacio Real plenty of plans to landscape the area were put forward, but it wasn't until 1842 that Pascual y Colomer got things underway. Based around two monumental fountains, *Las Conchas* and *Los Tritones,* the grassy gardens are very English in style, featuring shady paths and ornamental pools, and provide an excellent refuge from the summer heat, at the same time as affording a splendid view of the palace. They were first opened to the public during the Second Republic in 1931, but closed under Franco and not reopened until 1983.

A short walk south along Paseo de la Virgen del Puerto is the early eighteenth-century **Ermita de la Virgen del Puerto**, Pedro de Ribera's Baroque-style fairytale chapel with its original octagonal slate cupola. Set in grounds right beside the River Manzanares, the Ermita stands alongside the oldest bridge in Madrid, the **Puente de Segovia**, designed by Juan de Herrera and completed in 1584. The bridge is an imposing structure, but the river below doesn't really match up. A French aristocrat once remarked, "with such a fine bridge, they really ought to get a river", while the German ambassador Rhebines called it the best river in Europe because it had the advantage of being "navigable by horse and carriage".

PLAZA DE ORIENTE AND BEYOND

Map 3, D4. Metro Ópera.

With the completion of a major pedestrianization project, entailing the diversion of the busy c/Bailén beneath the square, the aristocratic **Plaza de Oriente** has become one of the most pleasant open spaces in Madrid. The showpiece **fountain** in the centre was designed by Narciso Pascual y Colomer, who also transferred the bronze equestrian statue of Felipe IV here from the garden of the Buen Retiro Palace near the Prado. The statue was based on designs by Velázquez, and Galileo is said to have helped with the calculations to make it balance. Other **statues** in the square depict Spanish kings and queens. These were originally designed to adorn the palace facade, but were too heavy or, according to one version, were removed on the orders of Queen Isabel of Farnese, second wife of Felipe V, who dreamt they had fallen on her during an earthquake.

There is a very French feel to the buildings facing the Palacio Real, with their glass-fronted *terrazas* and decorated balconies, underlined by the elegant neo-Baroque **Café de Oriente**, whose summer *terraza* is one of the stations of Madrid nightlife. The café looks as traditional as any in the city, but was in fact opened in the 1980s, by a priest, Padre Lezama, who ploughs his profits into various charitable schemes.

The bulky, rather squat **Teatro Real** (open for visits

Tues–Fri 1pm; Sat, Sun & holidays 10.30am–1.30pm; 500ptas, 250ptas concessions; tickets on sale from 10am at the box office) straddles the area between Plaza de Oriente and Plaza de Santa Isabel. Designed by Antonio López Aguado and opened in 1850, it was once the hub of fashionable Madrid and staged highly successful operas by Verdi and Wagner. Plagued by municipal wrangling and pure incompetence, the opera house has only recently been reopened after a ten-year refurbishment that should have lasted four and which ended up costing a mind-boggling $150 million.

For more information on opera in Madrid see p.200.

Calle de Arenal

Map 3, F4–H5. Metro Ópera/Sol.

C/Arenal, stretching from the Teatro Real to Puerta del Sol, was once a stream which frequently dried up to leave a sandy channel (*arena* means "sand"). Today, it's lined with shops, but does contain a few, easily missed sights. The Palacio de Gaviria (no. 9) was originally an ornate palace constructed in 1851 by the Marquis of Gaviria, and now houses a disco, nightclub, dance school and cocktail bar all rolled into one. Further along, the *Joy Madrid* disco occupies the site of the former Teatro Eslava, established in 1872 to provide popular light entertainment. Behind it, the **Chocolatería San Ginés**, a Madrid institution, which at one time catered for the early-rising worker, now churns out *churros* and hot chocolate for the late nightclub crowd (see box p.189). Nearby stands the ancient church of **San Ginés** (Fri–Sun 7–10pm), one of the original ten parishes included in the 1202 Madrid charter, which granted Madrid its own *fueros*, legally established privileges, and divided the city into parishes. The neighbouring seven-teenth-century **Capilla de Cristo** (daily during services 9am–1pm & 6–9pm; entrance in c/Bordadores) contains an El Greco canvas showing the moneychangers being chased from the temple.

CONVENTO DE LA ENCARNACIÓN

Map 3, D2. Compulsory tours (some in English) Tues, Wed, Thurs & Sat 10.30am–12.45pm & 4–5.45pm, Fri 10.30am–12.45pm, Sun 11am–1.45pm; 425ptas, concessions 225ptas; joint ticket with Monasterio de las Descalzas 750ptas/350ptas, valid for a week; Wed free for EU citizens. Metro Ópera.

North of Plaza de Oriente, the **Convento de la Encarnación** is worth a visit for its reliquary alone – one of the most important in the Catholic world. Founded in 1611 by Felipe III and his wife Margarita de Austria, the convent was intended as a retreat for titled women. The solemn granite facade is the hallmark of architect Juan Gómez de Mora and was modelled on the Iglesia de San José de Ávila, built by his uncle, Francisco de Mora. Much of the painting contained within is uninspiring artistically, but there are some interesting items, including an extensive collection of royal portraits and a highly prized collection of sculptures of Christ, with an extremely gory post-crucifix-ion one by Gregorio Fernández. The library-like **reliquary** is lined with a cupboard full of more than 1500 sixteenth-to eighteenth-century saintly relics from around the world: skulls, arms encased in beautiful ornate hand-shaped con-tainers, and bones from every conceivable part of the body. The most famous relic of all is a small glass bulb said to contain the blood of St Pantaleón, a fourteenth-century doctor martyr whose blood supposedly liquifies at midnight on the eve of his feast day (July 28). The tour ends with a visit to the Baroque-style church which features a beautifully frescoed ceiling by Bayeu and the González Velázquez brothers, depicting scenes from the life of the monastery's patron, St Augustine, and a jasper- and marble-columned altarpiece.

··

Note that visitors with rucksacks and large bags are not allowed into the Convento de la Encarnación or the Monasterios de las Descalzas, and there is nowhere to leave them.

··

MONASTERIO DE LAS DESCALZAS

Map 3, H3. Compulsory tours (some in English) Tues–Thurs & Sat 10.30am–12.45pm & 4–5.45pm, Fri 10.30am–12.45pm, Sun & holidays 11am–1.45pm; 650ptas, concessions 250ptas; joint ticket with Convento de la Encarnación, 750ptas/350ptas, valid for a week; Wed free for EU citizens. Metro Ópera/Sol.

Just north of c/Arenal in Plaza de las Descalzas, behind an unobtrusive wooden door, stands one of the hidden treasures of Madrid, the **Monasterio de las Descalzas Reales** (Monastery of the Barefoot Royal Ladies). Originally the site of a medieval palace, then the residence of Emperor Carlos V's royal treasurer, Alonso Gutiérrez, the building was transformed by Juana de Austria, born here in 1535, into a convent in 1564, and the architect of El Escorial, Juan Bautista de Toledo, was entrusted with its design. Juana was daughter of the Emperor Carlos V, sister of Felipe II, and already, at the age of 19, the widow of Prince Don Juan of Portugal. The original nuns were from Gandía, near Valencia, but were later joined by a succession of titled ladies, who, not wanting to leave behind all evidence of earthly delights, brought with them a whole array of artistic treasures. As a result, the monastery accumulated a fabulous collection of paintings, sculptures and tapestries.

The place is unbelievably opulent and also beautiful and tranquil. It's still in use as a monastery, housing 26 shoeless nuns of the Franciscan order. Unfortunately, the quality of the guides is variable and a number seem intent on doing the tour at record speed, so you'll have to do your best to slow them down if you want a chance to properly admire the monastery's treasures.

The **main staircase**, connecting a two-levelled cloister lined with small but richly embellished chapels, is truly magnificent, with floor-to-ceiling frescoes painted at the end of the seventeenth century by José Ximénez Donoso and Claudio Coello. Felipe IV and his family are pictured gazing down at visitors from a balcony at the very top.

The **Coro** (Choir) contains the tomb of Empress María of Austria, sister of Felipe II, who had fifteen children and later died in the convent. Juana de Austria is also buried here. Look out for the moving sculpture of the *Doloroso*, with its incredibly realistic tears and misty eyes. There is also a small waist-high chapel that was built especially for the children of the ladies. One of the most outstanding features of the monastery is the **Tapestry Room**, containing a magnificent collection of early seventeenth-century Flemish tapestries based on designs by Rubens – now in the Prado – and representing the Triumph of the Eucharist. A mass of royal portraits and beautiful painted wooden sculptures, most of which are of unknown origin, decorate other rooms. Keep an eye out for the little spiked slippers worn by the nuns to mutilate their feet, and for a marvellous painting by an artist of the Bosch school, *Ship of Salvation*, full of devilish mutant figures. On your way out you pass screened windows which hide the orchard and gardens still tended by the nuns.

MONASTERIO DE LAS DESCALZAS

The Rastro, Lavapiés and Embajadores

The areas south of Plaza Mayor have traditionally been tough, working-class districts, with tenement buildings thrown up to accommodate the huge expansion of the population in the eighteenth and nineteenth centuries. In many places these old houses survive, huddled together in narrow streets, but the character of the area is beginning to change as their inhabitants become younger and the districts themselves more fashionable. Built on land that slopes down towards the River Manzanares, **Lavapiés** and **Embajadores** were traditionally called the *barrios bajos* (lower districts) and developed their own identity separate from the rest of Madrid. The city's early industrial and commercial centre, now known as the **Rastro**, was concentrated here and its inhabitants became known as **castizos** – authentic *Madrileños* – renowned for their sharp native wit and fierce pride.

Castizo

The word **castizo** is used to signify anything authentically *Madrileño*, and bears many similarities to the Cockney tradition in London, with the inhabitants of the *barrios* of Lavapiés and La Latina, as well as Chamberí, all laying claim to the label. Community life in these working-class districts, which grew up in the nineteenth century, was based around *corrales* (balconied tenement blocks with a central courtyard), and it was here that the strong sense of *castizo* identity began to develop. Quick-witted, sarcastic, sharp dressers, intensely proud, and often described as being *chulo* or "cocky", the *castizos* were immortalized in many of Goya's paintings and are celebrated in *zarzuelas*, Madrid's own form of operetta (see box on p.43). Today, their traditional dress of black-and-white-checked caps, waistcoats and black trousers for the men, embroidered dresses, petticoats, shawls and headscarfs plus red carnation for the women, is most likely to be seen during the festivals of San Isidro, the summer *verbenas* of San Cayetano, San Lorenzo and La Paloma or at the *zarzuela*. Also associated with the *castizos* and often heard at the *verbenas*, is the *chotis*, a sort of upbeat Wild-West saloon type of music played on a barrel organ and said to have descended from the Scottish jig.

The area covered by this chapter is shown in detail on colour map 5.

THE RASTRO

Map 5, C5. Metro La Latina/Puerta de Toledo.

The best starting point for an exploration of the **Rastro** is the church of San Isidro on c/Toledo (see p.24). From here take the signposted route down c/Estudios to Plaza de Cascorro where the main thoroughfare **Ribera de Curtidores** begins. This area was formerly the site of two large slaughterhouses and the resulting blood that flowed down the hill gave the area its name (*rastro* means "stain"). The establishment of the slaughterhouses acted as a magnet for other traders and craftsmen: tanners, after whom Ribera de Curtidores is named, leather workers and food sellers all soon set up in the area. These days, Ribera de Curtidores is lined with furniture shops, antique dealers (some extremely upmarket) and outdoor pursuits equipment suppliers, but the best day to visit is Sunday, when it's taken over by Madrid's most famous market, **El Rastro** (see box opposite).

At the southern end of Ribera de Curtidores on your right, you'll see a large arch, the **Puerta de Toledo**, an eloquent testament to the political vicissitudes that Madrid endured in the nineteenth century. Originally commissioned by Joseph Bonaparte to commemorate his accession to the Spanish throne, the arch ended up being a celebration of his defeat when it was completed in 1827.

Just in front of the arch, the **Mercado Puerta de Toledo**, once the city's main fish market, has pretensions to being a stylish arts and crafts centre, but in fact many of the sites allocated for shops haven't been occupied and it stands practically empty, apart from an underused tourist office. Below, past the lines of anonymous apartment blocks, lies the **Puente de Toledo**, a pedestrian bridge designed by Pedro de Ribera for Felipe V and built between 1718 and 1732. The arched construction spanning the rather sad-looking River Manzanares and the hopelessly congested M30 ring road can still be crossed to reach the summer *terraza* on the other side. As you cross, on your right you'll see the M30 disappearing underneath the main stand of the huge **Vicente Calderón** football stadium, home to Atlético Madrid.

The Flea Market

Madrid's flea market, **El Rastro**, is as much part of the city's weekend ritual as Mass or a *paseo*. This gargantuan, thriving shambles of a street market sprawls south from Metro La Latina along Ribera de Curtidores to the Ronda de Toledo. Crowds flood through the market between 10am and 3pm every Sunday and increasingly on Friday, Saturday and public holidays too. On offer are secondhand and pseudo-designer clothes, military surplus items, T-shirts, sunshades, razor blades, Taiwanese radios, cutlery, canaries, and coke spoons – in fact just about anything you can imagine. The serious antique trade has now mostly moved off the streets and into the adjacent shops, while the real junk is found only on the fringes. The atmosphere is always enjoyable and the bars around these streets are as good as any in the city.

One **warning**, however: keep a tight grip on your bags, cameras (best left at the hotel) and jewellery. The Rastro rings up a fair percentage of Madrid's tourist thefts.

LAVAPIÉS AND EMBAJADORES

Lavapiés and **Embajadores** stretch south and east from Plaza Tirso de Molina (Metro Tirso de Molina). Just to the south of the plaza at c/San Pedro Mártir 5 is the house where the young Pablo Picasso stayed during his visits to Madrid at the time he was painting *The Woman in Blue* (now hanging in the Reina Sofía). From here you can follow **c/Mesón de Paredes**, stopping for a drink at the darkly panelled *Taberna Antonio Sánchez* at no. 13, which dates back to 1830. Now owned by an ex-*torero*, it's decked out with two bull's heads and numerous taurine paintings. The street is buzzing, colourful and cosmopolitan, lined with ethnic shops, cafés, an Arab tea house and small plazas.

On c/Caravaca, a side street off c/Mesón de Paredes, is the *Pastelería Licorería El Madroño* (closed July & Aug), where you can sample Madrid's native liquor made from the berries of the *madroño* tree.

Halfway down c/Mesón de Paredes on the right is **La Corrala**, built in 1839 and restored in the 1980s, one of many traditional *corrales* (tenement blocks) in the quarter, built with balconied apartments opening onto a central patio. The cramped housing means that much of the drama of everyday life is played out on the balconies or in the courtyard below – neighbours conducting long-distance conversations with each other, children crying, dogs barking, old men arguing over the football. The ruined building alongside was a church and religious school, destroyed in the Civil War and left as a monument. Plays, especially farces and **zarzuelas**, used to be performed regularly in Spanish *corrales*, and the open space here usually hosts a number of performances in the summer as part of the Veranos de la Villa cultural programme (see "Festivals" chapter, p.216). Some of the audience come dressed up in traditional *castizo* costume (see box on p.39) and sit, eating, drinking and chatting at the tables set up in the courtyard here.

Running parallel and to the west of Mesón de Paredes is **c/Embajadores**, one of the oldest streets in Madrid, brimming with traditional traders, shops and markets. The name of the street originated in the fifteenth century, when a number of ambassadors fled to the area in order to escape an outbreak of the plague in the city centre. The elaborately sculpted and ornamented church of **San Cayetano**, patron of one the area's most important festivals in August,

The zarzuela

Madrid is the birthplace of the **zarzuela**, Spain's very own brand of opera, incorporating features of classical opera, as well as the more bawdy elements of music hall. The name originates from the royal palace and hunting lodge just to the north of Madrid where entertainments were laid on for Felipe IV. The *zarzuela* developed in the early nineteenth century and is usually centred on a local community, with small-time protagonists, minor romances and soap-opera type plots. The most famous work is *La Revoltosa* ("The Rebellious Daughter") by Ruperto Chapí which tells the story of a young girl who refuses to desert her true love to marry for money. The season runs throughout the summer (June–Sept), with *zarzuela* perfomances taking place at several venues in the city, including the open-air *La Corrala* in Lavapiés, the most authentic backdrop for this *castizo* artform (see p.201 for further details of venues).

dominates the upper part of the street. José de Churriguera and Pedro de Ribera, both renowned for their extravagant designs, were involved in the design of the facade, constructed in 1761. Most of the rest of the church was destroyed in the Civil War and has since been reconstructed. The remainder of the street is a jumble of traditional shops, many with tiled frontages, and dilapidated dwellings, while at the bottom is the oldest **tobacco factory** in Europe. Originally built as a distillery, but modified to produce tobacco in 1809, its austere, unornamented facade is a classic example of early nineteenth-century industrial architecture. Its workforce was overwhelmingly female and constituted, by the end of the century, about twenty percent of Madrid's working population. The flamboyant *cigarreras*, as they were called, were renowned for their independence, solidarity and strength. They bargained with the management to achieve

LAVAPIÉS AND EMBAJADORES

the establishment of special schools, crèches and improvements in working conditions.

Just east of here, along c/Miguel Servet, you'll reach **Plaza Lavapiés**. This district was the core of the **Jewish quarter** in medieval Madrid, with the synagogue situated on the site now occupied by the Teatro Olimpia. In 1492, the Jews were given the choice of expulsion or conversion to Christianity by the fanatically Catholic Spanish monarchs; those that converted took Christian names, traditionally using Manuel for the eldest son, which led to the area being dubbed "*El Barrio de los Manolos*". Meanwhile, the converted Muslims (*Moriscos*) tended to congregate in the zone around c/Ave María. With its Chinese, Arabic and African inhabitants, Lavapiés remains a cosmopolitan place to this day. The plaza is a very colourful and animated spot, with a variety of bars and cafés in various states of decay. There are *terrazas* and more bars along the cool, tree-lined c/Argumosa, which leads out to Atocha and the Centro de Arte Reina Sofía (see p.81).

Calle de Atocha

Map 5, E1–I4. Metro Tirso de Molina/Atocha.

Lavapiés is bounded to the northeast by **Calle de Atocha**, one of the old ceremonial routes from Plaza Mayor to the *basílica* at Atocha. At its southern end it's a mishmash of fast-food and touristy restaurants, developing, as you move north up the hill, into a perverse mixture of cheap hostels, fading shops, bars, lottery kiosks and sex emporia. The huge sex shop, El Mundo Fantástico, at no. 80, with its brash neon lighting and shiny black facade, stands unashamedly opposite a convent and the site of an old printing house that produced the first edition of the first part of *Don Quixote*. Further up, just before you reach Plaza Antón Martín, you'll pass Pasaje Doré, a narrow alley on the left, bordered by an indoor market crammed with miniature stores. At the end is the **Cine Doré**, the oldest cinema in Madrid, dating from 1922. It has been converted to house the Filmoteca Nacional, an art-house cinema with bargain admission prices and a pleasant, inexpensive café/restaurant (Tues–Sun 1.30pm–12.30am).

For more information on Madrid's cinemas see p.213.

Back on c/Atocha, **Plaza Antón Martín** is named after the founder of a sixteenth-century hospital for the treatment of venereal diseases, once situated here, and now the site of the Teatro Monumental, where Prokofiev premiered his second violin concerto in 1935. Around the plaza are a variety of great-value bars, cafés and flamenco joints, including *Casa Patas* in c/Cañizares (see p.202).

LAVAPIÉS AND EMBAJADORES

Sol, Santa Ana and Huertas

The **Puerta del Sol** marks the western tip of the **Santa Ana/Huertas** area, a triangle bordered to the east by the Paseo del Prado, to the north by c/Alcalá, and along the south by c/Atocha. The city expanded into this area in the 1560s during the Spanish golden age, and this *barrio de las letras* is steeped in **literary tradition**. It was home to many of the great Spanish authors and playwrights, including Lope de Vega, Cervantes and Góngora. Theatres, bookshops and literary cafés proliferate and the *barrio* also contains the **Ateneo** (literary, scientific and political club), **Círculo de Bellas Artes** (Fine Arts Institute), **Teatro Nacional** and the **Congreso de Los Diputados** (Parliament). Just to the north, there is also an important museum and art gallery, the **Real Academia de Bellas Artes de San Fernando**. For most visitors, though, the major attraction of the district are its beautiful **bars** and *tascas* (tavern-type bars) – some of the best in the city. They are concentrated particularly around **Plaza de Santa Ana**, which, following a rather seedy period, has been smartened up by the council and is now one of the finest squares in the city.

....

The area covered by this chapter is shown in detail on colour map 6.

....

PUERTA DEL SOL

Map 6, A3–B3. Metro Sol.

The best place to start exploring this part of Madrid (and many other areas of the centre) is the **Puerta del Sol**. This square marks the epicentre of the city - and, indeed, of Spain. It is from here that all distances are measured, and on the pavement outside the clock-tower building on the south side of the square, a stone slab shows Kilometre Zero. In front of the department store El Corte Inglés stand a statue of the city's emblem, the bear and *madroño* (arbutus) tree, and an equestrian bronze of King Carlos III. For most *Madrileños*, however, the square's most renowned landmarks are the Tío Pepe sign perched above the buildings to the east and the sweet-smelling Mallorquina cake shop, just outside the metro station entrance to the west.

Puerta del Sol's most important building, the **Casa de Correos**, was built in 1766 by Jaime Marquet and served as the city's post office until 1847, when it became home to the Ministry of Interior and later the headquarters of the much-feared security police under Franco. It now houses the main offices of the Madrid regional government, the Comunidad de Madrid. The Neoclassical building is crowned by the nation's most famous **clock** which officially ushers in the New Year: on New Year's eve, *Madrileños* pack into the square below and attempt to scoff twelve grapes, one on each of the chimes of midnight to bring themselves good luck for the succeeding twelve months. There was a national outcry recently when the chimes were mistimed so that the majority of Spain was left still holding its grapes.

The square has been a popular meeting place since the mid-sixteenth century, when the steps of the former monastery San Felipe (on the site now occupied by *McDonald's*) acted as one of the officially recognized *mentideros* or gossip mills. Citizens came here to catch up on all the latest news and scandals. Later, the square was the site of the *Café Pombo*, where regular *tertulias* (see box on p.172) were held in the 1920s – a typical session is portrayed in José Gutiérrez Solana's famous painting *La Tertulia del Café Pombo*, now hanging in the Reina Sofía. The square has also witnessed several events of national importance. On May 2, 1808, troops of Napoleon's marshal, Murat, aided by the infamous Egyptian cavalry (the "Mamelukes"), cold-bloodedly slaughtered a rioting crowd, an event depicted in Goya's canvas *Dos de Mayo*, now hanging in the Prado. Just off Puerta del Sol, in c/Carretas, the liberal prime minister of Spain, José Canalejas, was assassinated in 1912 while browsing in a bookshop. The communist Julián Grimau also met his end here in 1963 in even more sinister fashion: he was thrown out of a window of the Casa de Correos and later finished off by a firing squad. Just north of the plaza, on c/Tetuán, is *Casa Labra*, famous for its tapas of fried *bacalao* (cod) and where the Spanish Socialist Party, the PSOE, was founded in 1879.

The road leading from the southeast corner of Puerta del Sol is **Carrera de San Jerónimo**, a route laid out in 1538 to provide access to the San Jerónimo Monastery. Although now a rather anonymous street it does contain the marvellous **Lhardy** restaurant and shop, founded by Frenchman Emilio Lhardy in 1839. Entering the shop you take a step back into the nineteenth century – the shelves are packed with ancient preserves, patés and soups; crystal decanters and glasses grace silver salvers; and customers are greeted by impeccably mannered ancient staff dressed in aprons. Help yourself to the consommé from the giant silver urn, select a savoury cake or vol au vent from the octagonal glass display case and pay at the till on your way out. The restaurant upstairs is famous for its *cocido madrileño* (meat and chickpea stew), but is only for those with large wallets.

PLAZA SANTA ANA

Map 6, C5. Metro Sol.

Plaza Santa Ana lies southeast of Puerta del Sol; head along c/San Jerónimo and take any of the streets off to the right. Recently renovated, **Plaza Santa Ana** was one of the series of squares created by Joseph Bonaparte, whose passion for open spaces led to a remarkable remodelling of Madrid in the six short years of his reign. The plaza is dominated by two distinguished buildings at either end: to the west, the *Reina Victoria*, a giant cream cake of a hotel which looks as though it would be more at home in Nice or Cannes, and to the east, the nineteenth-century Neoclassical **Teatro Español**. The theatre, the facade of which is decorated with busts of famous Spanish playwrights, is the oldest in Madrid and there has been a playhouse on the site since 1583. The main reason for visiting the area, however, is to explore the mass of **bars**, **restaurants** and **cafés** on the square itself and in the nearby streets.

··

**Places to eat and drink in Santa Ana
are reviewed on pp.154–156 and 169–171.**

··

HUERTAS

The **Huertas** area, east of Plaza Santa Ana, has a highly schizophrenic identity. By day, it's rather dull and sleepy with doors closed, windows shuttered and the odd stray cat and dog roaming the empty streets, but at night, the buildings metamorphose into an astounding variety of **bars** – cocktail, jazz, karaoke, disco – and the place is a hive of activity, with people thronging the streets and car horns hooting until 2 or 3am. North of c/Huertas, and parallel to it, are two streets named after the greatest figures of Spain's seventeenth-century literary golden age, **Cervantes** and **Lope de Vega**. Bitter rivals in life, both are probably spinning in their graves now, since Cervantes is interred in the Convento de las Trinitarias on the street named after Lope de Vega, while the latter's house, the Casa de Lope de Vega, finds itself at c/Cervantes 11. Two sites that have played a significant role in the political history of the city are also to be found in this area. The **Ateneo** was the focus of political debate and discussion in the turbulent years of the early nineteenth century, while the **Congreso de Los Diputados** was the scene of the most dramatic event in recent political history: the Tejero Coup attempt.

Casa de Lope de Vega

Map 6, E5. Tues–Fri 9.30am–2pm, Sat 10am–1.30pm; 200ptas, concessions 100ptas, Wed free. Closed mid-July to mid-Aug. Metro Antón Martín.

The reconstructed home of the great golden age Spanish dramatist merits a visit if only for what it shows of life in seventeenth-century Madrid. **Lope de Vega** lived here for 25 years until his death in 1635 at the age of 48. He was a prolific writer and had a tangled private life. His first wife died in childbirth, his second also died and he had five children with his actress mistress. His ordination as a priest in 1614 did not diminish his appetite for romantic liaisons, and one of his mistresses moved into the house after the death of her husband. Gradually turning blind and then insane, she remained here, cared for by the play-wright, until her death in 1632. The house itself has been furnished in authentic fashion using the inventory left at the writer's death. A number of family possessions have survived, preserved by Lope de Vega's daughter, who became a nun at the nearby Convento de las Trinitarias. Other pieces of period furniture in the house are from the Prado and other museums. The highlights include a chapel containing some of Lope de Vega's original relics, the writer's study with a selection of contemporary books, and an Arabic-style harem complete with silk cushions and a *brasero* (an open pan in which hot coals were placed to warm the room). The garden, with its orange tree, vine, well and courtyard, has been replanted and designed according to references found in the writer's correspon-dence.

Ateneo Artístico, Científico y Literario

Map 6, D4. Mon–Sat 9am–1pm, Sun & public holidays 9am–10pm. Metro Sevilla.

The **Ateneo** (literary, scientific and political club), c/Prado 21, was founded after the 1820 Revolution and provided a home for some of the new liberal political ideas circulating at that time. It was accordingly closed down by the myopi-cally conservative Fernando VII on his return from exile after the French occupation. However, it reopened after his death on its present site in 1835, once again establishing itself as one of the focuses of cultural and political life in nineteenth-century Madrid. The exterior is Neoplateresque in style, while the inside features a neo-Greek lecture the-atre and a splendid reading room, with individual desks, lights and green leather writing boards. There's also a good-value cafeteria.

El Congreso de Los Diputados

Map 6, E4. Sat 10.30am–1pm. Closed Aug & public holidays. Metro Sevilla.

A short stroll down c/Prado from the Ateneo to Plaza de las Cortes, takes you past an unprepossessing nineteenth-century building where **El Congreso de Los Diputados** (the lower house of the Spanish parliament) meets. Sessions can be visited by appointment only, though anyone can turn up (with a passport) and queue for a tour on Saturday mornings – this takes in several of the most important rooms and the chamber itself where the bullet holes left by mad Colonel Tejero and his Guardia Civil associates in the abortive coup attempt of 1981 are pointed out (see "Contexts", p.299).

CALLE DE ALCALÁ AND PLAZA DE LA CIBELES

Calle de Alcalá, the original road to the Roman University town of Alcalá de Henares, runs west–east from Puerta del Sol to Plaza de la Cibeles at the junction with Paseo del Prado and on past the Retiro. Lined with gargantuan buildings, its architectural highlights include the colonnaded Neoclassical **Banco Central Hispano** designed by Antonio Palacios and Joaquín Otamendi in 1910, the more severe **Banco del Comercio** and the **Ministry of Education and Culture**. The pastel-pink building at no. 25, down towards Puerta del Sol, is the Baroque **Iglesia de las Calatravas**, a seventeenth-century church built for the nuns of the Calatrava, one of the four Spanish military orders. Look out for the splendid early twentieth-century wedge-shaped **Banco Español de Crédito**, adorned with elephant heads and plaques listing all the branches of the bank in Spain; the **Banco de Bilbao Vizcaya**, with its Neoclassical concave facade complete with charioteers on top; and the classic Baroque **Ministerio de Hacienda**. Yet more delights await with the **Casino de Madrid**, constructed according to the design of Luis Esteve after an international competition in 1903, organized by the business and intellectual elite who wanted a more upmarket setting for their meetings. It has a suitably opulent central staircase and main salon – ask the doorman if you can have a look.

Museo de La Real Academia de Bellas Artes de San Fernando

Map 6, C2. Tues–Fri 9am–7pm, Mon, Sat, Sun & public holidays 9am–2.30pm; 300ptas, concessions 150ptas, free Sat & Sun. Free guided visits Mon–Fri 10am–2.30pm for organized groups. Metro Sevilla.

Two hundred metres east of Puerta del Sol on c/Alcalá, art buffs who have some appetite left after the Prado, Thyssen and Reina Sofia, should head for the **Real Academia de Bellas Artes de San Fernando**, c/Alcalá 13. One of the most important art galleries in Spain, it has sections dealing with painting, sculpture, architecture and music. Its extraordinary collection of Spanish painting includes work by Velázquez, Murillo, Zurbarán, Goya, Sorolla and Picasso, as well as interesting French and Italian work. The Real Academia was set up by Felipe V at the request of his state secretary and his court sculptor, with the present building being acquired in 1773. The Goya section includes, among other gems, two revealing self-portraits, the contemptuous depiction of the royal favourite *Don Manuel Godoy*, and the desolate representation of *The Madhouse*. There are some supremely ugly royal portraits such as De la Calleja's *Carlos III*, and a variety of sculptures including, scattered throughout the museum, a dismembered *Massacre of the Innocents* by sculptor José Ginés. Look out, too, for the penetrating, rather haunting, portrait of *Haile Selassie* by Delgado. The gallery is also home to the national chalcography collection which includes some Goya etchings.

Círculo de Bellas Artes

Map 6, E2. Café daily 8am–2am; exhibitions Tues–Fri 5–9pm, Sat 11am–2pm & 5–9pm, Sun 11am–2pm; 100ptas. Metro Banco España.

As c/Alcalá descends towards Plaza de la Cibeles you will pass the **Círculo de Bellas Artes** at c/Marqués de Casa Riera 2, a strange-looking 1920s building crowned by a statue of Pallas Athene. This is Madrid's best arts centre, and includes a theatre, music hall, exhibition galleries, cinema and a very pleasant café – all marble and leather decor, with a nude statue reclining in the middle of the floor. For many years a stronghold of Spanish culture, it attracts the city's arts and media crowd, but it's not in the least exclusive, nor expensive, and there's an adjoining *terraza*, too. The Círculo is theoretically a members-only club, but it issues day membership on the door, for which you get access to all areas. Pick up the centre's *Minerva* magazine to find out what's on or ask the helpful staff.

Plaza de la Cibeles

Map 6, G1. Metro Banco de España.

Encircled by four of the most overstated monumental buildings in Madrid – the Palacio de Comunicaciones (the Post Office), Banco de España (the Central Bank), the Palacio de Buenavista (the Army HQ) and the Palacio de Linares (the Casa de América) – **Plaza de la Cibeles** must be the most glorified roundabout in the city. Awash by a sea of traffic, the centre is dominated by a **fountain** and statue of the goddess Cibeles riding in a chariot drawn by two lions. It was designed, as were the two other fountains gushing magnificently on the Paseo del Prado, by Ventura Rodríguez, who has a metro station and a street named after him. It survived the Civil War by being swaddled in sandbags, but was damaged in celebrations after one of the victories of the national football team in the 1994 World Cup. Fully repaired, it still hosts celebrations for victorious Real Madrid fans (Atlético supporters bathe in the fountain of Neptune just down the road).

The wedding cake building on the eastern side of the square is Madrid's main post office, the aptly named **Palacio de Comunicaciones**. Constructed between 1904 and 1917, it is vastly more imposing than the parliament and runs the Palacio Real pretty close. A fabulous place, flanked by polished brass postboxes for each province, it preserves a totally byzantine system within, with scores of counters each offering just one particular service, from telegrams to string, and until quite recently, scribes. The **Casa de América** (Tues–Sat 11am–7pm, Sun 11am–2pm) is used for concerts, films and exhibitions of Latin American art and has a good bookshop and fine café/restaurant.

The Museo del Prado

The **Museo del Prado**, or the Prado, is Madrid's premier tourist attraction, and one of the oldest and greatest collections of art in the world. The Prado houses all the finest works collected by Spanish royalty – for the most part avid, discerning and wealthy buyers – as well as Spanish paintings gathered from other sources over the past two centuries. Recently, major work has been carried out at the museum, with the installation of air conditioning and the remodelling of the roof to let in more light. The museum, however, is desperately short of space, with only about ten percent of its artistic holdings actually on permanent display (still a pretty daunting tally). A controversial plan is currently underway to modernize and extend the museum, adding three existing nearby buildings, which will enable the Prado to double the number of works on show. Rafael Moneo, the architect who refurbished both the Estación de Atocha and the Museo Thyssen-Bornemisza, won the competition to design the first stage of the plan, which involves an extension to the rear of the main building, incorporating the cloisters of the church of San

Jerónimo. However, completion of the whole scheme still looks to be a very long way off. The plan on p.59 outlines the position of the major schools and collections, though it's worth bearing in mind that paintings are sometimes moved around; any changes will be shown on the free maps available on your way into the museum.

The Museo del Prado (Map 6, H6) is open Tuesday–Saturday 9am–7pm, Sunday & holidays usually 9am–2pm, but closed on New Year's Day, Good Friday, May 1 and Christmas Day; 500ptas, concessions 250ptas, free on Saturday after 2.30pm & all day Sunday. Metro Banco de España/Atocha.

The museum's highlights are its Flemish collection – including almost all of **Bosch**'s best work – and its incomparable display of Spanish art, especially paintings by **Velázquez** (including *Las Meninas*), **Goya** (including the *Majas*) and **El Greco**. There's also a huge collection of Italian painters – **Titian**, notably – collected by Carlos V and Felipe II, both great patrons of the Renaissance, as well as a strong showing of later Flemish pictures collected by Felipe IV. Even in a full day you couldn't hope to do justice to everything here, and it's perhaps best to make a couple of focused visits. In summer, the crowds can become oppressive, with the incursions of large tour groups; it's best to hang back and let them sweep by on their whirlwind progress.

There are two main **entrances** to the museum: the **Puerta de Goya**, which has an upper and a lower entrance opposite the *Hotel Ritz* on c/Felipe IV, and the **Puerta de Murillo** on Plaza de Murillo, opposite the Botanical Gardens, which often has shorter queues. The upper entrance of the Puerta de Goya takes you to the first floor, where the seventeenth-century Flemish and Dutch art gives way to the main Spanish collections, while the lower entrance is the one to take if you want to embark on a chronological tour. The Puerta de Murillo is a ground-floor entrance which steers you towards the classical sculpture and on to the Italian Renaissance galleries. Thankfully, there is no prescribed or obvious route, which helps ease congestion, and rooms are numbered in Roman numerals above the doorways. A temporary exhibition space on the ground floor by the Puerta de Goya is used to show visiting exhibitions and selections from the museum holdings not on permanent view.

Illustrated **guides and catalogues** describing and explaining the paintings are on sale in the two museum shops (1100–2200ptas), one on each floor. Particularly helpful is the *Quick Visit Guide* which selects and explains the background to about fifty of the most important works. Useful **colour booklets** (100ptas) on Velázquez, Goya, El Greco, Titian and Bosch are also available in their respective galleries. The museum has a decent cafeteria and restaurant in the basement (closes at 1.30pm on Sun).

If you plan to visit all three art museums on the Paseo del Prado during your stay, it's well worth buying the under-advertised Paseo del Arte ticket (1275ptas), on sale at all three museums: this is valid for a year and allows one visit to each museum at a substantial saving.

SPANISH PAINTING

The Prado's collections of **Spanish painting**, not surprisingly the largest in the world, begin on the ground floor. Room 51c houses cycles of twelfth-century **Romanesque frescoes**, reconstructed from a pair of churches from the Mozarabic (Muslim rule) era in Soria and Segovia. In the

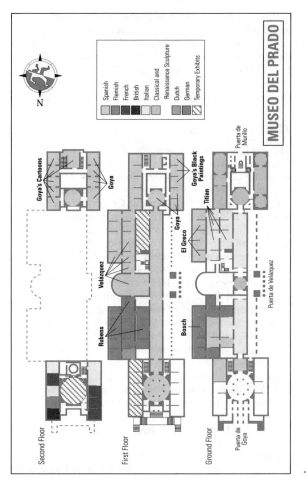

MUSEO DEL PRADO

Spanish
Flemish
French
British
Italian
Classical and
Renaissance Sculpture
Dutch
German
Temporary Exhibits

N

Goya's Cartoons

Goya

Goya's Black
Paintings

Titian

Goya

El Greco

Velázquez

Rubens

Bosch

Puerta de
Murillo

Puerta de Velázquez

Second Floor

First Floor

Ground Floor

Puerta de Goya

SPANISH PAINTING

59

rooms that follow, the remarkably well preserved **early panel paintings** – exclusively religious fourteenth- and fifteenth-century works – include a huge *retablo* by Nicolás Francés, the anonymous *Virgin of the Catholic Monarchs*, Bermejo's ornate portrayal of *Santo Domingo de Silos*, Pedro Berruguete's *Auto-de-Fé* and depictions of the lives and tortuous deaths of a variety of saints.

The golden age

The Prado's collections from Spain's golden age – the late sixteenth and seventeenth centuries under Habsburg rule – are prefigured, on the ground floor (rooms 60a, 61a and 62a), by a collection of paintings by **El Greco** (Domenikos Theotocopulos, 1540–1614), the Cretan-born artist who worked in Toledo from the 1570s. You really need to see the collection of El Greco's works in Toledo to fully appreciate his extraordinary genius, but the portraits and religious works here are a good introduction. The development of his Mannerist style can be traced from the early richly coloured, Italian-influenced *Trinity*, in which there is little sign of the distortions and exaggerations that characterize his later work, to the visionary *Adoration of the Shepherds*, painted 35 years later for his own burial chapel, with its ghostly elongated bodies and sombre oily colouring. His skills as a portrait painter are amply demonstrated in *The Nobleman with his Hand on his Chest*, where the depiction of the Mayor of Toledo with his pointed beard, ruffed collar and sleeve, austere black dress and stern expression has become an archetypal image of the sixteenth-century Spanish nobleman.

See p.268 for details on visiting the city of Toledo.

Nearby, in Room 63a, is a fine collection of imperious portraits of Felipe II's family by **Alonso Sánchez Coello**

(1531–88). Among them is a portrait of *El Príncipe Don Carlos*, the half-mad son of Felipe II's first marriage who died mysteriously in prison in 1568.

Upstairs on the first floor (rooms 12, 14, 15, 15a and 16), you confront the greatest painter of Habsburg Spain, **Diego Velázquez** (1599–1660). Born in Seville, Velázquez became court painter to Felipe IV, whose family is represented in many of the works. "I have found my Titian," Felipe is said to have remarked of the artist's appointment. Velázquez's masterpiece, **Las Meninas** (The Maids of Honour, 1656), is given pride of place in the large central gallery in Room 12. Manet remarked of it, "After this I don't know why the rest of us paint"; the French poet Théophile Gautier asked, "But where is the picture?" because it seemed to him a continuation of the room; while the Italian painter, Luca Giordano, identified it as "the Theology of Painting". The work captures a moment in the artist's study, featuring the artist himself, the Infanta Margarita, the court dwarfs, ladies-in-waiting, a butler, the palace marshal watching from the stairs at the back, and Felipe IV and his wife Mariana of Austria standing in the viewer's footsteps and reflected in the mirror on the wall. Velázquez's superlative brushwork and his mastery of colour, light and perspective mark the painting out as one of the all-time great works of art.

The painter's other canvases also merit attention. With the aid of light and loose brush strokes in *Las Hilanderas* (The Tapestry-Weavers), Velázquez again plays with simultaneous action in the foreground and background, depicting the story of Minerva, the goddess of the arts, challenging Arachne to see who can weave the most beautiful tapestry. In the foreground, yarns are being prepared for the weaving of the tapestries, while in the background, Minerva is preparing to turn Arachne into a spider for producing a work of superior quality to her own. Velázquez's

SPANISH PAINTING

portraits of Felipe IV are sympathetic and intimate representations of the monarch, with his childlike features and tired eyes, while that of the dwarf, *Don Sebastián de Morra*, focuses on his morose, pensive expression. Further magnificent works include *Christ Crucified*, with his bowed head and shimmering halo; *Los Borrachos* (The Drunkards), a clever corruption of which can be seen in the *Los Gabrieles* bar (see p.170); *Vulcan's Forge* and *The Surrender of Breda*. In fact, almost all of the fifty works on display (around half of the artist's surviving output) warrant close attention. Note also the two small panels of the *Villa Medici*, painted in Rome in 1650, in virtually Impressionist style.

In the newly refurbished adjacent rooms are examples of just about every significant Spanish painter of the seventeenth century, including many of the finest works of **Francisco Zurbarán** (1598–1664), **Bartolomé Esteban Murillo** (1618–82), **Alonso Cano** (1601–67) and **Juan Carreño** (1614–85). Murillo's soft, vaporous, almost mystical style is seen to best effect in *The Immaculate Conception of Soult* and *The Good Shepherd*. Look out for Carreño's portrait, rendered with terrible realism, of the last Habsburg monarch, the mentally retarded *Carlos II*, a product of chronic inbreeding. The contemporary obsession for the bizarre is also amply illustrated in Carreño's pair of paintings of the grossly overweight *La Monstrua Vestida* and *La Monstrua Desnuda*, forming an interesting contrast with Goya's *Majas* displayed upstairs. Here, too, are the Prado's holdings of **José Ribera** (1591–1652), who worked firstly in Rome, where he was influenced by Caravaggio, and then in Naples, where local fishermen and beggars acted as models for many of his works. His masterpieces are considered to be the dark, realist portrait of *Saint Andrew* and *The Martyrdom of St Philip*, where the artist uses light and shade to dramatic effect, highlighting the naked body of Philip who is being prepared for his ordeal of being skinned alive.

Goya

The final suite of Spanish rooms (32–39 and 85–94) which spans the first and second floor at the Puerta de Murillo-end of the building, provides an awesome and fabulously complete overview of the works of **Francisco de Goya** (1746–1828), the largest and most valuable collection of his works in the world, with some 140 paintings and 500 drawings and engravings. Goya was the greatest painter of Bourbon Spain and a chronicler of contemporary Spanish life, an artist whom many see as the inspiration and forerunner of Impressionism and modern art.

After an apprenticeship in Zaragoza, Goya studied in Italy in 1770–71, returning to Spain to draw cartoons for the Royal Tapestry Workshop, and later, in 1789, becoming court painter to Carlos IV. Illness in 1792 made him deaf and from then on his paintings became more intense, introverted and stylized. He left for France in 1824 and died there four years later.

Goya was an enormously versatile artist: contrast the voluptuous *Maja Vestida* and *Maja Desnuda* (The Clothed and Naked Belles) with the horrors depicted in *Dos de Mayo* and *Tres de Mayo* (on-the-spot portrayals of the rebellion against Napoleon in the streets of Madrid and the subsequent reprisals). Then again, there are the series of pastoral cartoons – designs for tapestries – and the extraordinary Black Paintings, a series of murals painted by the deaf and embittered painter in his old age. His many portraits of his patron, Carlos IV, are remarkable for their lack of any attempt at flattery, while those of Queen María Luisa, whom he despised, are downright ugly.

The **tapestry cartoons** (rooms 85–94) include a series dedicated to the seasons of the year; others feature toothless, starving peasants, dainty playful aristocrats, mischievous boys and a hunchback bridegroom. Most are produced in clearly separated pastel colours to help the weavers and are set against the Madrid landscape. The two **Majas** (Room 89) were painted at different times – the brushwork used in each of the paintings is quite different – and may have formed part of a game whereby the clothed figure was placed over the naked one. *The Family of Carlos IV*, hanging in the octagonal Room 32 alongside preliminary studies for the painting, provides a rather sardonic commentary on Goya's patron: the domineering María Luisa is clearly in charge, while the well-fed Carlos is pictured staring into space. In a clear tribute to Velázquez, Goya places himself staring out at the viewer from the left-hand corner. The two canvases portraying the events of the **Second and Third of May, 1808** (Room 39), and painted six years later, have immortalized the heroic resistance to the Napoleonic invasion of Spain, and also allowed Goya to reaffirm his somewhat compromised patriotic credentials, having worked for Joseph Bonaparte. Both works are incredibly powerful condemnations of the violence. *The Colossus* or *Panic* is also said to refer to the upheavals inflicted by the Napoleonic invasion, some claiming that the giant figure represents Napoleon wreaking havoc on Spain, while others claim it symbolizes Spain rising against her oppressor. The disillusioned *Self Portrait* in Room 89 bears a passing resemblance to that other famous deaf artist, Beethoven, with his deeply troubled demeanour and penetrating eyes seeking to make sense of the world around him.

The Black Paintings (1819–23) now displayed in the suitably gloomy rooms 36–38, were originally painted straight on to the wall of Goya's house, known as "*Quinta del Sordo*" (The Deaf Man's Villa), beside the Manzanares. The works were transferred to canvas in 1873 and donated to the Prado in 1881; they were given titles after Goya's death by people who had known him. The thoroughly disconcerting canvases are often hard to penetrate, but both

The History of the Royal Collection

The Paseo del Prado originally ran along the edge of the city by the *prado* ("meadow") of San Jerónimo. During the reign of Carlos III, plans were made to develop the area as a showcase for scientific knowledge, embodying the ideas of the Enlightenment. A botanical garden, observatory and natural history museum were to be sited here. The latter was to be housed in the Prado building, begun in 1785 and designed by Juan de Villanueva in matchless Neoclassical style. Work continued until 1808, when, during the Napoleonic invasion, it was ransacked by the French, who used it as a barracks and stables. The building was restored by Fernando VII, who decided to move the royal painting collection here. It was opened in 1819, becoming the property of the state in 1868. The collection's holdings were greatly enlarged by the incorporation of the Museo Nacional de la Trinidad, which contained works confiscated from dissolved ecclesiastical properties. During the Civil War, over 350 paintings were taken first to Valencia and then to Geneva under the protection of the League of Nations, but were returned at the beginning of World War II. Once democracy was restored after the death of Franco, the museum became home to the Picasso legacy, including *Guernica* (now in the Reina Sofía).

The nucleus of the Prado collection, however, is made up of paintings from the **Spanish royal family**, many of whom were enthusiastic collectors and dedicated patrons of the fine arts. Consequently the, at times rather eccentric, collection is best viewed as a faithful reflection of the changing tastes of the Spanish monarchs. Carlos V's favourite painter was Titian, and his son, Felipe II, continued to acquire his works, but also showed a penchant for Hieronymus Bosch. Felipe III favoured Rubens and Felipe IV Velázquez, while one of the few redeeming features of Carlos IV's reign was his patronage of Goya.

their style and their ability to shock the viewer mark Goya out as an artist well ahead of his time. They also provide a vivid image of an isolated, bitter and seriously ill old man living out his last years in a world of anguished silence. *Saturn Devouring One of his Sons* symbolizes the destruction of everything by time; *The Cudgel Fight* illustrates a fight to the death by two men; others feature ghoulish skull-like faces, witches and devils and a half-submerged dog.

ITALIAN PAINTING

The Prado's early **Italian galleries** (on the ground floor) are distinguished principally by **Fra Angelico**'s (1387–1455) devout and mystical *Annunciation* (c.1445) which originally hung in the Monasterio de Las Descalzas (see p.36), and by a trio of panels by **Botticelli** (1444–1510). The latter illustrate a story from the *Decameron* about the strange vision experienced by a young man who has been rejected by his lover. In his vision he sees a woman hunted by hounds and caught by a nobleman who tears her heart out and feeds it to his dogs; when the young man shows the prophetic vision to his disdainful lover she changes her mind and agrees to marry him. The wedding is shown in a fourth panel which is in a private collection in the US.

With the sixteenth-century Renaissance, and especially its Venetian exponents, the collection really comes into its own. The Prado is said to have the most complete collection of Titian and painters from the Venice school in any single museum. There are major works by **Raphael** (1483–1520), including a fabulous *Portrait of a Cardinal*, and masterpieces by **Tintoretto** (1518–94), including the beautifully composed *Lavatorio*, bought by Felipe IV when Charles I of England was beheaded and his art collection was auctioned off. **Veronese** (1528–88) and **Caravaggio** (1573–1610) are also represented. The most important group of works, however, is by **Titian** (1487–1576) and include portraits of the Spanish emperors, *Carlos V* and *Felipe II*. The magnificent equestrian portrait, *The Emperor Carlos V at Mühlberg,* depicts his triumph in 1547 over the Protestant armies of Germany, with Carlos resplendent in his armour – the suit is preserved in the Palacio Real – astride a huge black charger. Ironically, however, by the time Titian painted his subject some years later, he could hardly sit on a horse because of his gout. The collection also features a famous, and much-reproduced piece of erotica, *Venus, Cupid and the Organist* (two versions are displayed here), a painting originally owned by a bishop.

FLEMISH, DUTCH AND GERMAN PAINTING

The biggest name in the extremely rich early **Flemish** collection (rooms 55–58A) is **Hieronymus Bosch** (1450–1516), known in Spain as "El Bosco". The Prado has several of his greatest triptychs. The early-period *Hay Wain* features fish-headed monsters devouring humans. The middle-period *Garden of Earthly Delights* begins on the left with the Creation of Man, then in the centre, worldly pleasures and sins and, finally, Hell on the right; fantasy animals, sexual imagery and satanic visions abound. These and the late *Adoration of the Magi* are all familiar from countless reproductions, but infinitely more chilling in the original. Bosch's hallucinatory genius for the macabre is at its most extreme in these triptychs, but is reflected here in many more of his works, including three versions of *The Temptations of Saint Anthony* (though only the smallest of these is definitely an original). Don't miss the amazing table-top of *The Seven Deadly Sins*, showing devils, roasting, spanking and tormenting peasants, while ghostly skeletons creep around in the background. The Latin inscription reads "Beware, beware, God sees you."

FLEMISH, DUTCH AND GERMAN PAINTING

Bosch's visions find an echo in the works of **Pieter Brueghel the Elder** (1525–69), whose *Triumph of Death* must be one of the most frightening canvases ever painted. Death is pictured triumphing over all earthly things: riding on a wizened horse hauling cartloads of skulls, driving humanity against an army of skeletons shielded with coffin lids, dragging bloated bodies from the water, and preparing to slice off the head of a wretched figure on a hill. The grim unrelenting image is emphasized by the use of dark shades of brown and black and by the burning smoke in the background.

Another elusive painter, **Joachim Patinir** (1480–1524), precursor of landscape painting, is represented by four of his finest works, including the dream-like blue-green toned *Crossing the Styx Lake*. From an earlier generation, **Roger van der Weyden**'s (1400–1464) dramatic *Deposition* is outstanding, its monumental forms making a fascinating contrast with his miniature-like *Pietà*. There are also important works by Memling, Bouts, Gerard David and Massys, as well as a dramatic series of panels by Van der Stockt. The outstanding portraiture work of **Mor**, or "**Antonio Moro**" (1519–1567) as he was known when he worked in the Spanish court, is displayed amongst the royal portraits on the ground floor in rooms 55 and 55b, and includes his fine representation of the haughty gaze of *Mary Tudor*.

The collection of more than 160 works of **later Flemish and Dutch** art has been imaginatively rehoused in a new suite of twelve rooms on the first floor (rooms 7–11). Grouped by themes, such as religion, daily life, mythology, and landscape, the rooms have been tastefully decorated, while many of the paintings have been given a new lease of life by their restoration to their startling original colours.

Rubens (1577–1640) is extensively represented, though he supervised rather than executed the series of eighteen mythological subjects designed for Felipe IV's hunting lodge in El Pardo. The gruesome horror of his *Saturn*

Devouring a Child clearly influenced Goya, whose version can be seen with the Black Paintings. Typically, there is plenty of pearly white female flesh set amongst sensual landscapes in works such as *Nymphs and Satyrs* and the beautifully restored *Three Graces*.

There is, too, a fine collection of works by his contemporaries, for example **Van Dyck**'s dramatic *Piedad* and magnificent portrait of himself and Sir Endymion Porter. The minute detail of **Jan Brueghel**'s representations of the five senses and **David Teniers**' scenes of peasant lowlife also merit a closer look. For political reasons, Spanish monarchs collected few works painted in seventeenth-century Protestant Holland; an early **Rembrandt**, *Artemisia*, in which the artist's pregnant wife served as the model is, however, a notable exception.

The **German room** (54) on the ground floor is dominated by **Dürer** (1471–1528) and **Lucas Cranach the Elder** (1472–1553). Dürer's magnificent *Adam and Eve* was saved from destruction at the hands of the prudish Carlos III only by the intervention of his court painter, Mengs. The most interesting of Cranach's works are a pair of paintings depicting Carlos V hunting with Ferdinand I of Austria. The work of **Anton Raphael Mengs** (1728–79), who worked on the ceilings of the Royal Palace and directed the Royal Tapestry Factory, is to be found in the European galleries on the second floor. His portraits of the royal family are meticulous in their detail and possess an almost photographic quality.

FRENCH AND BRITISH PAINTING

Most of the **French** work held by the Prado is from the seventeenth and eighteenth centuries (rooms 76–84 on the second floor). Royal marriages and the establishment of the Bourbon royal house helped establish closer links between the two countries, although a large part of the collection was lost in the Peninsular War. Among the outstanding painters represented is **Nicolas Poussin** (1594–1665), with his classical Baroque style and intense colours shown to best effect in *Triumph of David*, *Bacchanal*, *Landscape with St Jerome* and *Parnassus*. The romantic landscapes and sunsets of **Claude Lorraine** (1600–82) are well represented by *The Port of Ostia with the Embarcation of Santa Paula Romana* and *Landscape with Tobias and the Archangel Raphael*. Look out, too, for the outrageously imperious portrait of Louis XIV by **Hyacinthe Rigaud** (1659–1743).

British painting is poorly represented, as a result of hostile relations between the Spanish and English from the sixteenth to the nineteenth centuries. There are, however, some examples of the aristocratic portraiture of Joshua Reynolds (1723–92), Thomas Gainsborough (1727–88) and Thomas Lawrence (1769–1830) in Room 83.

SCULPTURE AND THE DAUPHIN'S TREASURE

Various pieces of **sculpture**, from the classical era to the nineteenth century, are grouped around the entrance halls and scattered throughout the museum. The classical work is well preserved, and the marble representations of gods, goddesses and emperors are undeniably impressive. There's an interesting selection of busts of Carlos V and Felipe II by **Leone Leoni** and his son **Pompeo Leoni**. One of their most arresting works is a statue of *The Emperor Carlos V Subduing Rage* (Room 1), from which the emperor's armour can be removed to reveal his nude figure.

The basement houses a display of part of the **collection of jewels** that belonged to the Grand Dauphin Louis, son of Louis XIV and father of Felipe V, Spain's first Bourbon king. The collection features goblets, cups, trays, glasses and other pieces richly decorated with rubies, emeralds, diamonds, lapis lazuli and other precious stones. The collection was taken back to France during the Napoleonic invasion, but returned to Spain in 1815. One of the highlights is the onyx saltcellar with a gold mermaid, adorned with rubies.

CASÓN DEL BUEN RETIRO

Admission is included in the entrance ticket to the Museo del Prado.

Just east of the Prado is the **Casón del Buen Retiro** (currently closed for restoration) which used to be a dance hall for the palace of Felipe IV, but is now devoted to **nineteenth-century Spanish art**, in which Neoclassical, romantic and historical themes dominate. The Realist work of **Eduardo Rosales** in the melodramatic deathbed scene of *Queen Isabella's Will* and **Francisco Pradilla** in *Doña Juana la Loca* (Joanna the Mad) are perfect examples of this style. The latter depicts Carlos V's grief-stricken mother, Joanna, accompanying her dead husband's coffin on the long march from Burgos to Granada. **José de Madrazo Agudo**'s (1781–1859) *The Death of Viriato* is a characteristic epic piece; **Vicente López**'s portrait of the ageing *Goya* is certainly worth a look for its impressive depiction of the old master, looking rather disapproving, as is the luminescent Impressionist work *Children at the Beach* by **Joaquín Sorolla** (1863–1923; see p.111 for the Museo Sorolla).

Museo Thyssen-Bornemisza

O nly a step away from the Prado is another exceptional museum, the **Museo Thyssen-Bornemisza**, an ideal complement to the former establishment, as the Thyssen tends to excel in the areas that the Prado is particularly deficient in. The Thyssen collection houses important German Renaissance works, seventeenth-century Dutch painting, Impressionist, German Expressionist and Russian Constructivist art, Abstract and Pop Art. Although both museums are essentially personal – the Prado reflecting the tastes of the Spanish monarchy and the Thyssen those of the present baron and his father – the Thyssen also provides an unprecedented excursion through the history of Western art from the fourteenth to the late-twentieth century.

The Museo Thyssen-Bornemisza (Map 6, F4) is open Tuesday–Sunday 10am–7pm; permanent collection 700ptas, concessions 400ptas, under-12s free; temporary exhibitions 500ptas, concessions 300ptas. Metro Banco de España.

The Thyssen collection, whose eight hundred-odd paintings many would argue is the world's greatest private art trove after that of the British royals, was begun in the 1920s by German-Hungarian industrial magnate **Baron Heinrich Thyssen-Bornemisza**. On his death in 1947, the works were distributed amongst his heirs. The present baron, Hans Heinrich, tried to reunite the collection by buying back the paintings and later expanding it with the purchase of additional old masters and modern art. As his own Villa Favorita in Lugano in Switzerland could only accommodate about three hundred pictures, the baron sought a new home for his collection. Despite stiff competition from other suitors, including Prince Charles, the Swiss and German governments, and the Getty Foundation, Spain managed to secure the display of the collection for a knock-down $350m (£230m) in June 1993. The museum itself operates as a private institution, administered by the Thyssen Foundation, and proceeds from the entrance fees of the 700,000 visitors each year are ploughed back into the running of the museum.

The museum occupies the mid-eighteenth-century Neoclassical **Palacio de Villahermosa**, diagonally opposite the Prado, at the end of the Carrera de San Jerónimo. The building was brilliantly remodelled by architect Rafael Moneo, who redistributed the rooms and changed the ceilings in order to make the most of the natural light available. Without a doubt, the availability of this prestigious site played a large part in Spain's acquisition. Another trump card was Baron Thyssen's current (fifth) wife, "Tita" Cervera, a former Miss Spain, once married to Tarzan actor Lex Barker, who steered the works towards Spain. A kitsch portrait of Tita in fairy-like winged dress hangs in the great hall of the museum, alongside her husband, plus King Juan Carlos and Queen Sofía. Tita in fact has her own collection of some eight hundred works of art, and plans are afoot to extend the museum into the nearby buildings in order to accommodate some of them. The basement houses a handy, good-value **café/restaurant** which can be entered separately from the museum, and there's also a temporary exhibition space down here which has staged a number of interesting and highly successful shows, including recent ones on El Greco, Sorolla and August Macke. The museum **shop** sells an informative and well-illustrated guide (1800ptas), as well as the first instalments of the fifteen-volume catalogue of the baron's collection. It also has a good selection of postcards and children's art books. Re-entry to the museum is allowed as long as you get your hand stamped at the exit desk.

EUROPEAN OLD MASTERS: SECOND FLOOR

Cross to the far side of the building and take a lift or the stairs to the second floor and you'll find yourself at the chronological beginning of the museum's collections: European painting and some sculpture from the fourteenth to eighteenth centuries. The core of these collections was accumulated in the 1920s and 1930s by the present baron's father, Heinrich, who was a friend of the art critics Bernard Berenson and Max Friedländer.

Heinrich was clearly well advised. The early paintings include incredibly good, rare devotional panels by the Siennese painter **Duccio di Buoninsegna** and the Flemish artists **Jan van Eyck** and **Roger van der Weyden**. In rooms 1 and 2 the pilgrimage through the history of Western art begins with a fine exhibition of the evolving styles that prefigured the Renaissance. The development of spatial depth, inclusion of gestures and the increasing repertoire of artistic skills can be seen in the differences between the Master of Magdalen's *Madonna and Child* and Duccio's *Christ and the Samaritan Woman*, both painted in the first half of the fourteenth century. The International Gothic style is well represented by Johann Koerbecke's expressive and emotional *Assumption of the Virgin* (1457) and the eight panels dedicated to the four evangelists by Gabriel Maelesskircher (1478). In Room 3 **Jan van Eyck**'s highly original and remarkable *Annunciation Diptych* (c.1434–1441), in which he depicts the Angel, Virgin and Holy Spirit, draws the eye, as does Petrus Christus' *Our Lady of the Tree* (c.1450), where the Virgin is shown as a flowering shoot bringing life to the dry tree. One of the highlights in the room dedicated to the Italian Quattrocento is the haunting, translucent *Resurrected Christ* by **Bramintino** (c.1465–1530).

Moving on to Room 5, you come to a fabulous array of Early Renaissance portraits, showing a change from the portrayal of the supernatural to more worldly matters. **Ghirlandaio**'s *Portrait of Giovanna Tornabuoni* (1488) captures the serene beauty of the subject, the Latin epigram in the painting stating, "If the artist had been able to portray the character and moral qualities there would not be a more beautiful painting in the world." **Hans Holbein**'s portrait of the self-confident *Henry VIII*, the only one of many variants in existence which is definitely genuine, is accompanied by the austere, melancholic *Spanish Infanta* by **Juan de Flandes**, which may represent the first of Henry VIII's wives, Catherine of Aragón. The technical advancement in the art of portraiture and the beginnings of real characterization are seen to good effect in the *Portrait of a Stout Man* by Robert Campin (c.1425). Among the sixteenth-century Italian paintings, **Raphael**'s delicate and subtly coloured *Portrait of a Young Man* and **Titian**'s *Portrait of the Doge Francesco Vernier* stand out, while the *Young Knight* by **Carpaccio** (Room 7), with its symbolic plants and animals and various allegorical figures, is one of the earliest known full-length portraits. Beyond these, a collection of **Dürers** and **Cranachs** rivals that in the Prado, and includes Dürer's *Jesus Among the Doctors*, showing an effeminate-looking Christ hounded by decrepit old men. As you progress through this extraordinary panoply, display cases along the corridor contain scarcely less spectacular works of sculpture, ceramics and gold- and silverwork.

Next in line, in Room 11, is **Titian**, ushering in a stylistic revolution with his greater range of tones and almost Impressionistic brushwork, as evidenced in his masterpiece *St Jerome in the Wilderness*. The influence of Titian can be seen in the work of **Tintoretto** – his massive canvas of *Paradise* is exhibited in the central gallery on the ground floor – and in *The Annunciation* by **El Greco**, in which Mannerist influence is also apparent. In the same room, the anonymous *Last Supper* (previously attributed to El Greco), portrays a highly irreverent version of events, with a drunken apostle, dogs and cats greedily eyeing up the food and Christ being virtually ignored by all those present.

The Early Baroque fascination with light and shade is brilliantly demonstrated by **Caravaggio**'s *St Catherine of Alexandria* and by **José Ribera**'s *Lamentation over the Body of Christ*, in which the ghostly white body of Christ and the grieving faces are highlighted. The **Bernini** sculpture of *St Sebastian* heralds the more exuberant later Baroque work exemplified by **Murillo**'s *Madonna and Child with St Rosalina of Palermo*. **Claude Lorrain**'s *Pastoral Landscape with the flight into Egypt* is a characteristic romantic twilight landscape, full of nostalgia for the classical world, while **Tiepolo**'s *Death of Hyacinthus* uses monumental figures and rich colours to capture the drama of the moment. Catering to the eighteenth-century interest in architectural scenes and the demand for souvenirs of the Grand Tour of Italy, **Canaletto** is represented by three flawless views of Venice. The floor is completed with more classics, this time Flemish and Dutch. The richly coloured small oil of *Christ in the*

Storm on the Sea of Galilee by **Jan Brueghel the Elder**, **Van Dyck**'s marvellous portrait of the disdainful *Jacques Le Roy* and **Ruben**'s luxurious *Toilet of Venus* are amongst the highlights.

AMERICANS, IMPRESSIONISTS AND EXPRESSIONISTS: FIRST FLOOR

The collections on the first floor were largely brought together by the present baron, Hans Heinrich Thyssen, who began collecting, according to his own account, to fill the gaps in his late father's collection, after it was split among his siblings. He, too, began with old masters, but in the 1960s branched out into German Expressionists, closely followed by Cubists, Futurists, Vorticists and also American art of the nineteenth century.

The floor begins with a comprehensive round of seventeenth-century Dutch painting of various genres: still lifes, scenes from everyday life, landscapes and seascapes. Supreme technical skill and minute observation is demonstrated in still lifes such as **Willem Claesz Heda**'s *Rummer, Silver Tazza, Pie and Other Objects*, while **Frans Hals** introduces more lively subjects with his *Family Group in a Landscape* and his laughing *Fisherman Playing a Violin*. The characteristic Dutch landscape features in a number of pictures, including *View of Naarden* by **Jacob Isaacksz van Ruisdael**, where alternating patches of sunlight and shade are used to give the impression of depth. The British eighteenth-century painters **Thomas Gainsborough** and **Sir Joshua Reynolds** also get a look in with their contrasting portraits of English aristocrats.

In rooms 29 and 30 is displayed one of the largest and best collections of American painting outside the US. The theme of landscape seen to good effect in **Thomas Cole**'s

Expulsion, Moon and Firelight predominates, reflecting the nineteenth-century vision of America as an idyllic virgin land awaiting the settlement of the pioneers. The native population only feature as nostalgic stereotypes in the later paintings, such as Frederick Remington's *Apache Fire Signal* and George Catlin's *Falls of Saint Anthony*. Works by James Whistler, Winslow Homer and John Singer Sargent are displayed, as is James Goodwyn Clonney's wonderful *Fishing Party on Long Island Sound*.

This is followed by a group of European **Romantics and Realists**, including Constable's *The Lock*, bought not so long ago for $14m; **Goya**'s *Asensio Julia* and his *El Tío Paquete* from his Black Paintings (see p.64 for more on this).

Impressionism and **post-Impressionism** are also strong points of the collection, with works by **Manet**, **Monet**, **Renoir**, **Gauguin**, **Degas**, **Lautrec** and **Cézanne** (Room 33). Monet and Pissarro indulge in some marvellous experimentation with light and reflections in their respective works, *The Thaw at Vétheuil* and *Saint-Honoré Street in the Afternoon. Effect of Rain*. The shimmering green dress of the *Swaying Dancer* and the pastel shades of the jockey's colours in *Race Horses – The Training*, both by Degas, are a real treat. The pioneering *Portrait of a Farmer* by Paul Cézanne foreshadows the Cubism of Braque and Picasso, seen on the ground floor, and marks him out as one of the most influential of this group of painters. The collection is especially strong on paintings by **Vincent van Gogh**, which includes the fiery *Stevedores at Arles* and one of his last and most gorgeous works, *Les Vessenots*. The influence of van Gogh is apparent in the work of the Fauvists, particularly *Waterloo Bridge* by André Derain and *Olive Trees* by Maurice Vlaminck.

The broad-ranging **Expressionist movement**, with its enunciation of powerful emotions and use of equally powerful colours, is fully represented. The stunningly vivid paintings of **Ernst Ludwig Kirchner**, **Wassily Kandinsky**, **Emile Nolde** and **Franz Marc** are fascinating, as is the apocalyptic work, *Metropolis,* by **George Grosz**.

AVANT-GARDES: GROUND FLOOR

Works on the ground floor run from the beginning of the twentieth century through to around 1970. The good baron doesn't, apparently, like contemporary art: "If they can throw colours, I can be free to duck," he explained, following the gallery's opening. The most interesting work in his "experimental avant-garde" sections is from the **Cubists**. There is an inspired, side-by-side hanging of parallel studies by **Picasso** (*Man with a Clarinet*), **Braque** (*Woman with a Mandolin*) and **Mondrian** (*Grey–Blue Composition*). Picasso's range is fully demonstrated by the inclusion of the classical *Harlequin with a Mirror* next to the more abstract *Bullfight*.

The **Synthesis of Modernity** section includes the minimalist work *Catalan Peasant with a Guitar* by **Joan Miró**, the chaotic *Brown and Silver* by **Jackson Pollock**, and the explosive *Picture with Three Spots* by **Wassily Kandinsky**. There are also some superbly vivid canvases by **Max Ernst** and **Marc Chagall**. Surrealism is, not surprisingly, represented by **Salvador Dalí** with his *Dream caused by the Flight of a Bee Around a Pomegranate a Second before Awakening*, in which the artist's wife is depicted sleeping naked in the centre of a fantastic landscape populated by dream images of elephants on stilts and tiger-eating fish. Following on in the Surrealist tradition is **Francis Bacon**'s painfully distorted image *Portrait of George Dyer in a Mirror*. More down to earth are the stark *Hotel Room* by **Edward Hopper** and the cartoon iconography of **Roy Lichtenstein**'s *A Woman in A Bath*. Sharing the same room is a fascinating **Lucian Freud**, *Portrait of Baron Thyssen*, in which the baron is depicted standing in front of Watteau's *Pierrot*, hanging upstairs. To finish, there is a clever play on light and reflections in Richard Estes' *Telephone Booths*, while downstairs by the café is the series of five extensive flowing, colourful canvases that make up *The Blinding Exile* cycle by Roberto Matta.

Centro de Arte Reina Sofía

The final essential stop on the Madrid art circuit (or *Paseo del Arte*) is the **Centro de Arte Reina Sofía**, an immense exhibition space covering some 12,505 square metres and providing a permanent home for the Spanish collection of contemporary art, acquisitions of modern art, the twentieth-century collections from the Prado, and Miró and Picasso legacies including the jewel in the crown of the museum's collection – **Guernica**.

The Centro de Arte Reina Sofía (Map 5, I5) is open Monday & Wednesday–Saturday 10am–9pm, Sunday 10am–2.30pm; 500ptas, concessions 250ptas, free on Saturday after 2.30pm & all day Sunday. Metro Atocha.

The museum is housed in a vast building that was once the Hospital General de San Carlos. Constructed on the initiative of Carlos III and designed by Francesco Sabatini, the hospital was initially envisaged as a gargantuan complex of seven quadrangles, of which this was the only one ever actually completed. It ceased functioning as a hospital in

1965, twelve years later it was declared a monument of historical and artistic interest, and work began on transforming it into a museum of modern art. The initial conversion took until 1986, when Queen Sofía opened the space for staging temporary exhibitions. It was not until 1990 that the final renovation work was completed and it was opened as a museum with a permanent collection, and in July 1992, *Guernica* was brought here from the Casón del Buen Retiro.

Although it's rather sombre-looking from the outside, inside, the light from the central courtyard, the white walls, vast galleries and high ceilings create a sensation of spaciousness ideally suited to the display of so many large-scale works. Transparent lifts designed by British architect, Ian Ritchie, shuttle visitors up the outside of the building. As well as its collection of twentieth-century art on the second and fourth floors, the museum has a **cinema**, excellent art book and design **shops**, a print, music and photographic **library**, a **restaurant**, **bar** and **café** in the basement and a peaceful inner courtyard garden, as well as temporary exhibition halls on the first and third floors. An informative and well-illustrated catalogue is available from the shop, priced 1295ptas. At the second-floor entrance, there are audioguide headphones in English, which give a good introduction to Spanish art.

....

The museum keeps different opening hours and days from its neighbours and is one of the few museums open on Monday, so don't make the mistake of trying to cram in a visit after a Prado–Thyssen overdose.

....

THE SECOND FLOOR

The permanent collection traces the development of artistic movements in the twentieth century from the perspective of Spanish art, whilst at the same time providing an international context through the display of key works by foreign artists. Although the collection is a little erratic in its coverage of some of the major artists and developments, through it you can really appreciate how the artists interreacted, cooperated, competed and responded to each other's work. The collection begins on the second floor with a selection of work entitled "A Change of Century", examining the origins of modern Spanish art mainly through the two artistic nucleii that developed in Cataluña and the Basque Country at the end of the nineteenth century.

Picasso's *Mujer en Azul* (1901), a study of a bourgeois woman in all her finery, with piercing eyes and over-the-top make-up, is one of the early highlights, painted during one of the artist's brief stays in Madrid at the beginning of the twentieth-century and given an honorary mention at the National Exhibition of Fine Arts in 1901. Picasso failed to reclaim it and it was mislaid for a number of years before being rescued. Look out too for the luscious *Retrato de Sonia de Klamery* (1913) by Anglada Camarasa and the vivid Expressionist work *La Comulgante* (1914) by María Blanchard. Impressionist influences are clear in the work of the landscape artists Santiago Rusiñol and Joaquín Mir, while Francisco Iturrino's pleasant pastel *Jardin de Málaga* (1916) owes much to Fauvism. There is a room dedicated to the Madrid painter, **José Gutiérrez Solana**, whose highly idiosyncratic work reflects his obsession with death. Works include the solemn *La Visita del Obispo* (1926), the melancholic *La Procesión de la Muerte* (1930) and his famous portrayal of *La Tertulia del Café de Pombo* (1920), which features a range of leading Spanish artistic and literary figures including Solana himself on the far right.

Sculpture is well represented, with the Cubist-influenced ironwork of Julio González and the innovative studies by Pablo Gargallo, such as the mysterious *Máscara de*

Greta Garbo con Mechón (1930), the semi-religious semi-dictatorial figure of *El Gran Profeta* (1933), and the plump-faced head of *Picasso* (1913). This is followed by strong sections on Cubism, including fine work by **Juan Gris**, notably his *Retrato de Josette* (1916), and a masterly still life, *Los Pájaros Muertos* (1912), by fellow Parisian resident Picasso. The early Cézanne-influenced *Paisaje de Cadaqués* (1923) by Salvador Dalí features amongst other works of the Paris School.

Midway round the collection is Reina Sofía's main draw – **Picasso's Guernica** (see box p.86). Superbly displayed and no longer protected by bullet-proof glass and steel girders, this icon of twentieth-century Spanish art and politics carries a shock that defies all familiarity. The sheer size of the monumental work at 3.5m high and over 7.5m long is the first thing that impresses. The preliminary studies, displayed around the room, deserve equal attention as they show how Picasso developed its symbols – the dying horse, the fallen soldier, the mother and dead child, the bulls, the blacked-out dove, the grief-stricken woman, the sun, the flower, the burning figure plummeting to its death – making their incorporation into the painting all the more marvellous. Picasso's notorious reluctance to talk about the painting has led to decades of debate by art historians about its exact meaning. Common interpretations view the screaming horse as symbolizing the suffering of the people and the bull the overthrow of reason and the rise of animal passion. Whatever the arguments, this disturbing monumental work certainly lives up to expectations.

The post-*Guernica* halls feature rooms devoted to the heavyweights **Dalí** and **Miró**, as well as a host of lesser-known Spanish artists representing the main currents in Spanish art in the 1920s and 1930s. The development in Dalí's work and his variety of technique are clearly displayed in the classic portrait of his sister gazing out of the window, *Muchacha en la Ventana* (1925), the Cubist-influenced *Arlequín* (1925), and his more famous Surrealist work such as *El Gran Masturbador* and *El Enigma de Hitler* replete with dream landscapes, sexual imagery, insects and symbols of putrefaction. A large range of Miró's rather impenetrable but pleasing canvases and sculptures are exhibited with their characteristic images of dots, spots and crescents symbolizing the stars, sun, moon, birds and people.

Among the work of the **lesser-known Spanish artists** is a fine series of contrasting nudes by Aurelino Arteta, José de Togores and Roberto Fernández Balbuena. Angeles Santos's portrayal of four women in languid conversation in *Tertulia* (1929) and Alfonso Ponce de León's semi-comic *Accidente* (1936) also stand out. The final room on the second floor is used for rotating exhibitions of work from the museum's holdings.

THE FOURTH FLOOR

The permanent collection continues on the fourth floor, covering Spain's postwar years up to the present day and including Spanish and international examples of abstract and avant-garde movements such as **Pop Art**, **Constructivism** and **Minimalism**. Spanish artist José Guerrero adds a touch of Mediterranean colour to *Composición* (1956), a work which reflects his close connections with the leading figures of Abstract Expressionism, Rothko and Pollock. Antonio Saura's *Grito Nº 7* (1959) is an altogether more forbidding piece, with blacks, whites and greys combining to create a disturbing image of pain and desperation. There are some striking pieces by abstract sculptor, **Eduardo Chillida** and by Catalan surrealist painter **Antoni Tàpies**. Spanish-style Pop Art is represented by the Valencian group Equipo Crónica, whose *Pintar es como golpear* (1972) is one of their most memorable pieces.

The story of Guernica

When the **Spanish Civil War** broke out in July 1936, Picasso was living in France, continuing his rather hedonistic lifestyle detached from politics and public life, although he did accept the honorary post of Director of the Prado in support of the Popular Front government. Then in January 1937, he accepted a commission to paint a mural for the Spanish Republic's pavilion at the **World Fair** in Paris on a subject of his own choosing. By April he had still not started the work, but on April 26, 1937, the German Condor Legion, acting in concert with Franco's Nationalist forces, bombed and machine-gunned the Basque town of **Guernica**, celebrated home of Basque "liberties" and cultural traditions. Defenceless and without obvious military significance, the town was bombarded for three hours by wave upon wave of German planes and was almost completely destroyed, although the sacred oak before which Spanish monarchs had sworn to observe local Basque rights since medieval times was miraculously preserved. Despite initial denials, the Nationalists later admitted responsibility for the atrocity, and Göring, head of the German Luftwaffe, revealed in a chilling statement made shortly before his suicide that Germany had regarded Guernica as a testing ground for **aerial bombing**. Photo-journalists captured the horror of the atrocity, which sent shockwaves around Europe. The war had forced many intellectuals, especially in France, to take sides on the issue of Fascism versus Democracy and the time for sitting on the fence for Picasso was over. He began working on the commission and amid rumours that he was pro-Franco issued the following statement : "The Spanish struggle is the fight of reaction against the people, against freedom. My whole life as an artist has been nothing more than a continuous struggle against reaction and the death of art. How could anyone think for a moment that I could be in agreement with reaction and death. In the panel on which I am working and which I shall call *Guernica* and in all my recent works of art I clearly express my abhorrence of the military caste which has sunk Spain in an ocean of pain and death."

The resulting canvas, produced in little over a month, relied on allegory and metaphor, combined with the legacy of Cubism to produce a general commentary on the barbarity and terror of war itself. The Right criticized the painting as the degenerate work of a madman, while many on the Left were disappointed because of its inaccessibility and its failure to make an explicit rallying call for the forces opposed to Fascism. However, it soon came to be recognized as a timeless masterpiece. Herbert Read commented when it was shown in London in 1938: "It is a monument to destruction, a cry of indignation and horror intensified by the spirit of genius. Not only Guernica, but Spain, not only Spain, but Europe are symbolized in this allegory." Shortly after, the work was "loaned" to the **Museum of Modern Art in New York**, until such time, as Picasso put it, Spain had regained its democratic liberty. The artist never lived to see that time, dying as he did two years before Franco in 1973, but in 1981, following the restoration of democracy, the painting was, amid much controversy, moved to Madrid to hang (as Picasso had stipulated) in the **Prado**. Its transfer to the Reina Sofía in 1992 again prompted much soul-searching and protest, though for anyone who saw it in the old Prado annexe, it looks truly liberated in its present setting. More recently there have been calls to relocate the painting to the newly opened Guggenheim Museum in Bilbao, which is in the same province as the town of Guernica. However, after close examination by art experts it has been declared too delicate and too damaged by previous moves to be transferred once again.

THE STORY OF GUERNICA

The highlight of the international avant-garde work has to be **Francis Bacon**'s marvellous *Figura Tumbada* (1966), featuring one of his characteristic angst-ridden figures reclining on a bed, while pieces by **Graham Sutherland** and **Henry Moore** provide further reference points.

If the avant-garde work all gets too much for you, there are also offerings from the Spanish Realists. Xavier Valls' simple pastel-shaded still lifes *Bodegón con cerezas* (1980) and *Melocotones y Jarro* (1974) are soothing offerings, while **Antonio Lopéz Garcia** contributes with his dusty dry Madrid landscape *Visto desde del Cerro Tío Pío* (1962–63). The collection ends with galleries dedicated to contemporary art, using manufactured products and industrial materials, and range from the dizzying experience of Jesús Rafael Soto's *Extensión amarilla y blanca*, a floor full of yellow-tipped metal filaments, to the blinding display of fluorescent strip lighting by Dan Flavin.

The Retiro and around

I n addition to the heavyweight sites of the Prado, Thyssen-Bornemisza and Reina Sofía galleries, the area around the Paseo del Prado is home to a host of other minor attractions. These include the recently renovated **Estación de Atocha**, the fascinating **Real Fábrica de Tapices** (Royal Tapestry Workshop), a number of the city's smaller museums, the startlingly peaceful **Jardines Botánicos** and the **Parque del Retiro**, a delightful mix of formal gardens and wider open spaces – the perfect place to escape the city bustle for a few hours.

The area covered by this chapter is shown in detail on colour map 8.

PARQUE DEL RETIRO

Map 8. Metro Retiro/Atocha.

The origins of the **Parque del Retiro** go back to the early seventeenth century, when Felipe IV's royal adviser, the Conde Duque de Olivares, produced a plan for a new palace and playground for the court, the Buen Retiro (literally "Good Retreat"). Work began in 1630, and the architects Crescenzi, Gómez de Mora and Carbonell built a huge complex, of which only the ballroom (**Casón del Buen Retiro**, see p.71) and the Hall of Realms (**Museo del Ejército**, see p.92) survive to this day. Gardens were laid out at the same time and included a zoo for the exhibition of savage animals, an aviary for exotic birds and a large lake where mock battles and waterborne dramas could be staged. Other elements were added over the years, such as a French-style parterre during the reign of Felipe V (1700–46), a royal porcelain factory constructed by Carlos III (1759–88) and an astronomical observatory by Carlos IV (1788–1808). During the Peninsular War, the gardens, used by the French as a fortified barracks, were badly damaged, but restored under Fernando VII, who opened most of the park to the public. After the 1868 Revolution, the park became municipal property.

Although *Madrileños* jog, rollerblade, cycle, picnic and row on the lake (you can rent boats by the Monumento a Alfonso XII) in the park, their main activity here is to promenade. The busiest day is Sunday, when half of Madrid turns out for the **paseo**. Dressed for show, families stroll around, nodding at neighbours and building up an appetite for a long Sunday lunch. Strolling aside, there's almost always something going on in the park, including a good programme of concerts and *ferias* organized by the city council. The most popular of the fairs is the **Feria del Libro** (Book Fair), held from the end of May into early June, when every publisher and half the country's bookshops set up stalls and offer a 25 percent discount on their wares. In the summer months, at weekends there are **puppet shows** by the Puerta de Alcalá entrance (1pm, 7pm &

8pm), while on Sunday, you can often watch groups of Peruvian musicians or Catalans performing their counting dance, the *sardana*.

In addition, travelling art exhibitions are frequently housed in the beautiful **Palacio de Velázquez** (June–Sept Mon & Wed–Sat 11am–8pm, Sun 11am–6pm; Oct–May Mon & Wed–Sat 10am–6pm, Sun 10am–4pm), close to the southern end of the main lake; the nearby **Palacio de Cristal**; and **Casa de Vacas** (daily 10.30am–2.30pm & 4–8pm; closed Aug except for puppet shows), at the opposite end of the lake. Look out, too, for *El Angel Caído* (Fallen Angel), the world's only public statue of Lucifer, in the south of the park. Alongside is the very fine rose garden designed by municipal head gardener Cecilio Rodríguez, who died in 1953. His service spanning 75 years is commemorated by the well-groomed formal gardens that bear his name on the east side of the park (daily 8am–3pm). In the northeast corner, remains of Fernando VII's private recreational zone can be clearly seen around the pink folly, La Casita del Pescador, in the middle of an ornamental lake.

Although El Retiro has a very safe reputation by day, it's best not to wander alone in the late evening. Note also that the area east of La Chopera is known as a cruising ground for gay prostitutes.

PUERTA DE ALCALÁ TO LOS JARDINES BOTÁNICOS

Leaving the park at the northwest corner takes you into Plaza de la Independencia, in the centre of which is one of the two remaining gates of the old city walls. Built in the late eighteenth century by Francesco Sabatini to commemorate Carlos III's first twenty years on the throne, the **Puerta de Alcalá** was the biggest city gate in Europe at that time and, like the bear and bush, has become one of the city's monumental emblems.

South from here, you pass the **Museo de Artes Decorativas** (Tues–Fri 9.30am–3pm, Sat & Sun 10am–2pm; 400ptas, concessions 200ptas, free on Sun), a former nineteenth-century aristocratic residence, which has its entrance at c/Montalbán 12. The museum's highlight is its collection of *azulejos* and other decorative ceramics. The rest of the exhibits include an interesting but unspectacular collection of furniture, reconstructed sixteenth- and seventeenth-century rooms and *objets d'art* from all over Spain.

A couple of blocks west, in a corner of the Naval Ministry at Paseo del Prado 5 is the **Museo Naval** (Tues–Sun 10.30am–1.30pm; closed Aug; free). Beyond the impeccably turned-out saluting guards you'll find a well-presented array of models, maps and charts, paintings, weapons and navigational instruments grouped into periods of Spanish naval history. Notable exhibits include the first map to show the territories of the New World drawn by Juan de la Costa in 1500, cannons from the Spanish Armada, part of Cortés' standard used during the Conquest of Mexico and the giant globes made by Coronelli in the late seventeenth century.

The military theme continues with the **Museo del Ejército** (Tues–Sun 10am–2pm; 100ptas, concessions 50ptas, free on Sat; Metro Retiro) just to the south, at c/Méndez Núñez 1. A gloomily eccentric timewarp of a museum, it's crammed full of military memorabilia, often chaotically displayed, and, seemingly unaware of the changes over the past twenty years, it preserves a distinctly pro-Franco stance. The morbid, motley collection includes a piece of the shirt worn by Pizarro when he was assassinated, a death mask of Napoleon and part of the bomb thrown by anarchist Mateo Morral at the wedding procession of Alfonso XIII and Victoria Eugenie, all accompanied by curious piped music ranging from *Doctor Zhivago* to the theme tune from *Shaft*. Of more interest perhaps are the beautiful ceilings of the building itself, fragments of Don Juan's flag from the Battle of Lepanto (1571), mementos of Cervantes from the same battle and the tent used by Carlos I on his Tunis Campaign in 1535.

South again, past the Prado's Casón del Buen Retiro annexe, is **San Jerónimo el Real** (July–Sept Mon–Fri 8am–1.30pm & 6–8pm, Sat & Sun 9am–1.30pm & 6.30–8pm; Oct–June Mon–Fri 8am–1.30pm & 5–8pm, Sat & Sun 9am–1.30pm & 5.30–8pm). A monastery was founded on this site in the early sixteenth century by the Catholic monarchs, Fernando and Isabel, becoming an important destination for religious processions from the city, site of the swearing in of the heirs to the throne (the Princes of Asturias) and stage for royal marriages and coronations (including that of King Juan Carlos in 1975). Despite significant remodelling and the addition of two Gothic towers in the mid-nineteenth century, the old form of the church is still clearly visible. At some point in the future, the cloisters of the church and the Hall of Realms, which currently houses the Museo del Ejército (see opposite), will be taken over by the Prado and the museum will be moved elsewhere.

Opposite San Jerónimo is the Neoclassical **Real Academia Española de la Lengua** (Royal Language Academy), established in 1714 by Felipe V to "cultivate and establish the purity and elegance of the Castilian language". Its job nowadays is to make sure that the Spanish language is not corrupted by foreign or otherwise unsuitable words. The results are entrusted to their official dictionary – a work that bears virtually no relation to the Spanish you'll hear spoken on the streets.

A short distance to the west, on Paseo del Prado, is **Plaza de la Lealtad**, an aristocratic semicircular plaza that contains a war memorial, the Monumento a los Caídos por España. Originally a memorial to the *Madrileños* who died in the rebellion of the 2nd of May 1808 (the urn at the base contains the ashes of those killed by the French), it was later altered to commemorate all those who have died fighting for Spain, and an eternal flame now burns here. On one side of the plaza stands the palatial *Ritz Hotel*, work of the French architect Charles Mewès, who also designed the *Ritz* in Paris and London. If your wallet can stretch to it and you feel suitably attired, a drink on the summer *terraza* is a real treat.

Opposite is the elegant **Bolsa de Comercio**, the stock exchange (Mon–Fri 10am–2pm); here you can watch the dealing from the gallery on the first floor and visit the rather routine exhibition on the history of the place.

Los Jardines Botánicos

Map 8, A6. Daily: March & Oct 10am–7pm; April & Sept 10am–8pm; May–Aug 10am–9pm; Nov–Feb 10am–6pm; 200ptas. Metro Atocha.

Just below the Plaza de Murillo entrance to the Prado are the delightful, shaded **Jardines Botánicos**. Opened in 1781 by Carlos III, the gardens and buildings were developed by Juan de Villanueva and botanist Casimiro Gómez Ortega. The aim was to collect and grow species from all over the Spanish Empire, develop a research centre and supply medicinal herbs and plants to Madrid's hospitals. The gardens were abandoned after the Peninsular War, and although they were renovated later in the nineteenth century and a zoo was installed, they soon fell into disrepair once more. The nineteenth-century writer and traveller, Richard Ford, reported that they became so neglected they were inhabited by a pair of escaped boa constrictors who survived on a diet of stray cats and dogs. The gardens were eventually restored in the 1980s, using the original eighteenth-century plans, and are now home to some thirty thousand species from around the globe. Don't miss the state-of-the-art hothouse, with its collection of tropical plants and amazing cacti.

On the southern side of the botanical gardens is the sloping **Cuesta de Claudio Moyano**, lined with little wooden bookstalls. You can buy anything here, new or old, from secondhand copies of Captain Marvel to Cervantes or Jackie Collins. There's always something of interest, such as old prints of Madrid and relics from the Franco era. Although the street's at its busiest on Sundays, some of the stalls are open every day.

At the end of the Cuesta de Claudio Moyano stands the grandiose **Ministry of Agriculture**, a building of epic proportions designed by Ricardo Velázquez Bosco in 1893. Its exterior features decorative tile work, monumental caryatids representing industry and agriculture, and crowned by a striking figure of Glory, flanked by winged horses.

ESTACIÓN DE ATOCHA AND BEYOND

Map 8, A8. Metro Atocha.

At the bottom of the Paseo del Prado stands the impressive **Estación de Atocha**, worth a look even if you're not travelling out of Madrid. It's actually two stations, old and new, the former, a glorious 1880s glasshouse, revamped as a kind of tropical garden by Rafael Moneo in 1992. It's a wonderful sight from the walkways above, while on the platforms beyond sit the gleaming white high-speed AVE trains, built to ferry passengers to the 1992 Expo in Sevilla in two and a half hours.

Also in this area, at c/Alfonso XII, is the **Museo Nacional de Antropología/Etnología** (Tues–Sat 10am–7.30pm, Sun 10am–2pm; 500ptas, free Sat after 2.30pm & all day Sun), founded by the eccentric Dr Pedro González Velasco to house his collection. The unimaginatively displayed exhibits are designed to give an overview of different cultures of the world, in particular those inter-twined with Spanish history; the ground floor focuses on the Philippines and Asian religions, the first floor Africa and the second the Americas. The most interesting exhibits from the doctor's original collection are to be found in a side room on the ground floor – a macabre collection of deformed skulls, a Guanche mummy (the Guanche were the original inhabitants of the Canary Islands), shrivelled embryos and the skeleton of a circus giant (2m 35cm tall). It is said the old doctor embalmed his own daughter when she died and was regularly seen taking her out for meals and rides in his carriage.

On the hill opposite at the edge of the Retiro, the **Observatorio Astronómico** (Mon–Fri 9am–2pm) was another ingredient of Carlos III's academic complex (see box on p.65), although not actually finished until 1845. It's a beautiful Neoclassical building housing a poorly displayed collection of telescopes, chronometers, sundials and sextants.

Real Fábrica de Tapices

Map 8, F9. Mon–Fri 9am–12.30pm; 250ptas. Metro Menéndez Pelayo.

Ten minutes' walk southeast of the station, the fascinating **Real Fábrica de Tapices** (Royal Tapestry Workshop) on c/Fuentarrabia is well worth a visit. The original factory, situated in Plaza Santa Bárbara, was founded in 1721 by Felipe V, who wanted to emulate the Gobelins factory in Paris. The young Goya was employed to paint the cartoons that now hang in the Prado for a series of tapestries depicting everyday *Madrileño* life. The factory was moved to its present site at the end of the nineteenth century, but the processes have not changed for hundreds of years, and the eighteenth-century vertical looms are still in use. The workers, now numbering only 42 compared to four hundred fifty years ago, can be seen coolly looping handfuls of bobbins around a myriad of strings, sewing up worn-out masterpieces with exactly matching silk, and weaving together hundreds of different threads to produce different shades for a new tapestry. The intricacy of the work, the patience of the weavers and their artistic skill is astonishing. With progress being painfully slow – a square metre of tapestry every two months – the astronomical price of two million pesetas per square metre soon becomes believable. One of the giant sixteenth-century Flemish tapestries on display, produced before the era of the electric light, took more than two generations to complete.

Gran Vía, Chueca and Malasaña

The **Gran Vía**, Madrid's great thoroughfare, runs from just above Plaza de la Cibeles to Plaza de España, effectively dividing the old city in the south from the newer northern parts. Permanently jammed with traffic and crowded with shoppers and sightseers, it's the commercial heart of the city and, if you spare the time to look up, quite a monument in its own right, with its early twentieth-century, palace-like shops, offices and hotels.

C/Fuencarral heads north of the Gran Vía to the Glorieta de Bilbao, site of the *Café Comercial*, where many *tertulias* were held after the Civil War and still one of the most popular meeting places in Madrid. To either side of c/Fuencarral are two of Madrid's most characterful *barrios*: **Chueca** to the east, and **Malasaña** to the west. Their chief appeal lies in their amazing concentration of bars, restaurants and, especially, nightlife. However, the **Museo Municipal**, **Museo Romántico** and a number of beautiful **churches** provide a more than adequate excuse to look around here by day. Further to the east is the elegant area of

Las Salesas, while north lies the former working-class suburb of **Chamberí**, with its strong sense of identity, plentiful supply of bars, pleasant plazas and an excellent market.

....

**The area covered by this chapter is shown
in detail on colour map 7.**

....

GRAN VÍA

The **Gran Vía** (Great Way) was constructed in three stages over nearly half a century in order to link the two new districts of Argüelles and Salamanca. Its construction involved the destruction of fourteen other streets, the alteration of fourteen more, and the road itself became a symbol of the nation's arrival in the twentieth century. Financed on the back of the economic boom that Spain experienced as a result of its neutrality in World War I, the Gran Vía is a showcase for a whole gamut of architectural styles, from Modernist and Art Deco to neo-Rococo and Rationalist.

The finest section of the Gran Vía is the earliest, constructed between 1910 and 1924, stretching from c/Alcalá to the Telefónica building. Two buildings at the junction with c/Alcalá really stand out. The **Edificio Metrópolis**, built between 1905 and 1911 by the French architects Jules and Raymond Fevrier, with its cylindrical facade, paired columns, white stone sculptures, zinc-tiled roof, decorated with gold garlands and crowned by a winged statue, is suitably over-the-top, while the **Grassy building** (1916–17) just above it, is equally overblown, featuring curved balconies, colonnades and a dome. Look out for the Art Deco **Museo Chicote** at no. 12, where you can sample a rather overpriced cocktail in the bar founded back in 1931 by Perico Chicote, whose aim was to "mix drinks, lives and opinions" (see p.176 for more on this bar).

GRAN VÍA

This section of Gran Vía was known as "Shell Alley" during the Civil War, as the monumental **Telefónica building** was used as a reference point by Franco's Nationalist forces to bomb the Gran Vía from their trenches in Casa de Campo. The vast 81-metre slab of a building with its plain sand-coloured facade, decorated with touches of Spanish Baroque, was Spain's first skyscraper and prompted King Alfonso XIII to declare that Spain had finally entered the modern world.

The next stretch of the street down to Plaza de Callao is dominated by shops, cafés and cinemas with their massive old-fashioned hand-painted posters. The neon-lit Plaza de Callao is now the gateway to the shoppers' paradise of **c/Preciados**, home to the French store FNAC and to the ubiquitous department store El Corte Inglés. On the corner, just before the street begins to slope down towards Plaza de España, you'll see the classic Art Deco **Capitol** building (1930–33), its curved facade embellished with lurid neon signs.

CHUECA AND LAS SALESAS

The smaller streets immediately to the north of Gran Vía are shady hinterland areas home to all manner of vice-related activities and are notorious for petty crime, but this only becomes a problem at night. In the *barrio* of **Chueca**, east of c/Fuencarral, there's a strong neighbourhood feel, with kids and grannies on the streets during the day, and a lively gay scene around **Plaza de Chueca** at night. The area has experienced a rejuvenation in recent years, as boarded-up properties have been reopened and new businesses have been set up, taking advantage of the growing gay café–bar scene. The plaza (Metro Chueca) is fronted by one of the best old-style *vermút* bars in the city, *Bodega Angel Sierra* on c/Gravina at the northwest corner. To the south at c/Augusto Figueroa 35 is *La Tienda de Vinos* or "*El Comunista*", so called because it acted as a meeting place of left-wing critics of the old Franco regime.

For details of the bars and nightlife venues in Chueca, see pp.174–178, 184–185 and 189–191.

From Plaza de Chueca east to **Paseo de Recoletos** (the beginning of the long Paseo de la Castellana) are some of the city's most enticing streets. Offbeat restaurants, small private art galleries and odd corner shops are to be found here in abundance, and **c/Almirante** has some of the city's most fashionable clothes shops, too. Head south down c/Barquillo to the **Plaza del Rey** for a look at the **Casa de las Siete Chimeneas** (House of Seven Chimneys), which is supposedly haunted by a mistress of Felipe II who disappeared in mysterious circumstances. The sixteenth-century house has been heavily restored, but is still recognizable as the work of the two architects of El Escorial, Juan Bautista de Toledo and Juan de Herrera. Charles I of England stayed here when he came to Madrid to press his unsuccessful suit for marriage to the Infanta María.

To the north up c/Barquillo is the stately **Plaza de las Salesas**, dominated by the church and convent of Las Salesas Reales. The complex was founded in 1747 by Barbara of Bragança, Portuguese wife of Fernando VI, as somewhere she might go to escape from her mother-in-law, Isabella Farnese, should her husband die before she did. In the event, it was never needed, as Barbara was outlived by her husband. The church, with its impressive white granite Baroque facade decorated with marble statues, is set behind a very fine forecourt containing a rose garden, palm trees and magnolias. Inside, there's a grotto-like chapel, impressive frescoes and stained-glass windows, an extravagant pulpit and striking green marble altar decoration. The elaborate

CHUECA AND LAS SALESAS

tombs of Fernando VI and Barbara of Bragança lie in a side chapel, as does that of the military hero General O'Donnell. The convent behind the church now houses the Palacio de Justicia, the city's Law Courts, facing the elegant Plaza de la Villa de París.

West along c/Fernando VI, past the marvellous grocers and fishmongers, overflowing with fresh produce, are the Gaudiesque flowing lines of the cream-coloured **Sociedad de Autores** (Society of Authors), its dripping decoration of flowers, faces and balconies giving the appearance of a melting candle. The only really significant *modernista* building in Madrid, it was designed in 1902 by the Catalan José Grasés Riera. Just beyond is Plaza de Santa Bárbara and Alonso Martínez, one of the main centres of student nightlife in Madrid, with the nearby streets packed with trendy bars and nightclubs.

Museo Romántico

Map 7, H4. Tues–Sat 9am–2.45pm, Sun & public holidays 10am–2pm; closed Aug; 400ptas, concessions 200ptas, free on Sun. Metro Tribunal.

Nearby at c/San Mateo 13, the **Museo Romántico** aims to show the lifestyle and outlook of the late-Romantic era through the re-creation of a typical residence of the period. It's a successful attempt, with its musty atmosphere, creaking floorboards, cracking walls crowded with canvases and rooms overflowing with kitsch memorabilia and period furniture. Contributing to the pleasant aura of nostalgia are a series of idealized folk portraits of bullfighters, flamenco dancers and gypsies and some fine old engravings of Madrid at the end of the eighteenth century. The air of Romanticism is maintained by a pair of small paintings by Leonardo Alcázar satirizing the Romantic idea of suicide, and a case displaying the pistols which the satirist Mariano

José de Larra used to shoot himself in 1837 after being spurned by his lover. Weightier works of art on display are Goya's *St Gregory* hanging in the chapel, portraits by Federico de Madrazo and other canvases by Zurbarán, Murillo and Sorolla.

Museo Municipal

Map 7, G4. Mid-July to mid-Sept 9.30am–2.30pm, Sat & Sun 10am–2pm; mid-Sept to mid-July Tues–Fri 9.30am–8pm, Sat & Sun 10am–2pm; 300ptas, free Wed & Sun. Metro Tribunal.

Just around the corner from the Museo Romántico is the **Museo Municipal**, c/Fuencarral 78, opened on this site in 1929 in the former city almshouse, built in the early eighteenth century by Pedro de Ribera. True to form, he created a fantastically decorated Baroque doorway placed on an otherwise plain red-brick facade. Inside, the museum contains a chronologically arranged collection of paintings, photos, models, sculptures and porcelain, all relating to the history and urban development of Madrid.

The lower ground floor houses archeological finds from the banks of the Manzanares, and from nearby Roman villas. The ground floor contains displays relating to Habsburg Madrid, including Pedro Texeira's fascinating plan of Madrid dated 1656, and Pedro Berruguete's outstanding *Virgin and Child*, paintings of Plaza Mayor, Casa de Campo, the Retiro and other famous Madrid landmarks. Bourbon Madrid is the focus of the first floor, with some huge Bayeu canvases portraying *Madrileño* life, Goya's *Allegory of the City of Madrid* (see p.20), a great display of crude cartoons satirizing Napoleon and a supremely accurate model of Madrid in 1830 by León Gil de Palacio. A good selection of reasonably priced prints, posters and books is available in the museum shop.

MALASAÑA

To the west of c/Fuencarral is **Malasaña** district, named after the young orphan and seamstress, Manuela Malasaña, who became a heroine of the 1808 Rebellion. One version of the story states that French troops searched her on her way home from work and found the scissors she used for cutting cloth. Since they had forbidden the carrying of any weapons, she was summarily executed. The area, also known as the Barrio de Maravillas, became extremely poor and run-down after the Civil War; there were even plans to bulldoze it. However, the availability of cheap accommodation brought an injection of life with the arrival of students and young people in the 1960s. More recently, the quarter was the focus of the *movida Madrileña*, the "happening scene" of the late 1970s and early 1980s. As the country relaxed after the death of Franco and the city developed into a thoroughly modern capital under the leadership of the late lamented mayor, Tierno Galván, Malasaña became the mecca of the young. Bars appeared behind every doorway, drugs were sold openly in the streets, and there was an extraordinary atmosphere of new-found freedom. Today, the threatened takeover by drug addicts has been largely halted and the area immediately around **Plaza Dos de Mayo** has been redeveloped with a fantastic selection of **bars**, **restaurants**, **clubs** and **cafés** springing up, many of which have a very particular eccentric identity. The maze of dark and narrow streets to the south of the square, however, is best avoided at night.

Bars and restaurants aside, the streets have an interest of their own and there are some wonderful old shop signs and architectural details. Best of all is the old pharmacy on the corner of c/San Andrés and c/San Vicente Ferrer with its irresistible 1920s *azulejo* scenes depicting cures for diarrhoea, headaches and suchlike. Finally, two churches are worth a visit. The **Convento de San Plácido** (Mon–Fri 10am–noon & 5–6pm, Sat 5–6pm, Sun 11am–noon & 5–6pm) on c/San Roque was founded in the early seventeenth century, although the present building dates from 1661. It features a magnificent high-altar canvas of the *Annunciation* by Claudio Coello and frescoes by Francisco Rizzi. Scandal plagued the convent in the early seventeenth century, with rumours that the nuns had become possessed by devils, and of the sexual misdemeanours perpetrated by their confessor. The convent has hit the headlines more recently with the discovery of a mummified body within its precincts, claimed by some people to be the body of the painter Diego Velázquez. **San Antonio de los Alemanes** (daily 9am–1pm & 6–8pm) on Corredera de San Pablo was designed in 1624 by the Jesuit architect Pedro Sánchez and Juan Gómez de Mora. The subject of a recent restoration programme, the elliptical interior is covered with dizzying floor-to-ceiling fresco decorations, painted by Luca Giordano and featuring scenes from the life of St Anthony.

Salamanca

T
he elegant tree-lined Paseo del Prado continues beyond Plaza de la Cibeles as the aristocratic and palatial Paseo de Recoletos, until it reaches the cascading fountains of Plaza de Colón where it metamorphoses into the Manhattan-style urban landscape of the **Paseo de la Castellana**. Bus 27 will take you the full distance – an architectural odyssey spanning the eighteenth to the late-twentieth centuries. Spreading out to the east of the Castellana is the exclusive **Barrio de Salamanca**, Madrid's designer shopping district. There are also a scattering of other sights, museums and galleries that might tempt you up here, in particular the **Museo de Lázaro Galdiano** and the **Museo Sorolla**, the pick of Madrid's smaller museums.

The area covered by this chapter is shown in detail on colour map 9.

The grid-like *barrio* of **Salamanca** was developed in the second half of the nineteenth century as a new upmarket residential zone under the patronage of the Marquis of Salamanca. This flamboyant larger-than-life arch-capitalist became Minister of Finance at the age of 32, went on to establish the forerunner to the Bank of Spain, developed Madrid's first rail and tram lines and was the proud owner of the first flush toilets in Madrid. A generous patron of the arts, renowned party host and master of insider dealing and speculation, he made and lost a fortune on three separate occasions, the last time as a result of his massive investment in the Barrio de Salamanca. Today the area is still a smart address for apartments and even more so for shops. The streets are populated by the fur-coat and sunglasses brigade, decked out in Gucci and plenty of gold. The *barrio* is also the haunt of *pijos* – universally denigrated rich kids – and the grid of streets between c/Goya and c/José Ortega y Gasset contains most of the city's **designer emporiums**. Unsurprisingly, the bars and restaurants in this area tend to be rather pricey, although the quality is high (see pp.151–152, 163–165 and 179–180).

For a full rundown of Salamanca's best shops see p.230.

On the Paseo de la Castellana several modern buildings stand out, including the green-capped Torres Heron completed in 1976, La Pirámide at no. 31, the shiny black La Unión y el Fénix (no. 33) and further north, the Catalana Occidente, with its impressive opaque-glass finish. Look out, too, for the **Museo de Escultura al Aire Libre** (Metro Rubén Darío; free), an innovative use of the space underneath the Juan Bravo flyover, with its haphazard collection of sculptures, including a huge six-tonne suspended block titled *The Meeting* by Eduardo Chillida, *Mere Ubo* by Miró, and assorted cubes, walls, fountains and optical trickery. The Salamanca area is also home to a number of excellent **exhibition spaces** sponsored by a variety of companies and foundations (see box overleaf).

SALAMANCA

Exhibition spaces

A number of businesses and financial institutions have **exhibition spaces** scattered across the city – mainly around the Castellana and Salamanca districts – and they stage a variety of high-quality exhibitions and cultural events during the year. See press and the *Guía del Ocio* for details.

Fundación Arte y Tecnología, c/Fuencarral 3 (Metro Gran Vía; Tues–Fri 10am–2pm & 5–8pm, Sat & Sun 10am–2pm; free). This exhibition space, situated in the huge Telefónica building on Gran Vía, is used to display selections from the collection of twentieth-century Spanish art owned by the recently privatized telecommunication giant, as well as hosting frequently appealing temporary shows.

Fundación BBV, Paseo de la Castellana 81 (Metro Nuevos Ministerios; Mon–Sat 11.30am–1.30pm & 5.30–8.30pm, Sun 11am–2.30pm; free). Nestling below the skyscrapers in the AZCA complex, this fine exhibition space has hosted a variety of shows from Spain and abroad, including a recent display of work from the Dulwich Picture Gallery.

Fundación Banco Central Hispano, c/Marqués de Villamagna 3 (Metro Serrano; Tues–Sat 11am–2pm & 5–9pm, Sun 11am–2.30pm; free). A permanent collection spanning the sixteenth to twentieth centuries, along with temporary exhibitions.

Fundación La Caixa, c/Serrano 60 (Metro Serrano; Mon & Wed–Sat 11am–8pm, Sun 11am–2pm; free). Hosts a variety of prestigious exhibitions, which recently included a very popular display of Nigerian art.

Fundación Caja de Madrid, Sala de las Alhajas, Plaza de San Martín 1 (Metro Sol; Tues–Sat 11am–2.30pm & 5–8pm, Sun 11am–2.30pm; closed Aug; free). Situated in a beautiful old building opposite the Monasterio de las Descalzas, this exhibition space has hosted shows from Spain and abroad, including a critically acclaimed display of work by the German Expressionists.

Fundación Cultural MAPFRE, c/General Perón 40 (Metro Santiago Bernabéu; Mon–Sat 10am–9pm, Sun noon–8pm; free). A variety of enticing temporary shows by Spanish and international artists have appeared in recent years at this pleasant exhibition space opposite the Palacio de Congresos.

Fundación Juan March, c/Castelló 77 (Metro Núñez de Balboa; Jan–June & Sept–Dec Mon–Fri 10am–2pm & 5.30–9pm, Sat & Sun 10am–2pm; free). Situated in a garden full of modern sculptures, this outstanding cultural centre houses a collection of over 1300 works and is a venue for major art exhibitions. It was founded in 1955 by a Catalan businessman seeking to make amends after spending time in prison for embezzlement.

Sala del Canal de Isabel II, c/Santa Engracia 125 (Metro Rios Rosas; Tues–Fri 11am–2pm & 5–9pm, Sun 11am–2pm; free). This neo-*mudéjar* water tower has been turned into an exhibition space specializing in photographic displays.

AROUND PLAZA DE COLÓN

Map 9, B9–10. Metro Colón.

The first point of interest you come to in the *barrio* of Salamanca after emerging from the metro is **Plaza de Colón**, marking the point where Paseo de Recoletos becomes Paseo de la Castellana. The square is dominated by a neo-Gothic monument to Christopher Columbus (*Cristóbal Colón*), given as a wedding gift to Alfonso XII, and identical to the one in Barcelona. Directly behind are the Jardínes del Descubrimiento, a small park containing three huge stone blocks representing Columbus's three ships. Below the plaza, underneath the cascading wall of water facing the Castellana is the 1970s **Centro Cultural de la Villa**, a good place for film and theatre and occasional exhibitions. Across the plaza, at Paseo de Recoletos 41, you'll see the **Museo de Cera** (daily 10am–2.30pm & 4.30–8.30pm; 900ptas; Metro Colón), a pricey and pretty lamentable wax museum.

A better bet is the **Museo Arqueológico Nacional**, just off the plaza, entrance at c/Serrano 13 (Tues–Sat 9.30am–8.30pm, closes 6.30pm in summer; Sun 9.30am–2.30pm; 500ptas, concessions 250ptas, free Sat after 2.30pm and all day Sun; Metro Colón). The collections trace the evolution of human cultures from prehistory right up to the fifteenth century. There are even some pieces from the nineteenth century. Most exhibits are from excavations in Spain, and include some impressive pieces, among them the celebrated Celto-Iberian busts known as *La Dama de Elche*, *La Dama de Baza* and *La Dama del Cerro de los Santos*, and a wonderfully rich hoard of Visigothic treasures found at Toledo. Good coverage is given to Roman, Egyptian, Greek and Islamic finds. Rooms are, however, often closed for rearrangement, sometimes at very short notice. In the gardens, downstairs to the left of the main entrance, is a reconstruction of the prehistoric cave paintings discovered at Altamira in Cantabria. Given that the caves themselves are now closed to the public, this is the nearest you will get to the real thing.

In the same complex, but with entry from the Castellana, are the **Biblioteca Nacional** and **Museo del Libro** (Tues–Sat 10am–9pm, Sun & hols 10am–2pm; free), housed in a grand Neoclassical pile built over a twenty-five-year period in the late nineteenth century. The *biblioteca* contains over three million volumes, including every work published in Spain since 1716, while the museum displays a selection of some of the library's treasures, including Arab, Hebrew and Greek manuscripts and an exhibition on the development of written communication.

MUSEO SOROLLA

Map 9, A2. Tues–Sat 10am–2.30pm, Sun 10am–2pm; 400ptas, concessions 200ptas, free Sun. Metro Iglesia–Ruben Darío.

To the west of the Glorieta de Emilio Castelar on the Paseo de la Castellana, Paseo del General Martínez Campos leads to one of the hidden treasures of Madrid. Part museum and part art gallery, the **Museo Sorolla** gets little of the publicity of the mammoth collections to be found in the Prado and the Thyssen-Bornemisza, but this tribute to a single artist's life and work is in many ways just as rewarding. The museum is situated in Joaquín Sorolla's former home built in 1910 and donated to the nation by his widow after his death in 1923. It's a delight to stumble upon this oasis of peace and tranquillity, its cool and shady Andalusian-style courtyard and gardens decked with statues, fountains, assorted plants and fruit trees.

Sorolla himself was born in Valencia in 1863 and studied in Rome and Paris. Enormously successful during his lifetime and famous throughout Europe and the USA, he was dubbed the "Spanish Impressionist" and received countless prizes for his paintings, including first prize at the Paris Universal Exhibition of 1900. However, his work experienced a decline in popularity after his death and soon went out of fashion, and it's only more recently that it has experienced a revival. A video on the artist's life and work is shown Tuesday–Friday at 11am and noon. The ground floor has been kept largely intact, re-creating the authentic atmosphere of the artist's living and working areas. These rooms contain his **collection of popular jewellery**, including religious icons and charms, hair combs and earrings, garnered during his travels around the Iberian peninsula. The **studio** itself is bathed in the powerful Madrid sunlight from massive skylights and, amongst the artist's clutter, you'll see the *cama a la turca*, a small bed lined on three sides by cases of books, where Sorolla used to take his afternoon siesta.

The upstairs rooms, originally the sleeping quarters of the house, have been turned into a **gallery**, with works arranged chronologically from the far end. The development from his first darker, more sombre paintings such as *Trata de Blanca* (1894) and *An Investigation* (1897) to brighter, more optimistic works such as the lush green dreamlike *Siesta* (1911) and the vivid red *Puerto de Valencia* (1907) is striking. Powerful sunlight, sea, intense colours, women and children dominate his rather romantic paintings. On your way out, you'll see a small, tastefully displayed collection of his sketches and gouaches. Note that some of the galleries may be closed at weekends during the summer because of understaffing.

MUSEO LÁZARO GALDIANO

Map 9, E1. Tues–Sun 10am–2pm (July & Sept also open Thurs 7–11pm for guided tours); 500ptas, 750ptas guided tour, concessions 250ptas; free Sat. Metro Nuñez de Balboa.

Just east of the Glorieta de Emilio Castelar at c/Serrano 122 is the **Museo Lázaro Galdiano**. This former private collection of publisher and businessman José Lázaro Galdiano was given to the state after his death in 1947 and spreads over the four floors and 37 rooms of his former home. It's a vast treasure trove of paintings and *objets d'art*, with some very dodgy attributions, but includes some really exquisite and valuable pieces. The scope of the collections is enormous, comprising paintings, sculptures, ivories, enamels, jewellery, ceramics, arms, armour and furniture, ranging from the seventh century BC to the twentieth century. The museum provides informative leaflets in both Spanish and English.

The **ground-floor collection** contains some outstanding archeological pieces, beautifully decorated thirteenth-century Limoges enamels and a magnificent late sixteenth-century rock crystal and bejewelled drinking cup belonging to Emperor Rudolf II, the mad cousin of Felipe II. In the room on Renaissance sculpture is a superb little picture of *The Saviour* from the late fifteenth-century Lombard School, formerly claimed by the museum to be by Leonardo da Vinci.

The other floors contain an excellent collection of European paintings from the fifteenth to nineteenth centuries. Among the painters represented are Bosch, Dürer, Rembrandt, Lucas Cranach, Gainsborough, Reynolds, Turner and Constable. Unsurprisingly, there's a host of Spanish artists, including Berruguete, Murillo, Zurbarán, Velázquez, José de Ribera, El Greco and Goya.

MUSEO LÁZARO GALDIANO

Plaza de España and beyond

The northwest corner of the city, beyond Plaza de España, is a mixture of aristocratic suburbia, university campus and parkland, distinguished by the green swathes of **Parque del Oeste** and **Casa de Campo**. Sights include the downbeat **Museo Cerralbo**, the fascinating **Museo de América**, the **Ermita de San Antonio de la Florida**, with its stunning Goya frescoes and, further out, the pleasant royal residence of **El Pardo**, while the spacious **terrazas** along Paseo del Pintor Rosales provide ample opportunity for refreshment.

PLAZA DE ESPAÑA

Map 7, B5. Metro Plaza de España.

The **Plaza de España** at the west end of Gran Vía, is marked by two of what used to be the city's tallest buildings (their status has recently been usurped by the flurry of corporate construction along the Paseo de la Castellana). The grandiose apartment complex of the **Edificio de España** which heads the square, looking as though it has been transplanted from 1920s New York, was in fact completed in 1953. Four years later, the neighbouring thirty-two storey **Torre de Madrid** took over as the tallest building in Spain. Together they tower over an elaborate monument to Cervantes in the middle of the square, in which the seated author gazes intently into the distance while the bewildered bronze figures of Don Quixote and Sancho Panza stand below. The plaza itself can be a little seedy at night, although it does play host to occasional festivities and an interesting **craft fair** during the fiesta of San Isidro (on or around May 15), while behind the Edificio de España, on c/San Leonardo and c/San Bernardino, you'll find a host of multinational restaurants ranging from Mexican and Peruvian to Egyptian, Thai and Indian.

To the northwest, **c/Martín de los Heros** is a lively place, day and night, with three of the city's best original-language-version cinemas, and behind them the **Centro Princesa**, a complex of shops, clubs, bars and a 24-hour branch of the ubiquitous VIPS supermarket – just the place to have your film developed at 4am or get a bite to eat before heading on to a late club.

Museo Cerralbo

Map 7, A5. Tues–Sat 9.30am–2.30pm (July 10am–2pm), Sun 10am–2pm, closed Aug; 400ptas, concessions 200ptas, free Wed & Sun. Metro Ventura Rodríguez.

Just to the west of Plaza de España is the **Museo Cerralbo**, c/Ventura Rodríguez 17, an elegant nineteenth-century mansion endowed by the seventeenth Marqués de Cerralbo, a reactionary politician, poet, traveller and archeologist, who still had time to build up a substantial collection of paintings, furniture, armour and artefacts. He bequeathed his home and its eclectic contents to the state, although it didn't open as a museum until 1962. The cluttered nature

PLAZA DE ESPAÑA

of the exhibits is partly explained by the fact that he stipulated in his will that the collection should be displayed exactly as he arranged it. Among the chaos of objects and ornaments is a dark and moody *Francis of Assisi* by El Greco, work by José de Ribera, Zurbarán, Van Dyck and Tintoretto, a fascinating collection of clocks, pocket watches and mini sundials and some outrageously gaudy icing-sugar chandeliers. The highlight is a fabulous over-the-top mirrored ballroom with a Tiepolo-inspired fresco, golden stucco work and marbled decoration.

ARGÜELLES AND MONCLOA

Calle de la Princesa stretches northwest from Plaza de Espana into the *barrios* of Argüelles and Moncloa, the former home to some elegant apartment blocks, the latter a centre of student life. Up the steps opposite the Centro Princesa is **c/Conde Duque**, dominated by the massive former barracks of the royal guard constructed in the early eighteenth century by Pedro de Ribera. The barracks have been turned into a dynamic **cultural centre**, known as Centro Cultural Conde Duque, which stages concerts, plays and dance as part of the Veranos de la Villa season (see p.216). It's home to the city's collection of contemporary art and also hosts a variety of temporary exhibitions. Just to the east of this, the **Plaza de las Comendadoras**, a tranquil space bordered by a variety of interesting craft shops, bars and cafés, is named after the convent that occupies one side of the square. The nuns are from the military order of Santiago and the attached church is decked out with banners celebrating the victories of the order's knights. A large painting of their patron, St James the Moor-slayer, by Luca Giordano, hangs over the high altar.

About 400m from Plaza de España along c/Princesa, obscured by trees, stands the **Palacio de Liria**, the resi-

dence of one of the wealthiest and most important aristocratic families in Spain, the dukes of Alba. Housed within is
a vast private collection of artistic treasures, but visitors are
only allowed entry once a week, after a written request, and
the current waiting list is well over a year. The far end of
Princesa is dominated by the **Ministerio del Aire** (Air
Ministry), another product of the post-Civil War Francoist
building boom. Work on the mammoth edifice began in
1942, and even the Third Reich's architect, Albert Speer,
was consulted. However, with the defeat of the Nazis, plans
were soon changed and a Habsburg-style structure was built
instead, inspired by the work of Juan Gómez de Mora and
nicknamed the "Monasterio" del Aire because of its simi-
larity to El Escorial. Franco also had constructed the neighbouring Arco de la Victoria in 1956 to commemorate the
Nationalist military triumph in the Civil War. During term
time, the stretch of parkland by the arch often becomes the
scene of one big student party, with huddles of picknickers
under the trees and debris strewn across the grass.

The **Mirador del Faro** (Tues–Sun: June–Aug
11am–1.45pm & 5.30–8.45pm; Sept–May 10.30am–2pm &
5.30–8pm; 200ptas; Metro Moncloa), the futuristic 92-
metre-high viewing tower just past the **Arco de la
Victoria**, was opened in 1992 and provides stunning views
over the city and to the mountains beyond. Alongside, with
its main entrance at Avenida de los Reyes Católicos 6, is the
Museo de América (Tues–Sat 10am–3pm, Sun
10am–2.30pm; 500ptas, concessions 250ptas, free Sun).
This fabulous collection of pre-Columbian American art
and artefacts includes objects brought back at the time of
the Spanish conquest, as well as more recent acquisitions
and donations. The layout is thematic, with sections on
ideas and myths about America, geography and history,
social organization, religion and communication. Each of
the imaginatively displayed exhibits is introduced by a short

ARGÜELLES AND MONCLOA

video presentation in Spanish, but the lack of chronological development can be rather disconcerting. The Aztec, Mayan and Inca civilizations are all well represented and exhibits include the Madrid Codex (one of only three surviving hieroglyphic manuscripts depicting scenes from everyday Mayan life), the Tudela Codex, describing the events of the Spanish conquest, and the Quimbayas Treasure, a fabulous, breathtaking collection of gold objects and figures from the Quimbaya culture of Colombia.

Beyond the museum lies the campus of the **Ciudad Universitaria**, rebuilt after the Civil War when it was completely devastated in some of the fiercest fighting, lying as it did along the front line between the defending Republican forces and the besieging Nationalists. Alongside the campus, by the side of the road, is the **Palacio de la Moncloa**, the official residence of the Spanish prime minister since 1977.

THE PARQUE DEL OESTE

Map 2, B3. Metro Argüelles.

To the west of Plaza de España, the **Parque del Oeste** follows the railway tracks up to the suburbs of Moncloa and Ciudad Universitaria. Originally laid out by municipal gardener, Cecilio Rodríguez, at the beginning of the twentieth century, the park was devastated by the Civil War and had to be completely redesigned. It features a pleasant stream, assorted statues and shady walks, and in summer there are numerous *terrazas* overlooking the park on Paseo del Pintor Rosales. Also here is the **Teleférico** (April–Sept daily 11am–2.30pm & 4.30pm–dusk; Oct–March Sat, Sun & public holidays noon–2.30pm & 4.30–8pm; 360ptas one-way, 515ptas return), which shuttles its passengers high over the river with great views of the Palacio Real, the Almudena Cathedral and the city skyline, to the middle of

Casa de Campo (see overleaf). Below the Teleférico is the beautiful **Rosaleda** (at present being renovated and replanted), a vast rose garden, at its best and most sweet-smelling in May and June. On its south side is the **Templo de Debod** (Tues–Fri 10am–1.45pm & 6–8pm, Sat & Sun 10am–2pm; 300ptas), a fourth-century BC Egyptian temple given to Spain in 1968 in recognition of the work done by Spanish engineers on the Aswan High Dam. Reconstructed here stone by stone, it seems comically incongruous.

The Ermita de San Antonio de la Florida

Tues–Fri 10am–2pm & 4–8pm, Sat & Sun 10am–2pm (from 13th to 23th July daily only 10am–2pm); 300ptas, concessions 150ptas, free Wed & Sun. Metro Príncipe Pío.

Rail lines from commuter towns to the north of Madrid terminate at the recently renovated **Estación del Norte**, a quietly spectacular construction of white enamel, steel and glass which enjoyed a starring role in Warren Beatty's film *Reds*. About 500m from the station along the Paseo de la Florida stands the **Ermita de San Antonio de la Florida** at Glorieta de la Florida 5. This little church on a Greek cross plan was built by an Italian, Felipe Fontana, between 1792 and 1798 and decorated by **Goya**, whose **frescoes**, which took him only 120 days to complete, provided Carlos IV with enough evidence to appoint him court painter. The frescoes in the dome depict a miracle performed by Saint Anthony of Padua, while around it, heavenly bodies of angels and cherubs hold back curtains to reveal the main scene – the saint resurrecting a dead man. Beyond this central group, Goya created a gallery of highly realistic characters, modelled on court and society figures, while for a lesser fresco of the angels adorning the Trinity in the apse, he took prostitutes as his models. The church also houses the artist's remains. The mirror-image chapel on

THE PARQUE DEL OESTE

119

the other side of the Glorieta was built in 1925 for parish services so that the original could become a museum. On St Anthony's Day (June 13) girls queue up at the chapel to ask the saint to bring them a boyfriend; if the pins dropped into the holy water in the font stick to their hands, their wish will be granted.

CASA DE CAMPO

Metro Batán/Lago. Bus #33 from Príncipe Pío goes to the zoo and Parque de Atracciones or you can get here by cable car from Paseo del Pintor Rosales (see p.118) or on foot from the Estación del Norte via the Puente del Rey.

The **Casa de Campo**, an enormous expanse of heath and scrub, is in parts surprisingly wild for a place so easily accessible from the city. Founded by Felipe II in the mid-sixteenth century as a royal hunting estate, it was only opened to the public in 1931 and it later acted as a base for Franco's forces from which they shelled much of the city. Large sections have been tamed for conventional pastimes and there are picnic tables and café–bars throughout the park, the ones by the lake providing fine views of the Palacio Real, Cathedral, Plaza de España and San Francisco el Grande. There are also mountain-bike trails, a jogging track, open-air swimming pool (mid-June to Sept 11am–9.30pm; 500ptas. Metro Lago), tennis courts, and rowing boats for rent on the lake (again near Metro Lago). During the summer, open-air films are shown in the conference area. Other attractions include a popular, well-laid-out **Zoo** and a sprawling **Parque de Atracciones** (see "Kids' Madrid", p.243 for information on both). Be warned that many of the main access roads through the park have been taken over by prostitutes, both day and night (the council has banished them from the streets of the city) and can become crowded with kerb-crawlers – not particularly pleasant for picnics or excursions with the kids.

EL PARDO

Map 1, E5. April–Sept Mon–Sat 10.30am–6pm, Sun 9.30am–1.30pm; Oct–March Mon–Sat 10.30am–5pm, Sun 9.30am–1.30pm; 650ptas, concessions 250 ptas, free Wed for EU citizens. Closed for official events. Bus from Moncloa (services daily every 10–15min, 6.30am–midnight; 25min).

Nine kilometres northwest of central Madrid is Franco's former principal residence at **El Pardo**. A garrison still remains at the town, where most of the Generalísimo's staff were based, but the stigma has lessened over the years, and this is now a popular excursion for *Madrileños*, who come here for long lunches in the *terraza* restaurants along Avenida de la Guardia, or to play tennis and swim at one of the nearby country clubs. The tourist focus is the **Palacio del Pardo**, rebuilt by the Bourbons on the site of the hunting lodge of Carlos I. The present building is largely the work of Francesco Sabatini although traces of the old palace by Juan Gómez de Mora are still evident. The interior is pleasant enough and houses the chapel, where Franco prayed, and the theatre, built for Carlos IV's wife María Luisa, where the Caudillo and his cronies used to censor films. On display are a number of mementos of Franco, including his desk, a portrait of Isabel la Católica by her court painter, Juan de Flandes, and an excellent collection of tapestries, many after Goya's cartoons in the Prado. Tickets to the palace are valid also for the neighbouring pavilion, the **Casita del Príncipe**, though this cannot be entered from the palace gardens and you must return to the main road. Like the *casitas* at El Escorial, this was built by Juan de Villanueva and is highly ornate.

LISTINGS

Accommodation

Madrid has lots of **accommodation**, and most of it is pretty central. It is, on the whole, though, pretty functional. Few places, in any price range, have great character, and you're basically paying for location and facilities. At the lower end of the range, there are bargains to be had, with double rooms for as little as 3000ptas a night – and less if you're looking for an extended stay. Move upmarket a little and you can find plenty of places at 6000–8000ptas a night, offering comfortable rooms with a private bath or, more often, shower. The upper-range hotels regularly offer special deals, so it's well worth checking these out even if your budget is limited.

Although it is advisable to make **reservations** at all times of the year, especially during Spanish fiestas (see p.216), you will always be able to find something if you are prepared to spend time looking around. Alternatively, you could use an **accommodation service** – you'll find outlets at the airport, the Estación Sur de Autobuses and the train stations. Brújula (©91 559 97 05) is particularly helpful, with offices at Atocha and Charmartín train stations, Colón bus terminal and on the sixth floor of the Torre de Madrid in Plaza de España.

Much of the cheapest accommodation in Madrid is to be found in the wedge-shaped zone between **c/Atocha** and

Paseo del Prado and in the *barrios* of **Chueca** and **Malasaña**. Similarly, the huge old buildings on **Gran Vía** harbour a vast array of hotels and *hostales* at every price, often with a delightfully decayed elegance. After dark, however, the area can feel somewhat seedy.

In the very heart of the city – **Sol**, **Ópera** and **Plaza Mayor** – there is a surprising number of reasonably priced options, and if you want to be right in the thick of Madrid's nightlife, you'll find plenty of good choices around **Plaza de Santa Ana**.

North of Gran Vía, a number of *hostales* cluster on and around **c/Fuencarral** and **c/Hortaleza**, although the streets near the southern end of Fuencarral form a red-light district, so take care after dark. Further north towards Bilbao is another nightlife centre; the pleasantest options here are around **Plaza Santa Bárbara**.

The city's most expensive hotels are grouped around **Paseo del Prado**, **Recoletos** and in **Salamanca**, although even in these upmarket districts you'll find several more modest options.

Calling Madrid from abroad, dial your international access code, then 34, followed by the subscriber's number, which will nearly always start with 91.

HOTELS

Noise from the street can be a problem in the city centre, so it's a good idea to ask for a room on one of the higher floors or facing away from the street. In summer, air conditioning is advisable – all **hotels** in the ⑤ category and above will have it, while the hotel reviews will say if it is

Accommodation prices

Throughout this guide, accommodation is graded on a scale from ① to ⑧. These categories show the cost per night of the cheapest double room in each establishment. In Madrid there is no high or low season. However, many upper-range hotels offer good deals at weekends and during July and August. It's also worth enquiring about the *bonos* (hotel vouchers) on sale in all travel agents which often give substantial reductions on the more upmarket options.

① Under 3000ptas	⑤ 8000–12,000ptas
② 3000–4500ptas	⑥ 12,000–18,000ptas
③ 4500–6000ptas	⑦ 18,000–25,000ptas
④ 6000–8000ptas	⑧ Over 25,000ptas

available in any of the cheaper options. Swimming pools are a rarity, but you'll always be within striking distance of one of the public pools scattered around the city (see p.226). If you're arriving by car, a hotel with a garage is a must, given the city's parking and security problems. **Breakfast** is often not included in the price of a room, and anyway, it's usually much better value and more fun to go to a local café or bar.

ATOCHA AND PASEO DEL PRADO

Hotel Mediodía
Map 5, I5. Plaza del Emperador Carlos V 8 ✆91 527 30 60; fax 91 530 70 08. Metro Atocha.
Huge 165-roomed hotel right by the Reina Sofía and Estación de Atocha. Simple, but comfortable rooms, with bathroom and TV in all – a good bargain. Directly below, the *El Brillante* café does a good cup of coffee and some basic tapas. ④.

HOTELS

127

Hotel Mercator

Map 5, I4. C/Atocha 123 ℗91 429 05 00; fax 91 369 12 52. Metro Atocha.

Smart hotel, well geared up for tourists, with information leaflets, money-changing facilities and café–bar. A good option if you're coming by car, as it has its own car park and is easy to reach. Chintzy rooms have TVs and most have air condition-ing. ⑤.

Hotel Mora

Map 5, I2. Paseo del Prado 32 ℗91 420 15 69; fax 91 420 05 64. Metro Atocha.

Friendly, recently refurbished, 62-room hotel. All rooms have air conditioning, and some have pleasant views of the Paseo del Prado. Double–glazing helps to block out the noise of the traf-fic. Rooms are quite small, but the hotel is perfectly positioned for all the galleries on the Paseo del Arte. ④.

Hotel Nacional

Map 5, I3. Paseo del Prado 48 ℗91 429 66 29; fax 91 369 15 64. Metro Atocha.

Large, very plush hotel, part of the high-quality NH chain of Spanish hotels, attractively situated just opposite the Jardines Botánicos. Not that pricey, given the excellent facilities and luxurious surroundings. Special offers can reduce the price substantially. ⑦.

Hotel Palace

Map 6, F4. Plaza de las Cortes 7 ℗91 360 80 00; fax 91 360 81 00; *www.palacemadrid.com*. Metro Banco de España.

Colossal 440-room sumptuous hotel belonging to the Sheraton chain. It has every facility, including a hairdresser, beauty salon, conference rooms and business services – but none of the snootiness of the *Ritz* across the road. Doubles start at 56,500ptas. ⑧.

Hotel Asturias

Map 6, C3. C/Sevilla 2 ℂ91 429 66 76; fax 91 429 40 36; *jcrodri@cestel.es*. Metro Sevilla.

Comfortable well-appointed hotel housed in a beautiful building, only a stone's throw from Puerta del Sol. Rooms are quite
large, all have air conditioning and service is courteous. ⑤.

Hotel Carlos V

Map 3, H3. C/Maestro Vitoria 5 ℂ91 531 41 00; fax 91 531 37 61.
Metro Sol.

Large, recently refurbished early twentieth-century hotel,
belonging to the Best Western chain, in a pedestrianized part of
town, just off c/Preciados behind the Monasterio de las
Descalzas Reales. Some of the plush, air-conditioned rooms on
the fifth floor have quite large balconies with tables and chairs
(for which you pay extra), although there isn't much of a view.
There's an elegant lounge and café, and the hotel has a deal with
a nearby car park which guests can use at reduced rates. ⑤–⑥.

Hotel Ópera

Map 3, E3. C/Cuesta de Santo Domingo 2 ℂ91 541 28 00; fax 91
541 69 23; *hotelopera@sinix.net*. Metro Ópera.

In a very pleasant location near the Plaza de Oriente, this hotel
has good facilities at a pretty reasonable price. Rooms are comfortable and large, while, appropriately enough, the waiters in
the café downstairs also entertain diners with arias from operas
and *zarzuelas*. ⑥.

Hotel Paris

Map 6, B3. C/Alcalá 2 ℂ91 521 64 96; fax 91 531 01 88. Metro Sol.
Smart, old-fashioned hotel right on the Puerta del Sol with
spacious, pleasantly decorated rooms, half of which have air
conditioning. There's a nice interior patio and a laundry on the

premises. Very good value for its central position. Breakfast included. ⑤.

Hotel Persal
Map 6, B5. Plaza del Angel 12 ✆ 91 369 46 43 or 91 368 37 26; fax 91 369 19 52. Metro Sol.

Friendly hundred-room hotel superbly located between Sol, Santa Ana and Plaza Mayor. All rooms have air conditioning, bathroom and TV. Firm mattresses and surprisingly quiet rooms should make for a good night's sleep in this excellent-value hotel. ④.

Hotel Regina
Map 6, D2. C/Alcalá 19 ✆ and fax 91 521 47 25. Metro Sol.

Plush, well-located 142-room hotel between Sol and Cibeles, with very spacious rooms. Well set-up for tourists, with plenty of sightseeing information; popular with organized tour groups. ⑥.

Gran Hotel Reina Victoria
Map 6, C5. Plaza de Santa Ana 14 ✆91 531 45 00; fax 91 522 03 07. Metro Sol.

A giant cream cake of a hotel, perfectly placed at the top of Plaza Santa Ana, although it has lost a little of its character since it became part of the Tryp hotel chain. A favourite of bullfighters past and present, it has a taurine bar, where bull-fighting *tertulias* are still held during the San Isidro Festival in May, and a rather grand, elegant foyer. It comes complete with all the services you'd expect in this price range, including business services, currency exchange and a car park. ⑧.

Hotel Santander
Map 6, D4. C/Echegaray 1 ✆91 429 66 44; fax 91 369 10 78. Metro Sevilla.

Spacious, well-decorated and spotless rooms with large bathrooms and many with a small seating area. Classy old-fashioned decor and very friendly staff. Perfectly located for the bars and restaurants in the Santa Ana/Huertas area. ⑤.

PLAZA DE ESPAÑA, GRAN VÍA, CHUECA AND SANTA BÁRBARA

Casón del Tormes
Map 7, B6. C/del Río 7 ⓒ91 541 97 46; fax 91 541 18 52. Metro Plaza de España.
Plush 63-room hotel in a surprisingly quiet street off Plaza de España. The en-suite rooms are very comfortable and all are equipped with air conditioning. There is a bar, breakfast room (not included in price) and pleasant seating area. The staff are very helpful, speak English and more than willing to give advice and maps and help out with Spanish. Parking is available for 1700ptas per night. A very good mid-price option. ⑥.

Hotel Emperador
Map 7, D6. Gran Vía 53 ⓒ91 547 28 00; fax 91 547 28 17; *hemperador@sei.es*. Metro Callao/Plaza de España.
The only real reason to come to this hotel is the superb rooftop swimming pool, with magnificent views of the Palacio Real, Casa de Campo and the packed streets of Madrid. The hotel is geared up for the organized tour market and the atmosphere is rather impersonal, but the rooms are large and nicely deco-rated, many with recently refurbished bathrooms. ⑦.

Hotel Mónaco
Map 7, I6. C/Barbieri 5 ⓒ91 522 46 30; fax 91 521 16 01. Metro Chueca/Gran Vía.
In a city full of rather bland hotels this one stands out head and shoulders above the rest in terms of character. It was formerly a *casa de citas*: a place where lovers, in rather less liberal years, could arrange to meet. Since becoming a hotel in 1959 it has

HOTELS

retained much of its original decor, although this means that the fittings aren't always up to modern standards. The wonderful Art Deco double rooms are the ones to go for (the singles are nothing special); each is completely different, embellished with a variety of mirrors, chandeliers, canopies, oil paintings, and stuccoed ceilings. Room 20 with its raised bath tub was used by Alfonso XIII for his "appointments", but others have their own particular attractions and many have been used as sets for films or video shoots. Can be noisy at night though, with nearby disco bars. ⑤.

RECOLETOS, SALAMANCA AND CHAMBERÍ

Hotel Alcalá
Map 8, G1. C/Alcalá 66 ✆91 435 10 60; fax 91 435 11 05. Metro Príncipe de Vergara/Retiro.
Large classy hotel just to the north of the Retiro, with smart well-appointed rooms, laundry facilities and a car park. Very friendly staff and an attractive location right next to the park. The wider streets and avenues in this area give it a spacious and airy feel. Excellent deals during the summer and at weekends. ⑤–⑦.

Residencia Don Diego
Map 9, F8. C/Velázquez 45, 5° ✆91 435 07 60; fax 91 431 42 63. Metro Velázquez.
This is a comfortable, friendly, medium-sized hotel in an upmarket area of town. The rooms have full facilities, including air conditioning and satellite TV. ⑤.

Galiano Residencia
Map 9, B8. C/Alcalá Galiano 6 ✆91 319 20 00; fax 91 319 99 14. Metro Colón.
Hidden away in a quiet street behind the Heron building on the Castellana, this small hotel has a sophisticated air. There's a pleas-

ant well-furnished salon off the entrance lobby, staff are polite and the excellent rooms are air-conditioned. Car parking facilities. **⑥**.

Hotel Santo Mauro

Map 7, K1. C/Zurbano 36 © 91 319 69 00; fax 91 308 54 77; *santomauro@itelco.es*. Metro Rubén Darío.

A palace in the nineteenth century, later an embassy and now a small luxurious hotel situated in the quiet area of Chamberí, just to the west of the Castellana. The rooms have tasteful modern decor while the communal areas are more traditional, but very stylish. The excellent facilities include an indoor swimming pool, gym, sauna, beauty salon, car park and a babysitting service. Doubles start at 46,000ptas per night. **⑧**.

PENSIONES AND HOSTALES

Pensiones and **hostales** are small, no-nonsense, frequently family-run establishments, sometimes with shared bathrooms and fewer facilities than a hotel. They are housed in large centrally located apartment blocks and in the more popular areas, you'll find two or three separate establishments, each on their own floor, in the same building. **Floors** (*pisos*) are written as 1° (first floor), 2°, etc, and often specify *izquierda* (*izqda*) or *derecha* (*dcha*), meaning to the left or right of the staircase respectively. Some of the *hostales* in larger buildings – on Gran Vía, for example – don't always have an entryphone or doorbell at street level, making them inaccessible at night, unless you've been given a front-door key. If you book a room and intend to arrive after, say, 9pm, check that you will be able to get in.

ATOCHA AND PASEO DEL PRADO

Hostal Barrera

Map 5, H3. C/Atocha 96 2° ©91 527 53 81; fax 91 527 39 50;

snowy@accesocero.es. Metro Antón Martín.
Friendly, good value sixteen-room *hostal*, with an English-speaking owner. Rooms have a bath or shower, but most have no private toilet. There are plans to refurbish all rooms so that they have full bathrooms and air conditioning. Internet access available. ②.

Hostal Cervantes
Map 6, E5. C/Cervantes 34, 2° ©91 429 83 65 or 91 429 27 45; fax 91 429 83 65. Metro Antón Martín.
If you can't get in to the *Gonzalo* on the floor above, this is an equally friendly *hostal*, although slightly more expensive. All rooms have their own bathroom, TV and ventilator and are pleasantly furnished. ③.

Hostal Gonzalo
Map 6, E5. C/Cervantes 34, 3° ©91 429 27 14. Metro Antón Martín.
Very clean, recently renovated fifteen-room *hostal*; all rooms have bathroom, TV and ventilator. The charming owner, Antonio, runs a very smart place at an excellent price. Highly recommended. ③.

Pensión Mollo
Map 5, H3. C/Atocha 104, 4° ©91 528 71 76. Metro Atocha.
The closest reasonable *hostal* to the station, although it's up a steep hill and has no lift – not a good bet if you're heavily laden. There are seven clean rooms; all of the doubles have en-suite showers. ②.

SOL AND SANTA ANA

Hostal Aguilar
Map 6, D4. Carrera de San Jerónimo 32, 2° ©91 429 59 26 or 91 429 36 61; fax 91 429 26 61. Metro Sevilla.
Large *hostal*, with airy rooms all with bath, TV and air condi-

tioning. Specializes in multi-bed rooms offering very good prices for quadruples (8500ptas), making it an ideal budget place for families. ③.

Hostal Americano

Map 6, B3. Puerta del Sol 11, 3° ✆91 522 28 22; fax 91 522 11 92. Metro Sol.

Right beside the statue of Madrid's emblem, *El Oso y Madroño*, in Puerta del Sol – you couldn't get nearer to the city centre. This nicely furnished *hostal* has rooms with TV, bathroom and telephone, and there's a pleasant communal living room. ③.

Hostal Armesto

Map 6, E5. C/San Agustín 6, 1° dcha ✆91 429 09 40 or 91 429 90 31. Metro Antón Martín.

A small six-room *hostal*. All rooms have bathrooms and TV and the best ones overlook the pleasant little garden in the Casa de Lope de Vega next door. Very well positioned for the Huertas/Santa Ana area. ③.

Hostal Astoria

Map 6, D4. Carrera de San Jerónimo 30, 5° ✆91 429 11 88; fax 91 429 20 23; *hostalastoria@hotmail.com*. Metro Sevilla.

Friendly and well-appointed 26-room option in a building full of *hostales*. Decor is basic, but all of the large rooms have a bathroom, air conditioning, and satellite TV. Triples are available at 8000ptas a night. ③.

Hostal La Macarena

Map 4, F2. C/Cava de San Miguel 8, 2° ✆91 365 92 21; fax 91 364 27 57. Metro Sol.

Fine, family-run *hostal* in a recently pedestrianized characterful alley just off the Plaza Mayor. Rooms are quite small, but all have bathrooms, TV and ventilators. ④.

PENSIONES AND HOSTALES

Hostal Plaza D'Ort

Map 6, B5. Plaza del Angel 13, 1° ℗91 429 90 41; fax 91 420 12 97. Metro Sol.

Next door to the *Hotel Persal;* all rooms in this very clean *hostal* have a shower or bath, TV and telephone, and some rooms have air conditioning. There are also several self-catering apartments, sleeping five or six people for 16,000ptas a night, making it a good family or group option. ④.

Hostal Rifer

Map 3, H5. C/Mayor 5, 4° ℗91 532 31 97. Metro Sol.

Clean, bright rooms, all with en-suite facilities, in the highest – and therefore quietest – of three options in this block. The friendly owner is anxious to please. ③.

Hostal Villar

Map 6, C5. C/Príncipe 18, 1° ℗91 531 66 00 or 91 531 66 09; fax 91 521 50 73. Metro Sevilla.

Large *hostal* on four floors of a centrally situated building. Most of the standard rooms have small bathrooms, and all have TV and telephone. There are plans to install air conditioning in the near future. ②.

GRAN VÍA, CHUECA AND SANTA BÁRBARA

Hostal Asunción

Map 7, J3. Plaza Santa Bárbara 8 ℗91 308 23 48; fax 91 310 04 78. Metro Alonso Martínez.

In a pretty position overlooking the square, this *hostal* offers small but well-furnished rooms with bath, TV and mini-bar; two have air conditioning. ④.

Hostal Buenos Aires

Map 7, C6. Gran Vía 61, 2° ℗91 542 22 50 or 91 542 01 02; fax 91 542 28 69. Metro Plaza de España.

Plenty of facilities in this well-appointed *hostal* at the Plaza de España end of Gran Vía. Air conditioning, satellite TV, en-suite bathrooms and a bar, but the rooms are rather plain. **④**.

Hostal California

Map 7, F7. Gran Vía 38 ©91 522 47 03; fax 91 531 61 01. Metro Callao.

Well-placed, friendly but somewhat pricey *hostal*. Rooms are bright, new and relatively quiet, and all doubles have full bathroom, TV, telephone and air conditioning. It also has its own bar and café. **⑤**.

Hostal Kryse

Map 7, G7. C/Fuencarral 25, 1° izqda ©91 531 15 12; fax 91 522 81 53. Metro Gran Vía.

Compact ten-room *hostal*; all rooms have verandas and those above the street have double glazing. Small bathroom, TV, telephone and ceiling fans in all rooms. **③**.

Hostal Medieval

Map 7, G5. C/Fuencarral 46, 2° izqda ©91 522 25 49. Metro Chueca.

Small well-run and friendly family *hostal*. All of the airy rooms have showers, but toilets are shared. Well-maintained building with attractive plants trailing from the verandas. **③**.

Hostal El Pinar

Map 7, H7. C/San Bartolomé 2, 4° ©91 531 01 34. Metro Chueca.

Decent *hostal* charging some of the lowest rates in the city – perhaps because the building looks as though it's about to collapse. If you're on a tight budget and want to be right in the centre of town, this can't be beaten. Rooms have their own bathroom. Popular with students on long-term rates. **①**.

Hostal Santa Bárbara

Map 7, I3. Plaza Santa Bárbara 4 ©91 445 73 34; fax 91 446 23 45.
Metro Alonso Martínez.

Recently redecorated and refurbished, this is a rather upmarket
hostal in a good location. The nice rooms all have bathrooms
and there's a great Art Deco TV salon. Some rooms have air
conditioning. English-speaking Italian owner. ⑤.

Hostal Zamora

Map 7, H7. Plaza Vázquez de Mella 1, 4° izqda ©91 521 70 31.
Metro Gran Vía.

Seventeen simple rooms in this pleasant *hostal*, most of which
overlook the recently spruced-up plaza. All rooms have bathrooms, TV and air conditioning, and there are good-value
family rooms for 9500ptas. ④.

Eating

Eating out in Madrid is one of the highlights of any visit to the city. There's plenty to suit every pocket, from budget backstreet bars to high-class designer restaurants, and a bewildering range of cuisines encompassing tapas, traditional *Madrileño* and Spanish regional dishes, as well as international cooking.

Breakfast is a pretty light affair, usually a cup of coffee and a *tostada* (toast and marmalade), but the traditional *Madrileño* breakfast of *chocolate con churros* – a glutinous dark chocolate with deep-fried hoops of batter – is sometimes preferred, especially after a night out on the tiles (see p.189). A mid-morning snack of a *bocadillo* (a French bread sandwich) or a *sandwich mixto* (a toasted ham and cheese sandwich) should keep hunger at bay until *aperitivos* and a few tapas at any time from 1pm onwards. **Lunch** (*la comida*) is taken very late, with few *Madrileños* starting before 2pm, and is often a long, drawn-out affair. **Dinner** (*la cena*), which again may be preceded by some tapas, will usually begin around 10pm, though many restaurants will not admit customers much later than 10.30pm. There are quite a number of **late-night options**, however, and the listings magazines all have sections for restaurants open past midnight (*después de medianoche/de madrugada* – see box on p.158).

Opening hours have been given for all establishments listed on the following pages, but be warned that bars often open and close according to how busy they are or the mood of the staff working that night. Many restaurants close on Sunday and/or Monday and for all or part of August.

The streets around **Puerta del Sol** are packed with places to eat and drink. You should spend at least one evening sampling the historic, tiled bars of **Santa Ana/Huertas**, while to the south, in the tiny streets of **La Latina** and **Lavapiés** there's an appealing neighbourhood feel to the bars and restaurants. On **Gran Vía**, burger bars fill most of the gaps between shops and cinemas, but head a few blocks north, and there's plenty on offer, including a good cluster of ethnic restaurants on c/San Bernardino (north of the Plaza de España). **Chueca**, **Santa Bárbara** and **Malasaña** further north, have some superb traditional old bars and bright new restaurants, serving some of the most creative food in the city, while the smarter districts of **Recoletos and Salamanca** contain few bars of note, but some extremely good restaurants.

The recommendations given here include *bares*, *cafés*, *cervecerías* (beer halls), *marisquerías* (seafood bars) and *restaurantes*, but have been divided simply into "Tapas bars" and "Restaurants", depending on whether they concentrate more on bar food or sit-down meals; many will actually have a bar area where you can get tapas, and also a more formal *comedor* (canteen) or *restaurante* out the back or upstairs.

Children are nearly always welcome and most restaurants will make special arrangements for them. Restaurants are full to the brim at weekends, so it is vital to **book** at least a day ahead; even during the week it's advisable to reserve a table to avoid having to wait.

TAPAS

Madrid is renowned for its **tapas** (usually three or four chunks of fish or meat, or a dollop of salad), which traditionally were served up free with a drink. These days, you have to pay for anything more than a few olives (where you do get free food now, it will often be called a *pincho*), but a single helping rarely costs more than 200–400ptas unless you're somewhere very flashy. The procession from one bar to the next, sampling its speciality, has evolved into a culinary ritual in the city. Fortunately, the best tapas bars are clustered together, particularly in the streets between **Puerta del Sol** and **Plaza de Santa Ana**, **La Latina** and **Lavapiés**. One of the main advantages of tapas is that you can experiment, and in many places food is laid out in glass display cases, so you can eat whatever takes your fancy even if you don't know what it's called.

Madrid's own speciality tapas include *patatas bravas*, *orejas* and *callos* (see glossary overleaf).

Raciones are simply bigger plates of the same, and can be enough as a light meal in themselves; *pinchos morunos*, small kebabs, are often also available. When ordering, make sure you specify whether you want a *ración* or just a *tapa*. The more people you're with the better; half a dozen *tapas* or *pinchos* and three *raciones* can make a varied and quite filling meal for three or four people.

SOL, PLAZA MAYOR AND ÓPERA

El Anciano Rey de Los Vinos
Map 6, A4. C/Paz 4. Metro Sol.
Mon–Thurs & Sun 9.30am–4pm & 6.30–11.30pm, Fri & Sat
9.30am–4pm & 6pm–midnight. Closed Aug.

TAPAS

Tapas Glossary

Pincho	Mouthful
Tapa	Saucerful
Ración	Small plateful
Adobado	Marinated
Al ajillo	With olive oil and garlic
A la marinera	Seafood cooked with garlic, onions and white wine
A la parilla	Charcoal-grilled
A la plancha	Grilled on a hot plate
A la romana	Fried in batter
Asado	Roast

Standard tapas and *raciones* might include :

Aceitunas	Olives
Ahumados	Smoked fish
Albóndigas	Meatballs
Almejas	Clams
Anchoas	Anchovies
Bacalao	Cod (often salted)
Berberechos	Cockles
Boquerones	Small, anchovy-like fish, usually served in vinegar
Calamares	Squid
Callos	Tripe, often served in a spicy tomato sauce
Cangrejos de río	Freshwater crayfish
Carabineiros	Large red prawns
Caracoles	Snails
Champiñones	Mushrooms, usually fried in garlic
Chistorra	Sausage with paprika
Chorizo	Spicy sausage
Cocido	Meat and chickpea stew (a *Madrileño* speciality)

Croquetas	Croquettes
Empanada	Slices of fish/meat pie
Ensaladilla	Russian salad (diced vegetables in mayonnaise)
Gambas	Prawns
Hígado	Liver
Jamón serrano	Cured ham
Jamón de York	Regular ham
Langostinos	Langoustines
Mejillones	Mussels
Mollejas	Sweetbreads
Morcilla	Black pudding
Navajas	Razor clams
Nécora	Fiddler crab
Orejas	Pigs' ears
Ostras	Oysters
Patatas alioli	Potatoes in garlic mayonnaise
Patatas bravas	Spicy fried potatoes
Patatas a lo pobre	Slices of fried potato mixed with egg (and sometimes *chorizo*)
Pimientos	Peppers
Pincho moruno	Kebab
Pisto	Assortment of cooked vegetables, similar to ratatouille
Pulpo	Octopus
Riñones al Jerez	Kidneys in sherry
Salchicha	Sausage
Sepia	Cuttlefish
Sesos	Brains
Tortilla española	Potato omelette
Tortilla francesa	Plain omelette
Trigueros	Green asparagus
Zarajo	Grilled sheep's intestine wound around a stick, poached in brandy and wine and fried in olive oil.

TAPAS GLOSSARY

The "Old Man King of Wines" is a great old bar, near to the Puerta del Sol. The wines are excellent, and for the sweet-toothed, the *torrijas* (deep-fried bread doused in wine and sprinkled with sugar and spices) is a must. A host of other tapas is available, including fine *callos* and *albóndigas*.

Las Bravas

Map 6, C5 & B5. C/Alvarez Gato 3 and c/Espoz y Mina 13. Metro Sol. Daily noon–4pm & 7pm–midnight.

Standing-room only at both bars, and as the name suggests, *patatas bravas* is the thing to try; in fact, *Las Bravas* has patent-ed its own version of the spicy sauce. The *tortilla*, *pulpo* and *callos* are tasty, too. The outside of the bar is covered with novelty mirrors, which are said to have inspired a story by Valle-Inclán and are a hangover from when this was a barber shop. There's another branch just around the corner.

Casa del Abuelo

Map 6, C4. C/Victoria 12. Metro Sol. Daily 11.30am–3.30pm & 6.30–11.30pm.

Tiny, highly atmospheric bar serving sweet, rich red house wine and cooked prawns – try them *al ajillo* (in garlic) or *a la plancha* (grilled). Use your free wine voucher to get a drink at the bar's sister *El Abuelo*, nearby.

Casa Labra

Map 6, A3. C/Tetuán 12 ©91 531 00 81. Metro Sol. Mon–Sat 11am–3.30pm & 5.30–11pm.

A great, traditional place dating from 1869 and retaining much of its original interior. This is where the Spanish Socialist Party was founded in 1879. Order a drink at the bar and a *ración* of cod fried in batter (*bacalao*) and some of the best *croquetas* in town at the counter to the right of the door. There's also a restaurant through the bar on the right – an old panelled room, serving classic *Madrileño* food.

Lhardy

Map 6, C3. Carrera de San Jerónimo 8 ℗91 521 33 85. Metro Sol.
Shop: Mon–Sat 9.30am–3pm & 5–9.30pm, Sun 9am–2.30pm.
Restaurant: Mon–Sat 1–3.30pm & 9–11.30pm, Sun 1–3.30pm.

Lhardy is one of Madrid's most famous and expensive restaurants. Once the haunt of royalty, it's a beautiful place, but greatly overpriced – you can expect to pay upwards of 7000ptas per head for a three-course meal. On the ground floor, however, there's a wonderful bar/shop, seemingly preserved in aspic, where you can snack on canapés, *fino* and *consommé* – without breaking the bank – serving yourself from the glass cabinets and gleaming silver urn.

Mejillonera El Pasaje

Map 6, B4. Pasaje Matheu. Metro Sol.
Daily except Tues noon–midnight.

Mussels (*mejillones*) served in every way imaginable in a bar-packed pedestrian-only alleyway between c/Espoz y Mina and c/Victoria, south of Puerta del Sol.

Museo del Jamón

Map 6, B3. Carrera de San Jerónimo 6. Metro Sol.
Mon–Sat 9am–midnight, Sun 10am–midnight.

The largest branch of this Madrid chain, from the ceilings of which are suspended hundreds of *jamones* (hams). The best – and they're not cheap – are the *jabugos* from the Sierra Morena, though a ham croissant won't set you back more than 300ptas.

La Oreja de Oro

Map 6, C4. C/Victoria. Metro Sol.
May–July & Sept Mon–Sat 1–4pm & 8pm–1am; Oct–April
Tues–Sun 1–4pm & 8pm–1am. Closed Aug.

Standing room only in this bar just opposite *La Casa del Abuelo*. Go for the excellent *pulpo a la Gallega* (sliced octopus on a bed of potatoes fried in olive oil and seasoned with cayenne

TAPAS

145

pepper), washed down with Ribeiro wine served in terracotta bowls. Plenty of other seafood tapas on offer too.

El Oso y El Madroño

Map 6, A5. C/Bolsa 4. Metro Sol.
Mon–Sat 10am–midnight. Closed last two weeks in July.
A tiny *castizo* bar where you can have a drink to the accompaniment of the *Madrileño chotis* and chat to the traditionally attired barmen who appear to have been here forever. Speciality *cocido*, snails, sangría and Jerez.

SANTA ANA AND HUERTAS

Casa Alberto

Map 6, C6. C/Huertas 18 ✆91 429 93 56. Metro Antón Martín.
Tues–Thurs noon–1am, Fri & Sat noon–2am, Sun noon–4pm.
Traditional *tasca* with a zinc and marble bar which has resisted the passage of time since it was founded back in 1827. Good *caracoles*, *gambas* and a great anchovy canapé, ideally accompanied by a glass of house vermouth. There's a small dining room at the back.

La Costa de Vejer

Map 6, C5. Corner of c/Núñez de Arce and c/Alvarez del Gato. Metro Sol.
Tues–Sun noon–midnight.
The speciality here is prawns (*gambas*), grilled with garlic – an absolute must. Service is friendly and there's plenty of room to sit down at the back if you want to linger a little longer and try out some of the other tapas.

El Lacón

Map 6, D5. C/Manuel Fernández y González 8 ✆91 429 36 98. Metro Sol.
Daily noon–4pm & 8pm–midnight, Fri–Sun till 1.30am. Closed Aug.

Large Galician bar–restaurant, with plenty of seats upstairs. Great *pulpo*, *caldo gallego* (meat and vegetable broth) and *empanadas* (pastry slices filled with tuna and vegetables).

Prada A Tope
Map 6, C5. C/Príncipe 11 ©91 429 59 21. Metro Sevilla.
1.30–4.30pm & 8pm–midnight. Closed Tues & Aug.
Excellent-quality produce from El Bierzo in León. The *pimientos asados*, *morcilla* and *tortilla* are extremely tasty, while the smooth house wines provide the ideal accompaniment.

Viña P
Map 6, C5. Plaza de Santa Ana 3. Metro Sol.
Daily 1–4pm & 8pm–12.30am.
Very friendly staff serving a great range of tapas in a bar decked out with bullfighting mementos and posters. Try the asparagus, stuffed mussels and the mouthwatering *almejas a la marinera* (clams in a garlic and white wine sauce).

LA LATINA AND LAVAPIÉS

Almendro 13
Map 4, C4. C/Almendro 13. Metro La Latina.
Tues 1–5pm, Wed–Sun 1–5pm & 8pm–midnight.
Fashionable wooden panelled bar that serves great *fino* from chilled black bottles. Help yourself to the glasses from the racks on the wall and tuck into original tapas of *huevos rotos* (fried eggs on a bed of crisps) and *roscas rellenas* (rings of bread stuffed with various meats).

El Almendro
Map 4, E5. C/Almendro 27. Metro La Latina.
Daily except Tues 1–4.30pm & 8.30pm–midnight.
On the corner of the Plaza de San Andrés, this is just the place for tasty and highly original tapas. Fill in a card ticking your

TAPAS

orders and choose from, among other dishes, an excellent asparagus in avocado sauce, wafer-thin chips and *chorizo*, three-cheese salad and *tortilla de bacalao*.

Los Caracoles
Map 5, A5. C/Toledo 106. Metro Puerta de Toledo.
Tues–Sat 9am–10.30pm, Sun 9am–4pm. Closed July.
A continual supply of snails in spicy sauce is issued from the sizzling pan in this rough and ready local bar, all washed down with the local *vermút del grifo*.

La Chata
Map 4, F4. C/Cava Baja 24. Metro La Latina.
Daily 12.30–4.30pm & 8.30pm–12.30am. Closed Sun eve.
One of the most traditional and popular tiled tapas bars in Madrid, with hams hanging from the ceiling, and taurine and football mementos on the walls. Serves a good selection of *raciones*, including *cebolla rellena* and *pimientos del piquillo rellenos* (stuffed onions and peppers).

La Taberna Angosta
Map 4, C5. C/Mancebos 6. Metro La Latina.
Mon–Thurs 6pm–2.30am, Fri–Sun noon–3.30am.
Fantastic homemade patés – the *paté de ave al vino blanco* (white wine-flavoured paté) is especially good – accompanied by great wines in this friendly bar in the heart of the old Moorish quarter of Madrid. Also serves some mean *boquerones angosta* in a mustard sauce. There's a small *terraza* on the pavement opposite in the summer.

Taberna de Antonio Sánchez
Map 4, H6. C/Mesón de Paredes 13. Metro Tirso de Molina.
Mon–Sat noon–4pm & 8pm–midnight.
Said to be the oldest *taberna* in Madrid, this seventeenth-century bar has a stuffed bull's head (to commemorate Antonio

Sánchez, the son of the founder, who was killed by a bull) and a wooden interior. Lots of *finos* on offer, plus *jamón* and *queso* tapas or *tortilla de San Isidro* (omelette with salted cod) and *callos*.

La Taberna de los Cien Vinos
Map 4, E4. C/Nuncio 16. Metro La Latina.
Tues–Sun 1–3.45pm & 8–11.45pm.
A vast selection of Spanish wines plus plenty to choose from on the constantly changing tapas menu, including excellent leek pie, smoked salmon and *pinchos* of roast beef. Every month they sell a different selection of whites and reds. The owner also goes on regular journeys around Spain to discover new wines. Not suitable for the indecisive.

La Taberna de Zapatero
Map 4, E5. C/Almendro 22. Metro La Latina.
Tues–Sat 1–4pm & 8pm–midnight, Sun 1–4pm.
Excellent Ribera del Duero and original tapas in this friendly local haunt. Try the *pollo zapateado* (mild curry-flavoured chicken) and the delicious *canapé de revuelto de oricios* (sea urchin).

La Tasca de Jesús
Map 4, E5. C/Cava Alta 32. Metro La Latina.
Tues–Sun noon–5pm & 8pm–1am.
The staff ply you with a variety of excellent tapas while you wait at the minuscule bar for a table. When you do make it to the small brick-lined dining room the waiter is very happy to recommend dishes if you're unable to decide what to order – specialities include mini-steaks, grilled asparagus, shellfish and *patatas a lo pobre*.

TAPAS

GRAN VÍA, CHUECA AND SANTA BÁRBARA

El Bocaito
Map 7, I7. C/Libertad 4–6. Metro Chueca.
Mon–Sat 1–4pm & 8.30pm–midnight. Closed Sat lunch and for
two weeks in Aug.
You can watch the busy staff prepare the tapas in the
kitchen/bar as you munch away on a variety of delicious
canapés and tapas, washed down by a cold beer. Watch out for
the *Luisito*, the hottest canapé your taste buds are ever likely to
encounter.

Santander
Map 7, H6. C/Augusto Figueroa 25. Metro Chueca.
Mon–Sat 10.45am–4pm & 7.30–11pm. Closed Aug.
It's worth a visit to this bar in the heart of Chueca for its range of
tapas, including *empanadas*, *tortillas* and quiche lorraine, as well as
a huge variety of fresh homemade canapés at reasonable prices.

Stop Madrid
Map 7, G7. C/Hortaleza 11. Metro Gran Vía.
Mon–Sat noon–4pm & 7pm–midnight.
An old-time spit-and-sawdust bar specializing in dishes from
Extremadura, accompanied with Belgian, Mexican and
German beers as well as *vermút* on tap. Tapas consist largely of
jamón and *chorizo*, with the *Canapé Stop* of ham and tomato
doused in olive oil well worth a try.

Taberna de Sarmiento
Map 7, H6. C/Hortaleza 28. Metro Chueca.
Mon–Sat noon–4pm & 8pm–midnight (Fri & Sat 1am).
Closed Sat lunch.
One of the new wave of tapas bars that have sprung up in
recent years, specializing in artistically presented sit-down tapas.
Try the spinach croquettes, or the fantastically refreshing melon

TAPAS

salad served with prawns. The selection of canapés should not be missed, especially the paté with orange sauce, and there is an excellent selection of wines available from all over Spain.

Albur
Map 7, F2. C/Manuela Malasaña 15. Metro Bilbao.
Sun–Wed noon–midnight, Thurs–Sat noon–1.30am.
Wooden tables and rustic decor combine to make you feel that you're in a farm kitchen. The food is excellent, although the service can be a little slow. The *champiñones en salsa verde* and the *patatas albur* (potatoes fried with herbs and spices) are both worth sampling, and the good wines are the ideal accompaniment.

La Camocha
Map 7, G1. C/Fuencarral 15. Metro Bilbao.
Daily 7am–2am.
Asturian-cider bar serving splendid *pulpo* and *almejas a la sidra*. You can use the special cider-pouring instruments stuck to the wall to make sure the cider is properly aerated.

Chipén
Map 7, G1. C/Cardenal Cisneros 39. Metro Bilbao.
Daily noon–4pm & 7.30pm–midnight/1am.
A *castizo* bar, decorated with tiles portraying famous city sights and serving a range of tapas from a menu written in *Madrileño* slang. Specialities include *chipén* (smoked-salmon canapé) and *fetén* (blue cheese canapé). Also serves frog's legs and draught vermouth.

Alkalde
Map 2, K3. C/Jorge Juan 10. Metro Serrano.

TAPAS

Mon–Fri 1–4pm & 8.30pm–midnight, Sat 1–4pm.

This pricey, but very popular, bar serves up Basque tapas, a real treat which you could turn into a tasty meal. Look out for the *empanadas* and the *tortillas* filled with peppers.

Hevia

Map 9, E2. C/Serrano 118. Metro Núñez de Balboa.

Mon–Sat 9am–1.30am.

Plush venue and clientele for pricey but excellent tapas and canapés – the hot Camembert is a must.

José Luis

Map 9, E1. C/Serrano 89. Metro Núñez de Balboa.

Mon–Sat 9am–1am, Sun noon–11pm.

The best of this chain of smart bar–restaurants originally established by a Basque who came to the city in the late 1950s. An unstoppable success, with branches now in Seville, Valencia, Barcelona and Montréal. Dainty and delicious sandwiches are laid out along the bar, together with canapés of *cangrejo* (crab), *morcilla* (black pudding) and steak, but the bill quickly mounts up if you're not careful.

RESTAURANTS

Madrid's restaurants offer every regional style of **Spanish cooking**: Castilian for roasts (*horno de asar* is a wood-burning oven) and stews, *Gallego* for seafood, *Andaluz* for fried fish, Levantine (Valencia/Alicante) for paella and other rice-based (*arroz*) dishes, Asturian for winter stews such as *fabada* and Basque for the ultimate gastronomy (and high prices).

Over the last few years, dozens of **foreign cuisines** have also appeared. There are some good Peruvian, Argentinian and Italian places and a scattering of enjoyable Indonesian and Japanese restaurants. With few exceptions, though, Indian and Chinese restaurants are fairly dire, as, too, are most of the Mexican and Brazilian ones.

Restaurant prices

Restaurants have been graded as inexpensive (under 2000ptas a head for a three-course meal and wine), moderate (2000–3500ptas), expensive (3500–6000ptas) and very expensive (over 6000ptas). You can of course pay very different amounts at any restaurant depending on what you order and when. Fish and seafood generally boost the bill, while a set **menú del día** is often amazingly cheap (from as little as 900ptas for three courses and house wine), although it's usually only available weekday lunchtimes. If service is not included, a **tip** of somewhere between five and ten percent is sufficient, but never more than 500ptas in total.

Most – but by no means all – of the restaurants listed as "moderate" or above will accept **credit/charge cards** (*tarjetas*). If in doubt, phone ahead to check.

Traditional **Madrileño food** consists of robust mixed stews (such as the meat and chickpea *cocido*) and offal dishes, but the capital is also renowned for its quality seafood despite its distance from the sea – the best produce from Galicia is packed straight onto the train for Madrid each day.

SOL, PLAZA MAYOR AND ÓPERA

El Botín
Map 4, G2. C/Cuchilleros 17 ℡91 366 42 17. Metro Sol/Tirso de Molina. Daily 1–4pm & 8pm–midnight. Expensive.
Established in 1725, and highly picturesque, with its tiled and wooden panels, *El Botín* is cited in the *Guinness Book of Records* as Europe's oldest restaurant. Favoured by Hemingway among others, it's inevitably a tourist haunt, but not such a bad one. Highlights are the traditional Castilian roasts – especially *cochinillo*

(suckling pigs) and *cordero lechal* (lamb). Good house wine. The *menú del día* is around 4000ptas, but you could eat for less.

Casa Ciriaco

Map 4, C2. C/Mayor 84 ©91 548 50 66. Metro Ópera.
Daily except Wed 1.30–4pm & 8.30–1.30am. Closed Aug.
Moderate.

Attractive, old-style *taberna*, long reputed for its traditional Castilian dishes – trout *en escabeche* (marinated in vinegar and garlic), chicken *en pepitoria* (in almond sauce) and *cocido*, served up in old-style portions. The *menú* is 2500ptas; main *carta* dishes are a bit less. If you're not planning on a sit-down meal, you can still sample some of the excellent wine in the front bar.

Casa Gallega

Map 3, G5. C/Bordadores 11 ©91 541 90 55; Plaza San Miguel 8 ©91 547 30 55. Both Metro Ópera/Sol.
Daily 1–4pm & 8pm–midnight. Expensive.

An airy and welcoming *marisquería*, with a branch at Plaza San Miguel, that has been importing seafood on overnight trains from Galicia since it opened in 1915. Costs vary greatly according to the rarity of the fish or shellfish that you order. Gallego staples such as *pulpo* (octopus) and *pimientos de Padrón* (tiny, randomly piquant peppers) are brilliantly done and inexpensive, but the more exotic seasonal delights will raise a bill for two well into five figures.

SANTA ANA AND HUERTAS

El Cenador del Prado

Map 6, D5. C/Prado 4 ©91 429 15 61. Metro Antón Martín/Sevilla.
Mon–Fri 1.30–4pm & 9pm–midnight, Sat 9pm–midnight. Closed Aug. Expensive.

Set in a relaxing and stylish mauve-coloured room, with imaginative cuisine combining Spanish, Mediterranean and Far

Eastern influences. There's a *menú de degustación* (gourmet menu) at 3500ptas and some spectacular desserts.

Champagnería Gala

Map 6, E7. C/Moratín 22 ℗91 429 25 62. Metro Antón Martín. Daily 1.30–4.30pm & 9pm–1.30am, Fri & Sat eve bar only. Inexpensive–moderate.

Fantastic-value restaurant run by a group of women, specializing in paellas and *fideuás* (like paella, only made with noodles instead of rice) and with excellent *pan tumaca* (toasted bread with tomato and garlic). Book ahead and try to get a table in the verdant indoor patio at the back. It's best to avoid weekends when the crowds mean the paellas and service aren't quite up to the normal standard. In the evenings, champagne accompanied by chocolate is served. All in all, a sophisticated oasis of calm if you want to relax after a taxing bar crawl. No cards accepted.

Domine Cabra

Map 6, E6. C/Huertas 54 ℗91 429 43 65. Metro Antón Martín. Mon–Sat 2–4pm & 9–11.30pm, Sun 2–4pm. Closed Sat lunch & Sun in Aug and first half of Sept. Moderate.

Interesting mix of traditional and modern, with *Madrileño* standards given the *nueva cocina* treatment. Good sauces – a rarity in Spain – and look out for the *entrecot con crema de cabrales* (steak with blue-cheese sauce), the *vieiras gratinadas al vino Albariño* (roasted scallops in white wine) and the *berenjenas al horno* (roasted aubergines).

Donzoko

Map 6, D4. C/Echegaray 3 ℗91 429 57 20. Metro Sevilla. Mon–Sat 1.30–3.30pm & 8.30–11.30pm. Moderate.

Very reasonable-value Japanese restaurant with helpful service, decent sushi and delicious tempura. If you're in a group the *sukiyaki* (strips of meat and vegetables fried in a wok on the table) is a good bet.

RESTAURANTS

El Inti de Oro

Map 6, D4. C/Ventura de la Vega 12. ℗91 429 67 03. Metro Sevilla.
Daily 1.30–4pm & 8.30pm–midnight. Moderate.

The friendly staff at this Peruvian restaurant are more than ready to provide suggestions and give advice on those new to the cuisine. The *Pisco Sour*, a cocktail of Peruvian liquor, lemon juice, egg white and sugar is a recommended starter to clean the palate, while the *cebiche de merluza* (raw fish marinated in lemon juice) is a wonderful experience. Main courses include *papas rellenas* (potatoes stuffed with meat, olives and raisins) and chicken in a nut sauce.

La Sanabresa

Map 5, G2. C/Amor de Dios 12 ℗91 429 03 38. Metro Antón Martín.
Mon–Sat 1–4pm & 8–11.30pm, Fri & Sat till midnight. Closed Aug. Inexpensive.

A real local, with a TV in one corner and an endless supply of customers who come for its excellent and reasonably priced dishes. Don't miss the fried aubergines (*berenjenas a la plancha*).

La Vaca Verónica

Map 6, E7. C/Moratín 38 ℗91 429 78 27. Metro Antón Martín.
Mon–Sat 2–4pm & 9pm–midnight. Closed Sat lunch & Sun. Moderate–expensive.

Something to suit all tastes. Excellent Argentinian-style meat, really good fresh pasta in imaginative sauces, quality fish dishes and tasty vegetables. Try the *Filet Verónica* and the *carabinero con pasta*. The *menú del día* is a good deal at 1900ptas.

LA LATINA AND LAVAPIÉS

La Burbuja que Ríe

Map 4, C7. C/Angel 16 ℗91 366 51 67. Metro Puerta de Toledo.
Tues 1–5pm, Wed–Sun 1–5pm & 8pm–midnight. Moderate.

Very popular noisy Asturian restaurant, with a young clientele.

RESTAURANTS

Huge servings of mussels, an excellent selection of Asturian cheeses and a very tasty *mero a la crema de anchoas* (grouper in anchovy sauce). Get here early for a table.

Casa Lastra Sidrería

Map 5, E2. C/Olivar 3 ℗91 369 08 37. Metro Antón Martín/Tirso de Molina.
Mon, Tues & Thurs–Sat 1–5pm & 8pm–midnight, Sun 1–5pm.
Closed July. Moderate.

Very popular restaurant serving classic Asturian fare: *chorizo a la sidra* (*chorizo* in cider), *entrecot al cabrales* (steak in a strong blue cheese sauce), *fabada* (a warming winter stew of beans, *chorizo* and *morcilla*) and, of course, *sidra natural* (cider).

Casa Lucio

Map 4, F4. C/Cava Baja 35 ℗91 365 32 52. Metro La Latina.
Mon–Fri & Sun 1–4pm & 9–11.30pm, Sat 9–11.30pm. Closed Aug.
Expensive.

Madrileños come here for Castilian dishes such as *cocido*, *callos* (tripe) and roasts, cooked to perfection. Prices have gone up a bit since the king visited, but you can still eat well for under 4000ptas if you're careful. Booking is essential.

El Económico/Soidermersol

Map 5, F5. C/Argumosa 9. Metro Lavapiés.
Daily except Sat 1–5pm & 9pm–midnight. Closed mid-Aug to mid-Sept. Inexpensive.

Traditional family-run workmen's *comedor* set in what looks like the front room of a house, in a pleasant tree-lined street near the Reina Sofía. An unbeatable 800ptas lunchtime *menú* offering a surprisingly large choice, friendly service and very tasty food.

Viuda de Vacas

Map 4, F5. C/Cava Alta 23 ℗91 366 58 47. Metro La Latina.
Daily except Thurs 1.30–4.30pm & 9pm–midnight. Closed Sun eve

After Midnight

If you're desperate for that late-night stomach-filler to keep you going into the early hours, the following places are strategically situated in the key night-time areas of the city.

La Carreta, Map 7, I7. C/Barbieri 10 (Metro Chueca; ©91 532 70 42). The latest-opening of all – you can order up till 4.30am – and you get a show thrown in too. Tango dancing and grilled meats South American-style should satisfy even the most serious insomniac reveller. Daily 1–5pm & 9pm–5am. Moderate.

La Farfala, Map 6, E7. C/Santa María 17 (Metro Antón Martín; ©91 369 46 91). The place to go for late-night food and a lively party atmosphere in the Huertas area. Good range of tasty pizzas and Argentinian-style meat. Daily 9pm–3am; Fri & Sat till 4am. Inexpensive.

Palacio de Anglona, Map 4, D4. C/Segovia 13 (Metro La Latina; ©91 366 37 53). Italian-style dishes served up in this trendy joint situated in the cellars of an old palace. Daily 8.30pm–2.30am. Moderate.

and early Aug. Inexpensive–moderate.

Highly traditional, family-run restaurant serving quality Castilian fare. Better value, though more basic, than the more celebrated *tabernas* in Cava Baja. Try the *merluza al horno* (baked hake), the *callos* and the *rabo de toro* (ox-tail).

GRAN VÍA, CHUECA AND SANTA BÁRBARA

El 26 de Libertad
Map 7, I6. C/Libertad 26 ©91 522 25 22. Metro Chueca.
Daily 1–4pm & 9pm–midnight. Closed Sun eve in July & Aug.
Moderate.

RESTAURANTS

Imaginative cuisine served up in an attentive, but unfussy manner in this brightly decorated restaurant, popular with the Chueca locals. Peppers stuffed with seafood, mushrooms in blue cheese and ostrich steaks in raspberry are some of the highlights. A good-value *menú del día* for 1300ptas.

El Buey

Map 7, B7. Plaza de la Marina Española 1 ℗91 541 30 41 (Metro Santo Domingo); c/General Díaz Polier 9 ℗91 575 31 28 (Metro Goya).
Mon–Sat 1–4pm & 9pm–midnight. Moderate.
A meat-eaters' paradise, specializing in superb steak which you fry up yourself on a hotplate. Very good side dishes, too, including a great leek and seafood pie and excellent homemade desserts. Help yourself to wine and cheese in the tiny bar while you wait to be seated.

Carmencita

Map 7, I7. C/Libertad 16 ℗91 531 66 12. Metro Chueca.
Mon–Fri 1–4pm & 9pm–midnight, Sat 9pm–midnight. Inexpensive–moderate.
Beautiful old restaurant, dating back to 1830, with panelling, brass, marble tables – and a new Basque-influenced chef. Popular with politicians and the literary crowd. The lunch *menú* is a bargain at 1300ptas, with the speciality being the *cocido*, served on Thursdays only.

La Choco-Arroces

Map 7, I6. C/Barbieri 15 ℗91 521 00 23. Metro Chueca.
Daily 1.45–3.45pm & 9pm–1.30am. Closed Aug. Moderate.
High-quality Mediterranean rice dishes served up in this friendly and attentive restaurant. The *fideuá* (paella made with noodles) and the *paella con carbineros y langostinos* are particularly good.

RESTAURANTS

El Comunista (Tienda de Vinos)

Map 7, I6. C/Augusto Figueroa 35 ℗91 521 70 12. Metro Chueca.
Mon–Sat 1–4.30pm & 9.30–11.45pm, Sun 9.30–11.45pm. Closed
mid-Aug to mid-Sept. Inexpensive.

Long-established, popular *comedor* that has changed little since it
was given its unofficial (but always used) name as a student
haunt under Franco. The *sopa de ajo* (garlic soup) is particularly
recommended.

Momo

Map 7, I6. C/Augusto Figueroa 41 ℗91 532 71 62. Metro Chueca.
Daily 1–4pm & 9pm–midnight. Inexpensive.

Now a well-established feature on the Chueca scene, this is the
place to go for a *menú del día* with a little bit extra. For 1300ptas
you get three well-presented courses, with some imaginative
sauces, drinks and coffee, all served in an outrageously kitsch
decor. Very popular, so worth putting your name down before
you go for an apéritif at one of the local bars.

Nova Galicia

Map 7, C4. C/Conde Duque 3 ℗91 559 42 60. Metro Plaza de
España.
Mon–Sat 7am–midnight, Sun 7am–4pm. Closed second half of
Aug. Moderate.

Excellent-value Galician restaurant, specializing in seafood
tapas and *arroz con bogavante* (rice with lobster). Pass through
the ordinary-looking front bar and into the dining room hidden behind. For large parties they will do a special *queimada*
(flaming Galician liquor served in small terracotta bowls).

Salvador

Map 7, I7. C/Barbieri 12 ℗91 521 45 24. Metro Chueca.
Mon–Sat 1.30–5pm & 9pm–midnight. Closed Aug. Expensive.

Bullfighting decor and traditional specialities such as *rabo de toro*
(bull's tail), *gallina en pepitoria* (chicken fricassee), fried *merluza*

(hake) and *arroz con leche* (rice pudding), which are all excellent.

La Tasca Suprema

Map 7, J4. C/Argensola 7 ℅91 308 03 47. Metro Alonso Martínez.
Mon–Sat 1.30–4pm. Closed Aug. Inexpensive.

Very popular family-run local, only open at lunchtimes and worth booking ahead for. Perfect Castilian home cooking, including *callos*, and on Monday and Thursday, *cocido*.

MALASAÑA AND BILBAO

Balear

C/Sagunto 18 ℅91 447 91 15. Metro Iglesia.
Mon 1.30–4pm, Tues–Sat 1.30–4pm & 8.30pm–midnight, Sun 1.30–4pm. Moderate.

This relaxed Levantine restaurant serves only rice-based dishes – fifteen different types of paella – but they're superb. There's an inexpensive *cava* and you can turn up any time before midnight.

La Giralda

Map 7, G1. C/Hartzenbush 12 ℅91 445 77 79. Metro Bilbao.
Mon–Sat 1–4.30pm & 8pm–midnight. Moderate–expensive.

A little slice of Andalucía serving Andaluz fish and seafood of very high quality. Perfectly cooked *chipirones* (small squid fried in batter), *calamares* and all the standards, plus wonderful *mero* (grouper). A second branch, across the road, at no. 15, does a similarly accomplished job on *pescados fritos*.

La Glorieta

Map 7, E2. C/Manuela Malasaña 37 ℅91 448 40 16. Metro Bilbao.
Mon–Sat 1.30–5pm & 9pm–midnight. Closed Aug 10–25. Moderate.

Imaginative and tasty modern Spanish cooking, with Basque and French influences. Very good-value *menú del día* at 1100ptas, which includes a better-than-average bottle of wine,

RESTAURANTS

Madrid's Vegetarian Restaurants

Madrid can be an intimidating city for veggies, given the mass of pigs, fish and seafood on display in restaurant windows and on counters. However, you can order vegetables separately at just about any restaurant in the city – though make sure you specify that you do not want stray pieces of ham included – and there is good pizza and pasta to be had at a number of Italian places. You can even find the odd vegetarian paella. As for **tapas**, *champiñones*, *patatas bravas*, *patatas ali oli*, *pimientos de padrón* and *tortilla* are probably the best bets.

More crucially, the capital now has some decent and inexpensive **vegetarian restaurants** around the centre. These include:

Artemisa, Map 6, D4. C/Ventura de la Vega 4 (Metro Sevilla; ©91 429 50 92); c/Tres Cruces 4 (Metro Gran Vía; ©91 521 87 21). A popular place, best known for its veggie pizzas, stuffed aubergines and an imaginative range of salads. No smoking. Mon–Sat 1.30–4pm & 9pm–midnight, Sun 1.30–4pm. Moderate.

El Estragón, Map 4, D4. Plaza de La Paja 10 (Metro La Latina; ©91 365 89 82). Cosy atmosphere and a fine setting on the edge of this ancient plaza. Serves good vegetarian tapas, and a varied *menú del día* for 1000ptas. Daily 1–4.30pm & 8.30pm–midnight; closed Sun eve. Inexpensive-moderate.

El Granero de Lavapiés, Map 5, G5. C/Argumosa 10 (Metro Lavapiés; ©91 467 76 11). In a pleasant tree-lined Lavapiés street, serving excellent macrobiotic and vegetarian food. No smoking. Mon–Fri 1–4pm, Fri & Sat 8.30–11pm. Closed Aug. Inexpensive.

La Granja, Map 7, F3. C/San Andrés 11 (Metro Bilbao/ Tribunal; ©91 532 87 93). The good-value set menu at 950ptas changes daily, offering a choice of soup, salad, a main dish of vegetables, rice and fruits topped with sauce, dessert and drinks. Mon–Wed 1.30–4.30pm & 9pm–midnight, Thurs–Sun 1.30–4.30pm. Inexpensive.

zesty lemon cheesecake, coffee and a *copita* of high-powered Galician *orujo* (strong schnapps-like drink).

Ribeira Do Miño
Map 7, H5. C/Santa Brígida 1 ©91 521 98 54. Metro Tribunal.
Daily 1–5pm & 8pm–1am. Closed Mon. Moderate
Great-value *marisquería* near the Museo Municipal, serving a *mariscada* (shellfish platter) for two at only 3500ptas; go for the slightly more expensive Galician white wine, *Albariño*, to accompany it.

Taberna Griega
Map 7, E4. C/Tesoro 6 ©91 532 18 92. Metro Tribunal.
Tues–Sun 8.30pm–midnight and beyond. Closed Aug. Inexpensive.
Enjoyable Greek restaurant, with live *bouzouki* music most nights. A tasty *moussaka* and plentiful *metzes* are stalwarts of the menu. At weekends there's Greek dancing accompanied by obligatory plate smashing.

RECOLETOS AND SALAMANCA

Al Mounia
Map 7, K7. Paseo de Recoletos 5 ©91 435 08 28. Metro Banco de España.
Tues–Sat 1.30–3.30pm & 9pm–midnight. Closed Aug. Expensive.
Moroccan cooking at its very best at the most established Arabic restaurant in town, offering an atmospheric and romantic setting with impeccable service. The *bastilla* (pigeon pie) and desserts are a must.

El Amparo
Map 2, K3. Callejón Puigcerdá 8 ©91 431 64 56. Metro Serrano.
Mon–Fri 1.30–3.30pm & 9–11.30pm, Sat 9–11.30pm. Expensive.
Most critics rate this designer restaurant among the top five in

RESTAURANTS

Madrid, and you'll need to book a couple of weeks ahead to get a table. Faultless Basque cooking by Carmen Guasp, with main dishes around the 3000ptas mark. Expect a bill of at least 6000ptas a head.

Casa Portal

C/Dr Castelo 26 ℂ91 574 20 26. Metro Retiro.
Mon–Sat 1.30–4pm & 8.30–11.30pm. Closed Aug.
Expensive.

Superlative Asturian cooking – go for the *fabada* (beans, *chorizo* and *morcilla* stew) or *besugo* (bream), washed down with some natural cider. The shellfish is excellent too.

Paradis Madrid

Map 6, F3. C/Marqués de Cubas 14 ℂ91 429 73 03. Metro Banco de España.
Mon–Fri 1.30–4pm & 9pm–midnight, Sat 9pm–midnight. Closed Easter & Aug. Expensive.

Part of a chain of restaurants run by a Catalan duo, with branches in Barcelona and New York. Designerish details include a menu for olive oils. The cooking is light, Mediterranean and tasty; try the wonderful *arroz negro* (rice cooked in squid's ink) with seafood.

Viridiana

Map 6, H3. C/Juan de Mena 14 ℂ91 523 44 78 or 91 531 52 22.
Metro Retiro.
Mon–Sat 1.30–4pm & 9pm–midnight. Closed Easter & Aug. Very expensive.

Bizarre temple of Madrid *nueva cocina*, offering mouthwatering creations like *solomillo* (sirloin) with black truffles and *mero* with *crepes*, while also conducting pyrotechnic experiments – dishes often arrive decorated with small incendiary devices. Superb selection of wine. Main courses are around 2500ptas. No cards.

RESTAURANTS

Zalacaín

C/Alvarez de Baena 4 ©91 561 59 35. Metro Gregorio Marañon.
Mon–Fri 1.15–4pm & 9pm–midnight, Sat 9pm–midnight. Closed
Aug. Very expensive.

Luxurious setting for the best restaurant in town and the only
one with three Michelin stars. As you'd expect, the Basque-
style cooking of master chef Benjamín Urdaín is top-notch and
the wines are superb. You pay heavily for the pleasure, however, with a meal setting you back somewhere in the region of
11,000ptas per person.

ARGÜELLES

Casa Mingo

Paseo de la Florida 2 ©91 547 79 18. Metro Príncipe Pío.
Daily 11am–midnight. Closed Aug. Inexpensive.

Next to the Ermita de Antonio de la Florida, this is a great-
value, noisy and crowded Asturian chicken and cider house.
Tables on the pavement or in the barn-like interior are like
gold dust, so loiter close by with your bottle of *sidra natural* in
hand ready to jump in when someone finishes. The spit-roast
chicken is the practically compulsory main course, while the
chorizo cooked in cider and *cabrales* (blue cheese) are also very
good. You can also buy a takeaway for a picnic in the Casa de
Campo, if you prefer.

La Vaca Argentina

Map 2, A1. Paseo del Pintor Rosales 52 ©91 559 66 05. Metro
Argüelles.
Daily 1–5pm & 9pm–midnight. Moderate.

Good views and great grilled steaks (*churrasco*) at this
Argentinian restaurant overlooking the Parque del Oeste. Its
terrace is a very pleasant place to eat in summer.

Drinking

With over 12,000 **bars** in the city, it's clear that the bar – and its close cousins, the café and *terraza* – is a central feature of *Madrileño* life. There's a bewildering variety to choose from: *cervecerías* (beer specialists), *coctelerías* (cocktail bars), *champagnerías* (champagne bars), *tabernas* (old-style taverns), *bares de copas* (bars mainly serving spirits) and a new wave of Irish bars. You'll also find *disco-bares* and *pubs*, where music is the primary attraction; these are covered in a separate chapter (see "Nightlife", p.181).

"Bar hanging" is one of the best, and most pleasant, ways to get the feel of the city and its people, although you'll need to adopt *Madrileño* bar **customs** as quickly as possible. Don't get put off or feel uncomfortable if the barman or waiter appears to ignore you; just give a firm shout of "*oiga*", which, although it sounds rude to English-speaking ears, is in fact the polite way of calling the barman's attention. Once you have ordered don't be in a hurry to thrust your pesetas into the barman's hand; instead, wait until you are ready to go, and then ask for "*la cuenta*". Leave a few small coins as a tip if you wish, and remember that you normally pay a little more for sitting at a table with waiter service than for standing at the bar. You won't often find bins for your bar detritus of olive stones, paper napkins, toothpicks, etc, and it is usual to throw them on the floor.

Most cafés and bars serve some sort of food, but if this is their primary attraction we have listed them under "Tapas bars" in the "Eating" chapter. There is, however, no absolute dividing line, and you will often find excellent snacks in the places listed in this chapter. Many bars, and especially nightclubs, set up outdoor *terrazas* in summer. For details of these see p.192.

SOL AND SANTA ANA

Aloque
Map 5, F3. C/Torrecilla del Real 20. Metro Antón Martín.
Daily 7.30pm–1am. Closed Aug.
Relaxed wine bar where you can try top-quality wines by the glass. Its owner, Paco Parejo, is a science professor and expert on viticulture. Regular wine-tasting sessions and a wine connoisseurs' *tertulia* (Tues) are held here. The tapas, served up from the tiny kitchen at the back, are original and very tasty indeed.

El Anciano
Map 3, C6. C/Bailén 19. Metro Ópera.
Daily except Wed 10am–3pm & 5.30–11pm, Fri & Sat till 12.30am. Closed Aug.
Pleasant bar across the road from the Palacio Real, and just the place to refresh yourself after some hard work on the tourist trail. Tasty beer and a good range of wines in an old-fashioned establishment, dating back to 1907.

Café de Oriente
Map 3, D4. Plaza de Oriente 2. Metro Ópera.
Daily 8.30am–1.30am, Fri & Sat till 2.30am.
Elegant, traditional-style café, founded a decade or so ago by priest, Luis Lezama, to finance a charity rehab programme for ex-convicts. Plenty of mirrors, marble tabletops and candlesticks with occasional accompaniment from the pianist. A popular *terraza* in summer looks out onto Plaza de Oriente.

DRINKING

Drinking – The Essentials

Drinking out needn't be expensive, especially if you stick to the more down-to-earth local bars and, even better, get to know the barman. If you venture into cocktail bars and *bares de copas* you will pay a lot more for both beers and spirits, although measures are very generous indeed and it's usually up to you to tell the barman to stop pouring. It's worth remembering that imported beers and spirits (*importación*) are always a good deal more expensive than the Spanish equivalents (*nacional*).

BEER
Cerveza, lager-type beer, is generally of very good quality. It comes bottled in *tercios* (a third of a litre) or smaller *botellines*, and on draught (*de barril*), in *cañas* (small glasses), *dobles* (larger glasses), *jarras* (jugs) or even *pintas* (pints). Non-alcoholic beers (*cerveza sin alcohol*) are available by the bottle in all bars. The most popular local brand is Mahou, although practically every major international brand is now available in Madrid.

WINE AND LIQUEURS
Wines (*tinto* – red, *blanco* – white and *rosado* – rosé) are a very cheap option and many bars have a fine selection, so ask for it by name, as you will tend to get the cheapest if you don't specify. In addition to the internationally renowned Rioja, it is worth trying the red wines from Ribera del Duero, with their smooth blackcurrant flavour; 1989, 1995 and 1996 are particularly good years. Fine reds are also to be found from Navarra, Valdepeñas and Penedès. As for white wines, those from Rueda are recognized for their quality, while the Galician whites of Ribeiro and Albariño are refreshing and make an

excellent accompaniment to seafood. The light white wine, Barbadillo, from near Cádiz, is an excellent option in summer. A non-alcoholic alternative to wine is the sweet white *mosto*, which is available in most bars.

Sherries are also worth trying, especially the chilled dry *fino* or fuller bodied *palo cortado* served in many Andaluz bars, as is *vermút de barril* (draught vermouth), all of which make an ideal apéritif. Catalan champagne-like sparkling wine (**cava**) is good value and can be ordered at specialist wine bars and *champagnerías*. **Sangría**, a deceptively strong, but refreshing punch-like mixture of red wine, fruit and lemonade is common in summer. A variety of after-dinner drinks and **liqueurs** are available, including locally produced *anís* (aniseed), *pacharán* (another more fruity aniseed drink from Navarra) and *orujo* (a powerful schnapps-type drink).

SOFT DRINKS

As you'd expect, all the major brand-name soft drinks are available, but also worth trying are the specifically Spanish soft drinks such as *horchata* (a milky drink made from crushed nuts) and *granizado* (crushed ice with lemon, orange or coffee). When ordering water specify if you want it still (*sin gas*), sparkling (*con gas*) or from the tap (*del grifo*).

COFFEE AND TEA

Coffee is usually of excellent quality and generally served black in a small cup (*café solo*). If you want a larger, more dilute black coffee ask for an *americano*; with a drop of milk it's *café cortado*; and white with lots of hot milk it's *café con leche*. For decaffeinated ask for *descafeinado*. Tea (*té*) is usually poor, and ordering it with milk will often get you a glass of milk with a tea bag floating on top, so it's best to order the two separately.

DRINKING – THE ESSENTIALS

Cervecería Alemana

Map 6, C5. Plaza de Santa Ana 6. Metro Sol.

Daily except Tues 10am–12.30am, Fri & Sat till 2am.

Stylish old beer house, founded in 1904, with dark wooden panels, white marble tables and a packed bar. Frequented in times past by Hemingway and, these days, seemingly every other American tourist. Order a *caña* and go easy on the tapas, as the bill can mount up fast.

Cervecería Santa Ana

Map 6, C5. Plaza de Santa Ana 10. Metro Sol.

Daily 11am–1.30am, Fri & Sat till 2.30am.

Cheaper than the *Alemana*, with tables outside, but few inside. Good beer, friendly service and a fine selection of tapas. Always packed at night.

Los Gabrieles

Map 6, D5. C/Echegaray 17. Metro Sol.

Daily 2.30pm–2.30am.

This impressively tiled bar, which includes scenes from *Don Quixote* and a version of Velázquez's *Los Borrachos*, is a Madrid monument and it's worth going earlier than is cool to appreciate the fabulous tableaux, created by sherry companies in the 1880s. Drinks are reasonable, considering the venue. Live flamenco on Tuesdays. Very crowded after 10pm, especially at weekends.

Naturbier

Map 6, C5. Plaza de Santa Ana 9. Metro Sol.

Daily 8pm–3am.

Next door to the *cervecerías Alemana* and *Santa Ana*, the *Naturbier Bar* brews its own tasty, cloudy beer and serves a variety of German sausages to accompany it. There's usually room to sit in the cellar down below if the top bar is too crowded.

DRINKING

Salón del Prado
Map 6, D5. C/Prado 4. Metro Sol.
Daily 2pm–2am.
Elegant Parisian-style café–bar serving great coffee and hosting classical music concerts on Thursday night at 11pm. Turn up early if you want a table.

La Taberna de Dolores
Map 6, F6. Plaza de Jesús 4. Metro Antón Martín.
Daily 11am–midnight.
Splendid canapés at this popular and friendly tiled bar, decorated with beer bottles from around the world. The beer is really good, and the food specialities include roquefort and anchovy, and smoked-salmon canapés. Get here early if you want a space at the bar.

La Venencia
Map 6, D4. C/Echegaray 7. Metro Sol/Sevilla.
Daily 7pm–1.30am. Closed Aug.
This rather delapidated, narrow, wooden-panelled bar covered in yellowing advertising posters is great for sherry sampling. The whole range is here, served from wooden barrels, and accompanied by delicious olives and *mojama* (dry salted tuna). Atmospheric and authentic.

Viva Madrid
Map 6, D5. C/Manuel Fernández y González 7. Metro Antón Martín.
Daily noon–2am, Fri & Sat till 3am.
Another fabulous tiled bar – both outside and in – offering wines and sherry, plus basic tapas. Get here early if you want to see the tiles in their full glory, as it gets very crowded. Quite pricey, but certainly worth a stop.

DRINKING

Las Tertulias

Everywhere people meet to chat and argue, but only in Spain – a country where conversation is considered to be one of the fine arts – has this simple custom been converted into an established ritual. To earn the name **tertulia**, a regular time and place must be fixed – usually in a café or bar – and participants must come prepared to speak, interrupt, contradict and generally intensify the discussion. Subject matter can range from politics, philosophy and literature to bullfighting and flamenco.

The first *tertulias* began with the eighteenth-century Enlightenment and were largely political, with liberals and absolutists – supporters and opponents of the French Revolution – arguing out their differences. In the late nineteenth and early twentieth centuries, with the rise of the literary groups, the "Generation of '98" and subsequent "Generation of '27", they became a forum for intellectual and artistic ideas, with participants including the poet Federico García Lorca and painter José Gutiérrez de Solana (whose famous painting of the *tertulia* at the *Café del Pombo* hangs in the Centro de Arte Reina Sofía). Not all writers, however, enjoyed these literary gatherings: Hemingway, for one, hated them and regarded the people who attended them as "a load of show-offs".

Cafés such as *Gijón*, *El Lion* and *El Parnasillo* built their reputations on the standard of their *tertulias*, and as one old *contertulio* said, "In life there are only three fundamental choices: marital state, profession and café." However, many were silenced during the Civil War and afterwards under Franco, when meetings of more than five people were seen as suspect. They reappeared in the late 1940s, with the emergence of Juventud Creadora, a group of young writers who met in *Café Gijón*, headed by Nobel Prize Winner, Camilo José Cela, and to this day, although they have declined in importance and may not reach the intellectual heights of the past, they are still alive and well in a number of the city's old cafés and bars.

El 21
Map 4, G3. C/Toledo 21. Metro La Latina.
Daily 11am–3.30pm & 7–11pm. Closed Aug.
Excellent *chupito* (a thimbleful of spirits) bar, serving a vast
range of mini-cocktails (including non-alcoholic), with evocative names such as *Erótico*, *Medias de seda* (Silk stockings),
Terremoto (Earthquake) and *Volcán* (Volcano). The cheap and
cheerful alternative to a full-scale cocktail bar; all drinks are
150–200ptas.

Alquezar
Map 5, E4. C/Lavapiés 53. Metro Lavapiés.
Daily 1pm–1am, Fri & Sat till 3am.
An Arabian atmosphere is created with walls adorned with
camels and mosques, background music and sweet-smelling tea
served from silver-plated teapots. If you get peckish try the
Arab pastries.

Café del Nuncio
Map 4, E4. C/Segovia 9. Metro La Latina.
Daily 12.30pm–2.30am.
A great place for cocktails, alcoholic coffees and the house spe-
ciality, *Agua de Valencia* (a sort of bucks fizz). Good cakes and
biscuits, too, and a very pleasant *terraza* in summer.

María Panadora
Map 4, B4. Plaza Gabriel Miró 1. Metro La Latina.
Tues–Thurs 6pm–2am, Fri & Sat 6pm–3am, Sun 1pm–2am. Closed
second half of Aug.
An incongruous mixture of *champagnería* and library, where
quality *cava* can be enjoyed with the perfect accompaniment of
chocolates and mellow jazz – a decadent and highly enjoyable
outing.

DRINKING

Nuevo Café Barbieri

Map 4, F4. C/Ave María 45. Metro Lavapiés.

Daily 3pm–2am, Fri & Sat till 3am.

Ever so slightly seedy, well-known café with a vaguely intellectual reputation, situated just off the Plaza de Lavapiés. It's a relaxed place, with unobtrusive music, lots of wooden tables, old-style decor, newspapers and a wide selection of coffees.

Pastelería-Licorería El Madroño

Map 5, E4. C/Caravaca 10. Metro Lavapiés.

Tues–Sun 10am–2pm & 6pm–midnight, Fri & Sat till 2am. Closed Aug.

The place to go for Madrid's own liqueur made from the berries of the *madroño* tree; you can pick up a slice of seaweed cake, too, while you're here.

El Tempranillo

Map 4, E5. C/Cava Baja 38. Metro La Latina.

Daily noon–4pm & 9pm–2am.

Excellent little wine bar serving a vast range of Spanish wines by the glass. Although a relative newcomer, it feels as though it's been here for years and has already established a faithful clientele. A great place to discover your favourite Spanish wine, and the tapas are very tasty too.

GRAN VÍA AND CHUECA

Café Moderno

Map 7, D3. Plaza de las Comendadoras 1. Metro Noviciado.

Daily 3pm–2am, Fri & Sat till 3am; June–Sept from noon.

Hidden away in a quiet, hippyish square alongside the Convento de las Comendadoras is this mock Art Deco café. Activities include musical recitals, tarot-card reading, theatrical performances and Arabian dancing. Plenty of coffees and herbal teas.

DRINKING

Carpe Diem
Map 7, D5. Plaza Conde de Toreno 2. Metro Plaza de España/
Noviciado.
Tues–Sat 9pm–3am.
A part of the takings of this bar goes toward oversea projects
and it often stages markets in aid of developing countries. The
single-roomed bar is decorated with Pop Art and cartoons,
while noticeboards keep the clientele informed of upcoming
events. Happy hour goes on until midnight, with a variety of
Spanish pop and salsa played.

Círculo de Bellas Artes
Map 6, E2. C/Alcalá 42. Metro Banco de España.
Daily 8am–2am, Fri & Sat till 3am.
You pay 100ptas for day membership to the Círculo, which
gives access to the exhibitions (see p.54) and to a luxurious bar,
complete with reclining nude sculpture and sofas. Outside is a
year-round *terraza*.

El Cock
Map 7, H7. C/Reina 16, just behind Museo Chicote. Metro Gran Vía.
Daily 7pm–3am.
Formerly connected to the *Museo Chicote* (see overleaf)
by a secret corridor, this is now a smart and very *moda* bar,
styled like a gentlemen's club, and you have to knock
to get in. Attracts an arty crowd late at night, and the
music is good. *Cañas* or wine cost around 600ptas, cocktails
900ptas.

La Consulta
Map 7, J5. C/Belén. Metro Chueca/Alonso Martínez.
Daily 10pm–5.30am; Fri & Sat opens at 7.30pm.
Hidden away in a Chueca side-street is this dimly-lit, friendly
late-night bar with a thirty-something clientele. The joint
owners, Moncho and Chicho, who hail from Puerto Rico and

the Canary Islands respectively, serve up good-value cocktails and spirits with a smile.

Del Diego

Map 7, H7. C/Reina 12. Metro Gran Vía.

Mon–Sat 9pm–3am. Closed Aug.

Another stylish Art Deco cocktail bar set up by a former *Chicote* waiter who personally mixes all the excellent cocktails. Friendly, unhurried atmosphere and open until the early hours. The house special, vodka-based *Del Diego,* is the one to go for.

Museo Chicote

Map 7, H7. Gran Vía 12. Metro Gran Vía.

June–Sept 5pm–3am (Fri & Sat till 4am); Oct–May noon–3am (Fri & Sat till 4am).

The place to go if you've got a bit of imagination and want to wallow in nostalgia. Opened in 1931 and still full of Art Deco lines and pistacho-coloured booths, this bar was opened by Perico Chicote, ex-barman at the *Ritz*. At the back, he set up a museum to house his collection of over ten thousand special bottles, including original Napoleon brandy, Chinese chrysanthemum liquor and vodka from the Tsar. Sophia Loren, Frank Sinatra, Ava Gardner, Luis Buñuel, Orson Welles and the ubiquitous Hemingway have all passed through its doors. The collection has, alas, long gone, sold by Perico's descendants and then auctioned off bottle by bottle in 1984. Nowadays, they will mix you any (expensive) cocktail while you savour the memories. Busiest after midnight.

Net Café

Map 7, E2. C/San Bernardo 81. Metro San Bernardo.

Mon–Thurs 8pm–2am, Fri & Sat 4pm–3.30am, Sun 4pm–1am.

If you really can't bear to be away from the computer screen while you're on holiday, this is the place for you. Surf the Net, play the latest games and chat to other nerds.

DRINKING

Irish Pubs

Although a pint of the "black stuff" has long been available in the capital, specialist **Irish pubs** have sprung up all over the city in recent years. Having bought up the Spanish brewery, Cruzcampo, in 1991, Guinness has established its presence across the city, setting up and supplying pubs, whilst other individual ventures have followed in their wake. Theme pubs based on village shops, Dublin streets, country cottages and breweries have all appeared, while the Celtic music scene has taken off in a big way with a number of bands now firmly established on the pub circuit. Prices are high in comparison to most Spanish bars, but they are still popular with the city's large British community, and young *Madrileños* also form a substantial section of their clientele. If you want to be assured of a great St Patrick's night, catch up on the latest sport or just feel a little homesick you could try some of the following:

Finnegans, Map 7, J5. Plaza de las Salesas 9 (Metro Colón). Large bar with several rooms, complete with bar fittings and wooden floors brought over from Ireland. English-speaking staff and TV sports. Mon–Thurs & Sun 12.30pm–2am, Fri & Sat 1pm–3am.

O'Donnell's, Map 7, H3. C/Barceló 1 (Metro Tribunal). Right on the square behind the Museo Municipal – a popular venue for open-air student parties at weekends. Pub quiz on Mondays. Daily 10am–2am.

The Quiet Man, Map 7, G5. C/Valverde 44 (Metro Tribunal). One of the first on the scene, designed in the style of an early twentieth-century Dublin pub and full of authentic fittings. Mon–Thurs 5.30pm–2am, Fri–Sun 1pm–3.30am.

The Triskel Tavern, Map 7, G4. C/San Vicente Ferrer 3 (Metro Tribunal). Jazz nights on Tuesdays and the open mic session on Thursdays are worth a visit. There's a quiz on Mondays, and, to complete a typical pub night out, they even do curries.

Taberna Angel Sierra
Map 7, I6. C/Gravina 11, on Plaza Chueca. Metro Chueca.
Daily noon–1am.

One of the great bars in Madrid, with a traditional zinc counter. Everyone drinks *vermút,* which is on tap and delicious, accompanied by free, exquisite *boquerones en vinagre* tapas. *Raciones* are also available, though they're expensive.

MALASAÑA AND BILBAO

La Ardosa
Map 7, G5. C/Colón 13. Metro Tribunal.
Daily noon–3pm & 6.30pm–midnight.

A great selection of beers on offer in this classic *cervecería,* decorated with Goya reproductions. Over one hundred years old and serving Guinness years before the boom in Irish bars in Madrid, *La Ardosa* also serves great *tortilla* and a very tasty *salmorejo de Córdoba* (a substantial gazpacho with pieces of ham).

Café Comercial
Map 7, G2. Glorieta de Bilbao 7. Metro Bilbao.
Daily 8am–1am, Fri & Sat till 2am.

A *Madrileño* institution and one of the city's most popular meeting points. This is a lovely traditional café full of mirrors, substantial tables and the whole cross-section of Madrid society. Settle in, relax and listen to the pianist on Friday and Saturday nights. Regular *tertulias* on Monday at 6pm and bimonthly meetings for English writers on Saturday evening. Well placed for the Chueca/Santa Bárbara area.

Café del Foro
Map 7, F3. C/San Andrés 38. Metro Tribunal.
Daily 7pm–3am, Fri & Sat till 4am.

Expensive but enjoyable bar, with live music or some form of entertainment most nights. Attracts a slightly older, fairly smart

DRINKING

crowd. The decor, intended to look like a town square, is designed by Costus, Almodóvar's sidekick.

Café de Ruiz
Map 7, F2. C/Ruiz 11. Metro Bilbao.
Daily 3pm–3am.
Classic old-fashioned café in the midst of Malasaña – a great place to while away an afternoon reading the paper. Discreet background music and good cakes and biscuits.

Medina Magerit
Map 7, F3. C/Divino Pastor 21. Metro Bilbao.
Daily 7pm–2am.
Original bar with a friendly and enthusiastic owner serving an interesting and creative selection of drinks, including *Tisana India con zumos* (fruit juices with herbs and seeds), *Agua de Cebada* (a crushed ice and barley concoction) and delicious *mojito cubanos* (rum cocktails). A selection of board games is available to pass the time, and downstairs there's a very small, but atmospheric, cellar, where traditional flamenco is sometimes performed.

RECOLETOS AND SALAMANCA

Café el Espejo
Map 7, L6. Paseo de Recoletos 31. Metro Colón.
Daily 10am–2am, Fri & Sat till 3am.
Opened in 1978, but you wouldn't guess it from the antiquated decor. Mirrors, gilt and a wonderful, extravagant glass pavilion, plus a leafy outside *terraza*. Just the place to buy a coffee and watch the world go by.

Café Gijón
Map 7, K6. Paseo de Recoletos 21. Metro Banco de España.
Daily 8am–1.30am.
Famous literary café dating from 1888, decked out in Cuban

mahogany and mirrors. A centre of the intellectual/arty *movida* in the 1980s. Best for morning or late afternoon coffee, as tables are turned over for the set menu at lunchtime. There's also a cellar restaurant and a very pleasant summer *terraza*. Regular artistic *tertulias* are still held here (see box, p.172).

El Gato Persa
Map 7, K5. C/Bárbara de Braganza 10. Metro Colón.
Daily 10am–1am. Closed second half of Aug.
This tearoom, set in a small library with comfortable seats, soft lighting and Baroque music (jazz at night), makes a very relaxing escape from the bustle of the city. A wide range of fruit and floral teas is on offer, including *mil y una noches*, a combination of black tea and wild flowers.

Nightlife

Madrid's renowned **late-night scene** really took off with **la movida madrileña** in the late 1970s, when the end of the Franco era produced an explosion of artistic creativity combined with a long-suppressed desire to indulge in pure hedonistic enjoyment. Although the true *movida* has passed, and new laws have been introduced restricting opening times of some bars, nightlife still remains a pretty serious phenomenon – this is the only city in Europe where you can get caught in traffic jams at 4am, when clubbers are either going home or moving on to the dance-past-dawn discos. Madrid's bar and club scene has, if anything, got more frenetic over the past few years, largely owing to the appearance of **bakalao**, a Spanish (originally Ibizan) version of house music, which is especially prominent in the zone around Bilbao.

As with everything *Madrileño*, there is a bewildering variety of types of nightlife. The mainstays of the Madrid scene are the **discobares** – bars of all musical and sexual persuasion, whose unifying feature is background (occasionally live) rock, dance or salsa music and usually a small dance floor. These don't generally charge admission, but drinks are more expensive than in other bars; they get going around at 11pm and stay open till 2am or 3am. **Discotecas** are rarely worth investigating until around 1 or 2am, although queues often build up quickly after this time. They aren't always that different from *discobares*, though they tend to be bigger and flashier, with a lot of attention to lights, sound system and decor, and they stay open very late – most until 4am, some till 6am. If you're up for it, **"after hours" venues** open at between 5 and 6am and keep going until late morning when you can grab some *chocolate con churros* before finally heading home to bed (see box, p.189).

Venues with regular live music – rock, jazz, flamenco, salsa and classical – are covered in the "Live Music" chapter; see p.200.

In summer, many of the trendier clubs suspend operations and set up all-night outdoor **terrazas**, which are effectively open-air discos. They change location from year to year, as they are pursued by the local authorities for breaches of local by-laws on noise, traffic and obstruction, but they still pop up every summer in and around the Castellana.

DISCOBARES

Discobares are scattered all over the city, but each area has its own very particular identity. The magnet for the teenage crowd is **Alonso Martínez**, while **Argüelles** and **Moncloa** are student hangouts, and **Salamanca** is the place for chic bars and high prices. If you want to be at the cutting edge of trendiness, head for **Malasaña** and **Chueca**, while you'll find a more eclectic mix in the streets around **Sol** and **Santa Ana**.

La Comedia

Map 6, C4. C/Príncipe 16. Metro Sol.
Sun–Thurs 9pm–4am, Fri & Sat 9pm–9am.

Modern, relaxing bar for a quiet drink by day; gets livelier as
the night progresses. Good selection of varied and danceable
music, and it's a favourite haunt of staff from earlier-closing
bars, as it's open until 9am at the weekends. Entry charge of
1000ptas at night.

No se lo digas a nadie

Map 6, D4. C/Ventura de la Vega 7. Metro Sol.
Mon–Thurs 9pm–3am, Fri & Sat 9pm–5am.

Founded – and still run – by a women's co-op, though this
bar has mellowed a bit in recent years (the toilets no longer
proclaim *nosotras* and *ellos* – "us"and "them"). Nonetheless, it
retains a political edge, hosting benefit events from time to
time. There's no door policy or dress code and drinks are reasonably priced. Upstairs you'll find six pool tables and plenty
of places to sit; downstairs there's a disco playing mainly
dance music.

Villa Rosa

Map 6, C5. Plaza de Santa Ana 5. Metro Sol.
Mon–Sat 11pm–5am.

This dance bar was formerly a famous flamenco club which
later featured in Pedro Almodóvar's *High Heels*. The exterior is
adorned with beautiful *azulejos* of famous Spanish cities, and
the interior is straight out of the Alhambra, with its *Mudéjar*
arches and ceilings. Monday and Tuesday are salsa nights,
Wednesday flamenco and the rest of the week is mainstream
disco.

DISCOBARES

LA LATINA

El Viajero
Map 4, E6. Plaza de la Cebada. Metro La Latina.
Tues–Sun 2pm–2.30am.
A fashionable La Latina nightspot spread over a number of
floors. The summer *terraza* on the top floor affords great views
of San Francisco El Grande. Also has a restaurant serving good
pizzas and pastas.

GRAN VÍA, CHUECA AND SANTA BÁRBARA

Big Bamboo
Map 7, J7. C/Barquillo 42. Metro Alonso Martínez.
Daily 10.30pm–5am, Fri & Sat till 6am.
Reggae music and great cocktails, including an upside-down
margarita poured directly down the throat – mixing takes place
by vigorous shaking of the head before you swallow. Plenty of
room for dancing.

Impacto
Map 7, J3. C/Campoamor 3. Metro Alonso Martínez.
Daily 11pm–3am.
Inside, this place is a mini-labyrinth, with little rooms and bars
around every corner. A fairly trendy, slightly older crowd, reasonably priced drinks and a good variety of music, despite the
lack of a dance floor. Door policy of sorts.

Kingston's
Map 7, J5. C/Barquillo 29. Metro Chueca/Alonso Martínez.
Daily 10pm–5am.
Relaxed multicultural *discobar*, with colourful ethnic designs
portraying plants and exotic animals. Music ranges from soul
and funk to reggae and rap. At the weekend, professional
dancers get things going.

DISCOBARES

El Morocco

Map 7, D6. C/Marqués de Leganés 7. Metro Santo Domingo.
Daily 11pm–5am.

Latest venture by rock singer Alaska, long-time mover of the *movida* and mate of Pedro Almodóvar. The crowds here could well be from an Almodóvar movie and it's likely that some, at least, have acted in one. Cabaret show at 2am, the odd (and odd is the word) band, and a pulsing dance floor. There's an occasional entrance charge and you'll need to look the part to get past the doorman.

MALASAÑA AND BILBAO

Al Lab'Oratorio

Map 7, G5. C/Colón 14. Metro Tribunal.
Tues–Thurs 9pm–3am, Fri & Sat 9pm–6am.

Famous 1980s bar with very loud rock music on the sound system. Often stages live gigs for up-and-coming groups on a little stage downstairs. Young studenty clientele.

Lagata

Map 7, F4. C/San Vicente Ferrer 23. Metro Tribunal.
Daily 10pm–5am.

Despite a change of name and ownership this *discobar* remains a fixture on the Malasaña night scene. With plenty of room to dance, varied music at a volume that allows you to have a chat, and reasonably priced drinks, it's a recipe for a good night out.

Tupperware

Map 7, F6. C/Corredera Alta de San Pablo 26. Metro Tribunal.
Fri & Sat 8pm–5am.

The place to go for the latest on the indie scene, with a mixture of grunge, Britpop and old classics from the punk era.

DISCOBARES

La Vaca Austera
Map 7, F3. C/Palma 20. Metro Tribunal.
Daily 10pm–3.30am, Fri & Sat till 4.30am.
American-style rock bar playing punk/indie classics, with pool tables, mixed clientele and friendly atmosphere.

Vía Lactea
Map 7, F3. C/Velarde 18. Metro Tribunal.
Daily 8pm–3am.
Call in here to see where the *movida* began. A Malasaña classic, *Vía Lactea* was a key meeting place for Spain's designers, directors, pop stars and painters in the 1980s, and it retains its original decor from the time, billiard tables included.

Warhol's Club
Map 7, H1. C/Luchana 20. Metro Bilbao.
Wed & Thurs 7pm–1am, Fri & Sat 7pm–10am.
Very popular *discobar* spread over two floors, with lots of chrome, glass, video screens and ultra-violet lighting. Attracts an early-20s crowd.

SALAMANCA

Teatriz
Map 9, E9. C/Hermosilla 15. Metro Serrano.
Mon–Sat café noon–3pm, bars 9pm–3am. Closed Sat lunch & Aug.
This former theatre, redesigned by the Catalan, Mariscal, together with Philippe Starck, is as elegant a venue as any in Europe. There are bars on the main theatre levels, overlooked by a restaurant in the circle which serves tapas and pasta dishes. Down in the basement there's a library-like area and small disco; look out too for the futuristic toilets. Drinks are fairly pricey (1500ptas for spirits), but there's no entrance charge.

DISCOBARES

Vanitas Vanitatis

Map 9, G1. C/Velázquez 128. Metro Avenida América.

Daily 8.30pm–2am, Fri & Sat till 5am.

Upmarket hangout with a pretty strict door policy. Loud British and US dance music, but with a pleasant interior terrace if it all gets too much for you.

DISCOTECAS

Discotecas are usually the last stop on a *Madrileño* night out, visited long after the metro has closed, hence public transport can be a problem. Fortunately, most are situated in the central areas, so the best bet is to hop into a taxi or go on foot. Although **dress codes** are not, in general, particularly strict, some of the more upmarket joints are fairly selective about who they let in and you may at times need to ingratiate yourself with the doorman. Being foreign, oddly enough, seems to make it easier to get in. Long queues are also frequent, so it may be worth arriving slightly earlier than is cool. **Entry charges** are quite common and pretty hefty (600–3000ptas), but ususally include the first drink. You might, however, be able to pick up a free entry pass from the public relations staff who often hang around the entrance. Be aware that many *discotecas* in Spain are fairly ephemeral institutions and frequently only last a season before opening up somewhere else under a different name, so it's a good idea to consult *La Guía del Ocio* (see p.7) for the very latest information.

SOL, ÓPERA AND SANTA ANA

Joy Madrid

Map 3, G4. C/Arenal 11. Metro Sol.

Daily 11.30pm–5.30am, Fri–Sun till 6am; 2000–2500ptas.

This big-name disco is frequented by musicians, models, media folk and footballers. Home to the thirty-something yuppie crowd. If you can't get in (3–5am is the hippest time to come), console yourself at the *Chocolatería San Ginés* (see box opposite), on the street behind.

Kapital

Map 5, I4. C/Atocha 125. Metro Atocha.
Thurs–Sat midnight–5.30am; 2000ptas.
Seven floors catering for most tastes, with two dance floors, a cinema and a top-floor *terraza*. Varied musical menu of disco, merengue, salsa, *sevillanas* and even some karaoke.

Palacio de Gaviria

Map 3, H5. C/Arenal 9. Metro Ópera/Sol.
Daily 11pm–late; Mon–Thurs 1500ptas, Fri–Sun 1800ptas including first drink.
Aristocratic, nineteenth-century palace where you can wander through a sequence of extravagant Baroque salons, listen to a chamber concert in the ballroom, watch a live show or simply dance the night away. It hosts regular "International Parties", has dance classes and is a fantastic setting in which to have a late drink. A frequent stopping-off point before going into *Joy Eslava*, just down the road. Expect to pay 1500ptas a drink.

LA LATINA

Amnesia/Deep Dance Club

Map 5, A6. Puerta de Toledo 1. Metro Puerta de Toledo.
Wed–Sun 11.30pm–5am; 1500ptas including first drink.
Situated in the under-used Mercado Puerta de Toledo. Wednesdays are for funk and disco; Thursdays for hip-hop and live acts; Fridays and Saturdays play the latest house sounds; and on Sundays it's house and techno at the "after hours" *Friends' Club*.

Chocolate Before Bed

If you stay up through a Madrid night, then you must try one of the city's great institutions, the **Chocolatería San Ginés** on Pasadizo de San Ginés, off c/Arenal between the Puerta del Sol and Teatro Real. Established in 1894, this *chocolatería* serves *chocolate con churros* (dark chocolate with deep-fried hoops of batter) to perfection – just the thing after a night's excess. There's an almost mythical *Madrileño* custom of winding up at San Ginés after the clubs close (not that they all do any longer), before heading home for a shower and then off to work.

San Ginés is open Tues–Sun 1am–7.30am, also Fri–Sun 7–10pm for weekend shoppers when the *chocolate* is half-price.

GRAN VÍA, CHUECA, MALASAÑA AND SANTA BÁRBARA

Arena
Map 7, B5. C/Princesa 1. Metro Plaza de España.
Wed–Sun midnight–6am; 1500–2000ptas including first drink.
One of the "in" places to be seen at, this is a big, modern and very popular converted cinema, with a VIP lounge upstairs. Reggae and funk progresses to house music during the night.

El Calentito
Map 7, D7. C/Jacometrezo 15. Metro Callao.
Daily 11pm–5am.
A fine place to experience wild, abandoned Madrid. It's tiny and cramped with strictly South American sounds: be prepared to dance with anyone! The entrance is easily missed, however – look out for the painted window. Drinks are modestly priced.

DISCOTECAS

Davai

Map 7, C6. C/Flor Baja 1, cnr Gran Vía 59. Metro Santo Domingo/Plaza de España.

Wed–Sat 11pm–5am, Sun 9am–2pm & midnight–6am; 800–1000ptas including first drink.

A multi-club operating under several different names during the week and catering for a wide range of musical tastes with everything from house to 70s disco.

Midday/Midnight/Nature

Map 2, D2. C/Amaniel 13. Metro Plaza de España.

On Thursdays it's the Nature Session with techno and drums 'n' bass; Fridays is the Spirit Session with jungle/dub; while on Sundays you can really test your stamina by sampling one of Madrid's best "after hours" clubs, opening at 9am and closing at 3pm!

Pachá

Map 7, H3. C/Barceló 11. Metro Tribunal.

Wed–Sat 12.30am–5am; 1500–2000ptas including first drink.

An eternal survivor on the Madrid disco scene. Once a theatre and still very theatrical, it is exceptionally cool during the week, less so at the weekend when the out-of-towners take over. Good if you like techno.

El Sol

Map 7, G8. C/Jardines 3. Metro Gran Vía.

Daily 11.30pm–5am, Fri & Sat till 5.30am; 1000–2000ptas.

Hosts around twenty live concerts a month, but continues afterwards (usually at about 1.30am) as a disco with danceable house, soul and acid jazz. Very good acoustics and well ventilated.

Speakeasy

Map 7, I4. C/Fernando VI 6. Metro Alonso Martínez.

Mon–Wed 8pm–1am, Thurs–Sat 8pm–5am; free or 1000ptas
including first drink.

Good-value, friendly disco that holds "International Parties"
for foreigners new to the city. Good resident DJ.

OUT OF THE CENTRE

Cats

C/Julián Romea 4. Metro Guzmán El Bueno.

Daily 10pm–5.30am.

Situated in Moncloa, a popular student area, towards the end of
c/Princesa, with a good range of bars and discos, *Cats* is a large
bar surrounded by various dance floors, podiums and chill-out
areas. Attracts a young crowd and the emphasis is firmly on
dancing to a varied selection of music.

Galileo Galilei

C/Galileo 100. Metro Ríos Rosas.

Mon–Fri 3.30pm–3am, Sat 3.30pm–4am.

Bar, concert venue and disco all rolled into one. Check the
Guía del Ocio to find out whether it's the night for cabaret, salsa
or a singer-songwriter.

Space of Sound

Estación de Chamartín. Metro Chamartín.

Sat, Sun & public holidays 6.30am–noon.

If you've still got energy left, this "after hours" club on top of
the Chamartín train station will allow you to strut your stuff all
morning – if you can take the constant bombardment of
bakalao, lasers and smoke, that is.

DISCOTECAS

Terrazas and Chiringuitos

Madrid is a different city during summer: temperatures soar, and life moves outside and becomes even more late-night. In July and August, those *Madrileños* who haven't headed for the coast meet up with each other from 10pm onwards at one or other of the city's immensely popular **terrazas**. These can range from a few tables set up outside a café, or alongside a **chiringuito** (a makeshift bar) in one of the squares, to extremely trendy, and very expensive, designer bars, which form the summer annexe of a club or *discoteca*.

Paseo de Recoletos and Paseo la Castellana

The biggest concentration of *terrazas* is to be found up and down the grass strip in the middle of the Paseo de Recoletos and its continuation, Paseo de la Castellana. On the nearer reaches of Paseo de Recoletos are *terrazas* of the old-style cafés *Gran* (no. 8), *Gijón* (no. 21) and *Espejo* (no. 31), all popular meeting points.

Past Plaza de Colón – in the region known as "La Costa Castellana" – the trendier *terrazas* such as *Bolero* (no. 33) and *Boulevard* (no.37), begin. Most pump out music, and some offer entertainment, especially midweek, when they need to attract custom. They are extremely posey places, where clubbers dress up for a night's cruise along the length – an expensive operation, with cocktails at 1000ptas a shot, and even a *caña* costing 600ptas.

Elsewhere in Madrid

Jardines de Conde Duque, Map 7, C3. Corner of c/Conde Duque 11 and c/Santa Cruz del Marcenado. Metro Ventura Rodríguez. Close to the Centro Cultural where the Veranos de Villa concerts are based in the summer months.

Jardines de las Vistillas, Map 4, B4. C/Bailén, on the south side of the viaduct. Metro La Latina. This area, due south of the Palacio Real, has a number of *terrazas* and *chiringuitos*. It's named for the "little vistas" to be enjoyed in the direction of the Guadarrama Mountains to the northwest.

Paseo del Pintor Rosales, Map 2, A2. Metro Argüelles. There's a clutch of late-night *terrazas* at the base of the Teleférico, with views over the river to the Casa de Campo.

Plaza de las Comendadoras, Map 7, D3. Metro San Bernardo. One of the city's nicest squares, this has a couple of *terrazas* attached to the *Café Moderno* and a Mexican restaurant.

Plaza Dos de Mayo, Map 7, F3. Metro Tribunal. The *chiringuito* on Malasaña's main square is always diverting.

Plaza de Olavide. Metro Quevedo. An attractive neighbourhood square, with more or less year-round *terrazas* attached to four or five cafés and tapas bars.

Plaza de Oriente, Map 3, D4. Metro Ópera. The *Café de Oriente terraza* is a popular café on the Madrid nightlife scene.

Plaza San Andrés/Plaza Humilladero, Map 4, E6. Metro La Latina. In the heart of old Madrid, this square is particularly lively during the summer *verbenas*.

Plaza de Santa Ana, Map 6, C5. Metro Sol. Several of the *cervecerías* here have seats outside and there's a *chiringuito* in the middle of the square from June to September.

La Vieja Estación, Map 2, J9. Avda Ciudad de Barcelona. Metro Atocha. A massive multi-*terraza* just behind Estación de Atocha, this attracts a glamorous clientele ranging from football stars to TV personalities. If you don't fancy people-watching, there are concerts, talent contests and exhibitions.

TERRAZAS AND CHIRINGUITOS

Gay Madrid

Recent years have witnessed a significant expansion in the **gay scene** in the capital. The area around Plaza Chueca remains at the heart of the action, but gay clubs are beginning to open up in other areas too. The **lesbian scene** has experienced a similar expansion and shares many of the places listed with gay men. There are, however, a few exclusively lesbian clubs listed separately on p.199. Madrid nightlife in general, though, has a strong gay presence and most of the clubs and bars listed in the "Nightlife" chapter have a very mixed clientele.

Around Plaza Chueca, graffiti-plastered walls proclaim the existence of a **zona gay**, and the surrounding streets, especially c/Pelayo, harbour at least a dozen exclusively gay bars and clubs, plus a well-known gay café, the *Café Figueroa*. During *Carnaval* (the week before Lent), Chueca is especially lively, with the gay community joining in the fancy dress parades and general over-indulgence.

Despite the high level of integration in Madrid's nightlife and social scene, there is a remarkably reactionary attitude from many quarters of Spanish society towards homosexuality in general. As a result, the gay community is becoming more organized and groups such as **Coordinadora Gay de Madrid** are actively involved in pushing for gay rights. They also help organize **Gay Pride Week** held at the end of June.

Information Services

Berkana, Map 7, I6. C/Gravina 11 (Metro Chueca). Gay and lesbian bookshop. One of the best places to find out what's happening on the gay scene. Mon–Sat 10.30am–2pm & 5–8.30pm.

Centro de La Mujer, Map 7, J5. C/Barquillo 44, 1° izq ©91 319 36 89 (Metro Alonso Martínez). Feminist and lesbian groups all share this centre, and it's the best stop for information on anything to do with the lesbian community.

Coordinadora Gay de Madrid, Map 7, G6. C/Fuencarral 37 ©91 522 45 17 (Metro Chueca). The main gay organization in Madrid, giving information on health, leisure and gay rights. Mon–Fri 5–9pm; Aug from 7pm.

Two **publications** are worth picking up while you're in the city: *Revista Mensual*, a gay listings magazine covering the whole of Spain, available from most newspaper stands, and *Shangay Express*, a free newspaper avaliable in most gay clubs and bars.

CAFÉS AND RESTAURANTS

A Brasileira
Map 7, H6. C/Pelayo 49 ©91 308 36 25. Metro Chueca.
Mon–Sat 1–5pm & 9pm–2am.
Small Brazilian restaurant offering a very tasty selection of South American dishes. Expect to pay around 2000ptas per person.

Café Acuarela
Map 7, I6. C/Gravina 10. Metro Chueca.

Daily 4pm–2am, Fri & Sat till 4am.

Very comfortable café, stylish decor and the perfect place for a quiet drink.

Café Figueroa

Map 7, I6. C/Augusto Figueroa 17. Metro Chueca.

Mon–Sat noon–1am, Fri & Sat till 2.30am.

Opened in the early 1980s, this is an established institution on the *Madrileño* gay scene. Regulars of all ages. Pool table upstairs and great parties during *Carnaval*.

Gula Gula

Map 7, H8. Gran Vía 1 ©91 522 87 64 (Metro Gran Vía); c/Infante 5 ©91 420 29 19 (Metro Antón Martín).

Mon–Thurs 1–4.30pm & 9pm–2am, Fri & Sat 1–4.30pm & 9pm–3am.

Spacious salad-bar-type restaurant that does an eat-as-much-as-you-can self-service buffet for 1500ptas. Live shows featuring drag queens and dancers every night. Popular for "hen nights" as well as with the gay crowd.

La Sastrería

Map 7, H6. C/Hortaleza 74. Metro Chueca.

Mon–Thurs 8.30am–1.30am, Fri 8.30am–3am, Sat 10am–3am, Sun 10am–1.30am.

On the site of a former military tailor's shop, this popular two-floored café–bar is a great place for an afternoon coffee, tea or fruit juice, as well as an evening drink.

XXX Café

Map 7, H7. Corner of c/Clavel and c/Reina. Metro Gran Vía.

Daily 1pm–1.30am.

This pleasant café has a mainly gay clientele, but is open to everyone. A good place to read the paper while sampling some of the very good carrot cake and coffee.

CAFÉS AND RESTAURANTS

GAY BARS AND DISCOTECAS

Bar LL
Map 7, H6. C/Pelayo 11. Metro Chueca.
Daily 6pm–3am.
Upstairs, there's a bar which has live acts at the weekend (striptease and drag queens). Downstairs, there's a more intimate room, where people sit around and talk or watch hardcore gay porn on the video screen. Attracts a slightly older crowd, mainly singles.

Black and White
Map 7, I6. C/Libertad 34. Metro Chueca.
Daily 9pm–4am, Fri & Sat till 5am.
Very popular strip shows upstairs and a disco downstairs at this well-established nightspot.

Cruising
Map 7, H6. C/Pérez Galdós 5. Metro Chueca.
Daily 8pm–3.30am, Fri & Sat till 4.30am.
This *discobar* is strictly for leather boys, with a dark room showing porn films and a bar upstairs. Downstairs is a disco playing a good variety of danceable music.

Heaven
Map 3, G2. C/Veneras 2. Metro Santo Domingo/Callao.
Daily midnight–late; 1000ptas.
Just behind Plaza Callao, this mixed disco becomes very popular with the gay crowd as an "after hours" venue. Good DJs playing a selection of house music. During the week it organizes parties, live acts and strip shows.

La Lupe
Map 5, F3. C/Torrecilla del Leal 12. Metro Antón Martín.

Daily 9pm–2.30am.

Mixed gay and lesbian bar. Good music, cheap drinks and occasional cabaret.

New Leather Bar

Map 7, I5. C/Pelayo 42. Metro Chueca.

Daily 8pm–3am, Fri & Sat till 4am.

A bar on two floors with a mixed gay crowd. Dance floor, darkened rooms, erotic parties and strip shows.

OHM/Weekend

Map 7, E7. Plaza del Callao 4. Metro Callao.

OHM: Fri & Sat midnight–6.30am; Weekend: Sun midnight–5am; 1000–1500ptas.

Taking the place of the now defunct nightspot, *Angels of Xenon*, this new disco promises to become a fixture on the gay club scene. *Weekend* is the "after hours" club *par excellence* for those who still find their appetite for dancing isn't satisfied by midnight on a Sunday.

Ricks

Map 7, I7. C/Clavel 8. Metro Gran Vía.

Daily 11pm–5am.

Mixed straight/gay *discobar* which gets wild at weekends, when every available space is used for dancing. Open and light, with a friendly atmosphere and fine music ranging from house classics through disco to hi-NRG – plus table football at the back. Pricey drinks.

Shangay Tea Dance

Map 3, I2. C/Mesonero Romanos 13. Metro Callao.

Sun 9pm–2am; 1000ptas including first drink.

A compulsory Sunday night stop, featuring live shows and 70s disco hits.

LESBIAN BARS AND DISCOTECAS

Ambient
Map 7, H4. C/San Mateo 21. Metro Alonso Martínez.
Tues–Thurs & Sun 8pm–4am, Fri & Sat 9pm–5am.
Thriving lesbian bar, serving decent pizzas. Also pool, table
football, exhibitions, occasional live acts and a market on
Sunday.

Medea
Map 5, E2. C/Cabeza 33. Metro Lavapiés/Antón Martín.
Daily Tues–Sun 11pm–5am; 1000ptas.
The city's premier lesbian disco – though accompanied men
are admitted. Cabaret on Thursday & Sunday, smart decor,
great music and a pool table.

La Rosa
Map 6, B2. C/Tetuán 27. Metro Sol.
Daily 11pm–6am; 800ptas.
Lesbian disco run by a women's collective, although men are
admitted if accompanied. Good selection of music and friendly
atmosphere.

Live music

Madrid's **music** scene is as varied as anything else in the city and ranges from classical and opera to salsa and flamenco. Often, it's the smaller, offbeat clubs that are the more enjoyable, though there are plenty of large auditoriums – including the sports stadiums and bullring – for big-name concerts. In summer, events are supplemented by the council's Veranos de la Villa cultural programme, and in autumn, by the Festival de Otoño.

Forthcoming events are well covered in
Madrid's listings magazines; see p.7.

For **classical music** and **opera**, the **Teatro Real**, Plaza Isabel II (Metro Ópera; box office ✆90 224 48 24), the city's opera house, along with the **Auditorio Nacional de Música**, c/Príncipe de Vergara 146 (Metro Cruz del Rayo; box office ✆91 337 01 00), home of the Orquesta Nacional de España, are the two major venues. The **Teatro Monumental**, c/Atocha 65 (Metro Antón Martín; box office ✆91 429 81 19), also has regular classical music performances, while the **Teatro Calderón**, c/Atocha 18 (Metro Sol; box office ✆91 369 14 34) hosts a very popular annual opera season between September and July. Several smaller venues also present classical music recitals, including the **Círculo de Bellas Artes**, c/Marqués de Casa Riera 2 (Metro Banco de España; box office ℗91 531 77 00), and the **Fundación Juan March**, c/Castelló 99 (Metro Núñez de Balboa; box office ℗91 435 42 40). Chamber music is even played in a few **cafés and bars**; try the *Salón del Prado*, c/Prado 4 (Metro Sol) on Thursday night at 11pm and *La Fídula*, c/Huertas 57 (Metro Antón Martín) most nights at 11.30pm and 1am. Make sure you arrive on time, as the doors are closed during performances. The city's main venues for Spanish **operetta** (*zarzuela*) are the **Teatro de la Zarzuela**, c/Jovellanos 4 (Metro Sevilla; box office ℗91 429 82 25); the **Centro Cultural de la Villa**, Plaza de Colón (Metro Colón; box office ℗91 575 60 80) and during July and August, the open-air **La Corrala**, c/Tribulete and c/Sombrerete 13 (Metro Embajadores/Lavapiés; box office ℗90 210 12 12).

FLAMENCO

Flamenco has undergone something of a revival in Madrid in recent years, in large part due to the "new flamenco" artists, like Joaquín Cortés and Ketama, who are unafraid to mix it with a bit of blues, jazz, even rock. The following club and café listings span the range from purist flamenco to crossover experiments, and some host performances by the major stars. Opening hours are variable and those given below are only a rough guideline.

In addition, you can try the **Salas Rocieras**, places where the public get up and perform *sevillanas*, the complex and sensual courtship dance of southern Spain. Even if you don't want to have a go yourself, it's worth paying a visit just to watch the spectacle. Drinks and food are, however, very pricey. Good options are *Al Andalús*, c/Capitán Haya 19 (Metro Cuzco; Mon–Sat 11pm–6am; minimum bar/tapas charge of 2000–3000ptas) and *Almonte*, c/Juan Bravo 35 (Metro Núñez de Balboa; daily 9pm–6am).

FLAMENCO

Café de Chinitas

Map 3, E1. C/Torija 7 *℘*91 547 15 02. Metro Santo Domingo.
Mon–Thurs 9pm–2am, Fri & Sat 9pm–3am; 4300ptas.

One of the oldest flamenco clubs in Madrid, hosting a dinner-dance spectacular. Keep an eye on the prices, as it's very expensive and rather touristy, but the music is authentic.
Reservations are essential, though you may be able to get in late when people start to leave about an hour before closing (at this time you don't have to eat and the entrance fee includes your first drink).

Candela

Map 5, F3. C/Olmo 2 *℘*91 467 33 82. Metro Antón Molina.
Daily 10.30pm–late.

A legendary bar frequented by musicians, with occasional shows too. The late, great Camarón de la Isla is reputed to have sung here until 11am on one occasion. The cellar area is only accessible by invitation.

Caracol

C/Bernardino Obregón 18 *℘*91 530 80 55. Metro Embajadores.
Daily 9.30pm–2am; 500–4000ptas.

The top names tend to appear at this sometime club, sometime disco. Flamenco is often mixed with jazz and blues; pure flamenco is usually on Thursday night, but ring beforehand to check, because schedules are subject to change. Increasing numbers of indie-style bands now play here too, recent visitors including Super Furry Animals and Travis.

Casa Patas

Map 5, E2. C/Cañizares 10 *℘*91 369 04 96. Metro Antón Martín.
Daily midnight–3am; 1700–2500ptas.

Small club with bar and restaurant that gets its share of big names. The best nights are Thursday and Friday.

Corral de la Morería

Map 4, B4. C/de la Morería 17 ℗91 365 84 46. Metro La Latina.
Daily 9pm–3am; 4200ptas.

This is a good venue for some serious flamenco acts, but expensive at about 4200ptas for the show plus a drink. Worth staying until late in case there are any spontaneous contributions from the audience. Frank Sinatra and Ava Gardner are among the celebrities who have signed the guest book.

Peña Chaquetón

C/Canarias 39 ℗91 671 27 77. Metro Palos de la Frontera.
Fri 11.30pm only; 800–2000ptas.

The place for purists – just one show weekly, but it's a good one. Turn up early if there's a big name or you won't get in, and try and make yourself comfortable in the spartan surroundings (don't worry about the "Members Only" sign outside).

La Soleá

Map 4, F4. C/Cava Baja 27. Metro La Latina.
Mon–Sat 8.30pm–3am.

This brilliant, long-established flamenco bar is the genuine article. People sit around in the tiny salon, pick up a guitar or start to sing and gradually the atmosphere builds up until everyone is clapping or dancing. Has to be seen to be believed.

ROCK AND BLUES

Madrid is very much on the international **rock** tour circuit, and you can catch big (and small) American and British acts playing to enthusiastic audiences. In early summer, the Parque el Soto in Mostoles, to the south of the city, plays host to the Festimad rock festival, which features international groups ranging from heavy metal to indie and dance. Regular concerts are also held as part of the Veranos de la

ROCK AND BLUES

Villa season (see "Festivals" chapter, p.216) in the patio in the Centro Cultural Conde Duque, c/Conde Duque 11 (Metro Noviciado). **Tickets** for most big rock concerts, as well as for the Festimad and Veranos de la Villa concerts, are sold by Madrid Rock, Gran Vía 25; Fnac, c/Preciados 28 (both Metro Callao; daily 10am–10pm; all cards); and branches of El Corte Inglés.

You'll find a thriving Celtic music scene in many of Madrid's Irish pubs; see box on p.177.

Madrid has also long been the heart of the **Spanish rock** scene, and in the smaller clubs you'll see a very wide range of local bands. In most cases you can just turn up and pay on the door – keep an eye out for posters scattered around the city and check the *Guía del Ocio*.

CLUBS

Café Libertad 8
Map 7, I7. C/Libertad 8. Metro Chueca.
Mon–Thurs 5pm–2am, Fri 5pm–3am, Sat 7pm–3am, Sun 6pm–1am.
The place to go to listen to budding *cantautores* (singer-song-writers). Some big names such as Rosana and Pedro Guerra started off in this café, which has now been going for more than 25 years.

Chesterfield Café
Map 7, A2. C/Serrano Jover 5. Metro Argüelles.
Daily noon–3.30am.
As well as offering Tex-Mex food, this club is a live rock venue from Wednesdays to Sundays. Sets begin at midnight (1am on Fridays and Saturdays) and there is a happy hour between 8 and 10pm.

ROCK AND BLUES

La Coquette
Map 3, G4. C /Hileras 14. Metro Ópera.
Daily 8pm–2.30am. Closed Aug.
Small, smoky bar, where people sit around in the near dark, watching bands perform on a tiny stage. Wednesday and Thursday are the blues nights.

Maravillas
Map 7, F4. C/San Vicente Ferrer 33. Metro Tribunal.
Thurs–Sat 9pm–late.
Small, but usually uncrowded, indie venue, a favourite with the young crowd, where bands play anything from jazz to funk to reggae, often till around 4am.

Siroco
Map 7, D3. C/San Dimas 3. Metro San Bernardo/Noviciado.
Tues–Thurs 9.30pm–3am, Fri–Sun 10pm–6am.
Live local bands most nights at this popular little club/disco, just north of Gran Vía. Music ranges from soul and funk to rock and indie.

MAJOR CONCERT VENUES

La Cubierta
Plaza de Toros de Leganés ©91 765 18 90. On local train line from Atocha to Leganés.
Bullring in the southern industrial suburb of Leganés, increasingly used as a venue for heavy rock artists of the Iron Maiden, Megadeth variety.

La Katedral
C/Fundadores 7. Metro Manuel Becerra/O'Donnell.
A relatively new venue, which took over from the defunct Revólver, and kicked off with concerts by indie bands, includ-

ROCK AND BLUES

ing Echobelly and Supergrass. However, most of the big names now seem to be heading for La Riviera.

Palacio de Congresos
Paseo de la Castellana 99. Metro Santiago Bernabéu.
Large, comfortable, though somewhat sterile, venue used by a number of touring artists. Van Morrison was a recent visitor.

Palacio de Deportes
Avda Felipe II. Metro Goya.
Large indoor sports arena, home to Madrid's basketball teams, but increasingly used by the big-name artists on the Spanish leg of their European tours. Seats fifteen thousand, but the acoustics leave a lot to be desired. Oasis and the Spice Girls have appeared here, and more recently, the Cranberries.

Plaza de Toros de las Ventas
Las Ventas. Metro Ventas.
The bullring is a pretty good concert venue, put to use during the summer festival. Tickets are usually all one price, though the best reserved seats (*asiento reservado*) often carry an extra charge.

La Riviera
Map 2, A7. Paseo Bajo Virgen del Puerto s/n, Puente de Segovia. Metro Puerta del Angel.
Fri–Sun 11pm–5am.
Right next to the river, fun disco and concert venue that has hosted some of the big names in recent years, from the trendy Lenny Kravitz and Massive Attack to the not-so-trendy Lynyrd Skynyrd.

ROCK AND BLUES

LATIN MUSIC

Madrid attracts big-name **Latin** artists, and if you happen to coincide with the summer festival you'll stand a good chance of catching someone of the stature of Juan Luis Guerra from the Dominican Republic. Gigs by top artists tend to take place at the rock venues listed on pp.205–206. The local scene is a good deal more low-key, but there's enjoyable salsa, nonetheless, in a handful of clubs.

Las Noches del Cuplé
Map 7, E3. C/Palma 51 ©91 532 71 15 or 91 657 03 94. Metro Tribunal.
Daily except Wed 9.30pm–1am, Fri & Sat till 2am.
A 3000ptas entry charge will cover you for a drink and the show, while 6500ptas entitles you to food as well – good value as long as you're into traditional music-hall Spanish, French songs and tangos.

Oba-Oba
Map 3, G1. C/Jacometrezo 4. Metro Callao.
Daily 11pm–5.30am.
Live Brazilian music as you refine your samba and lambada technique with the help of lethal Brazilian caipirinhas from the bar.

Salsipuedes
Map 7, F6. C/Puebla 6. Metro Callao/Gran Vía.
Daily 11pm–6am; 1000ptas including first drink.
Serious salsa dancing to a live orchestra most weekdays in a "tropical" setting in this large venue. You need to be smartly dressed to get in.

JAZZ

Madrid doesn't rank with London, Paris or New York on the **jazz** front, but the clubs are friendly, unpretentious places. Look out for the annual jazz festival staged at a variety of venues in November.

Café Central
Map 6, B5. Plaza del Angel 10. Metro Sol.
Mon–Sat noon–1.30am, Fri & Sat till 2.30am; 800–1200ptas.
This was voted no. 6 in "Best Jazz Clubs of the World" poll in *Wire* magazine some time back. It's certainly an attractive venue – small, relaxed and covered in mirrors – and it gets the occasional big name, plus strong local talent. The Art Deco café is worth a visit in its own right.

Café Jazz Populart
Map 6, C6. C/Huertas 22. Metro Antón Martín.
Daily 6pm–2.30am; live music supplement 250–1000ptas.
Nightly sets from jazz and blues bands. Another friendly and relaxed venue. Tends to start a little earlier than the *Café Central*, which is a few minutes' walk away, so you can combine the two if you fancy an overdose of laid-back rhythms.

Downtown
Map 7, I1. C/Covarrubias 29. Metro Alonso Martínez.
Mon–Thurs & Sun 10pm–3am, Fri & Sat 10pm–3.30am.
Just north of Alonso Martínez, *Downtown* hosts good jazz nights on Mondays and Tuesdays, while blues bands often play here at weekends.

Segundo Jazz
C/Comandante Zorita 8. Metro Nuevos Ministerios.
Daily 7pm–3.30am.
Jazz on most nights of the week, but also some Latin sounds

(usually Wed & Thurs). Shows normally get going at around midnight. No entry charge, but you are obliged to buy a drink.

Triskel Tavern

Map 7, F4. C/San Vicente Ferrer 3. Metro Tribunal.
Daily 10am–3am.

This Irish bar hosts a jazz night on Tuesdays and it's worth popping in anytime from 11pm onwards to see what's on.

Theatre and cinema

I n a city that has been home to so many of the country's great writers and dramatists it is not surprising that Madrid's theatrical tradition is strong. In the golden age, writers such as **Cervantes**, **Lope de Vega** and **Tirso de Molina** all lived in the streets in and around Plaza de Santa Ana, and later, a number of great poets and writers such as **García Lorca** and **Antonio Machado** converged on the city, further contributing to Madrid's literary heritage. *Madrileños* have always been enthusiastic theatregoers, and today you can catch anything from the classics to contemporary experimental productions, cabaret and comedy acts.

Credit-card **bookings** can be made over the phone through La Caixa Catalunya and Caja de Madrid (see "Directory", p.255, for telephone numbers), or you can go directly to the theatre and buy the tickets on the spot. Prices range from 1000ptas to 4000ptas, but many venues operate a **día del espectador** (usually Mon or Wed), when prices are halved – demand for these is high, though, so you'll need to book as early as possible.

Details of performances, which usually begin after 9pm, are to be found in *La Guía del Ocio* and the Friday supplement of *El Mundo*. Look out also for what's on offer in the annual Festival de Otoño (late Sept to Nov), sponsored by the Comunidad de Madrid. This is often the time when international shows and performers visit the city. Madrid also hosts an alternative festival of theatre, dance and music, which is now in its tenth year and usually takes place around February.

Berlin Cabaret
Map 4, E4. Costanilla de San Pedro 11 ✆91 366 20 34. Metro La Latina.
Mon–Thurs 11pm–5am, Fri & Sat 11pm–6am.
Varied cabaret and comedy in a traditional, slightly seedy club setting. Admission is normally free, but drinks are expensive.

Centro Cultural de la Villa
Map 9, C9. Plaza de Colón ✆91 575 60 80. Metro Colón.
An arts centre directly under the waterfall in the plaza where you're likely to see some of the more experimental companies on tour, as well as popular works and *zarzuela* performances.

Círculo de Bellas Artes
Map 6, E2. C/Marqués de Casa Riera 2 ✆91 532 44 37 or 91 532 44 38. Metro Banco de España.
The Círculo (see p.54) houses a beautiful old theatre which puts on adventurous productions.

La Muralla Arabe
Map 4, B2. C/Cuesta de la Vega (no street number). Metro Ópera.
Atmospheric outdoor setting for plays from the Spanish golden age which are staged in the summer months as part of the Veranos de la Villa season. The play is performed on a traditional stage in the shadow of the old city wall, and there are

side shows and street entertainers, too. You'll need to arrive early if you want a table where you can eat and drink during the performance. Tickets are available from the booth outside the entrance during the summer season.

Teatro de la Abadía

C/Fernández de los Ríos 42 ©91 448 16 27. Metro Quevedo/Argüelles.

Beautifully decorated theatre, set in pleasant grounds just off the main street. The two stages, both with an intimate atmosphere, have put on some very successful productions and are especially popular venues during the Festival de Otoño. Steven Berkoff brought his studies of Shakespeare's villains here in 1999.

Teatro Albéniz

Map 6, A4. C/de la Paz 11 © 91 531 83 11. Metro Sol.

Another popular venue for Festival de Otoño productions. Also hosts small-scale dance performances.

Teatro Español

Map 6, C5. C/Príncipe 25 ©91 429 62 97. Metro Sol/Sevilla.

Classic Spanish theatre is performed in this majestic venue at one end of Plaza de Santa Ana. The theatre is built on the site of one of the original *corrales* (courtyards) where drama was first performed for ordinary *Madrileños* in the golden age. Works by Lope de Vega, Calderón de la Barca and Tirso de Molina often feature on the programme.

Teatro de Madrid

Avda de la Ilustración (no street number) ©91 740 53 74. Metro Barrio del Pilar.

Large, modern theatre next to the large La Vaguada shopping centre in the north of the city, presenting some excellent ballet, drama and touring cultural shows.

Teatro María Guerrero

Map 7, K6. C/Tamayo y Baus 4 ℂ91 319 47 69. Metro Colón.
This is the headquarters of the Centro Dramático Nacional which stages high-quality Spanish and international productions in a beautiful neo-*Mudéjar* interior.

Teatro Nuevo Apolo

Map 5, D2. Plaza Tirso de Molina 1 ℂ91 429 52 38. Metro Tirso de Molina.
An old music-hall-style venue with traditional decor and a good atmosphere, if a little cramped. Madrid's principal venue for major musicals and host to two highly successful tours by the Harlem Gospel Singers in the last few years.

CINEMA

Spaniards, and *Madrileños* in particular, are enthusiastic and knowledgeable movie devotees. They flock to the openings of Spanish and international films in the city, lap up the extensive press and TV coverage and seem to know all the latest gossip about the stars of the screen.

The city itself has been a star in its own right: the elegant apartment blocks on the edge of the Retiro, sleazy nightclubs and bars in the centre and the decaying slum areas on the outskirts have all featured as backdrops in the post-*movida* films of **Pedro Almodóvar**. While Almodóvar blazed the trail in the 1980s, a new generation of young directors followed in the 1990s, including Alex de la Iglesia, whose *El día de la Bestia* was a big box-office hit. More recently the young student, Alejandro Amenábar, with his thrilling debut *Tesis*, and Fernando León, with *Barrio*, a hard-hitting portrayal of working-class *Madrileño* youth, are the names to look out for.

Cinemas (*cines*) can be found all over the city centre. Major releases are dubbed into Spanish, though a number of cinemas have regular original-language screenings, with subtitles; these are listed in a separate *versión original subtitulada (v.o.)* section in the newspapers and *La Guía del Ocio*. Tickets for films cost around 750ptas, but most cinemas have a *día del espectador* (usually Mon or Wed), when admission is 500ptas. Be warned that on Sunday night half of Madrid goes to the movies and queues can be long – it's usually best to buy tickets early and then spend some time in a bar before the show starts.

Alphaville, Renoir & Lumière
Map 7, A4. C/Martín de los Heros ✆91 559 38 36, 91 559 57 60 or 91 542 11 72. Metro Plaza de España.
A trio of multiscreen cinemas, within 200m of each other just beside Plaza de España. Original-language-version new releases and old classics make up the majority of films. The Lumière has early sessions for children-oriented films, the Alphaville has a good basement café and the Renoir does informative film notes, although it doesn't allow food or drink inside.

Bellas Artes
Map 6, E2. C/Marqués de Casa Riera 2 ✆91 522 50 92. Metro Banco de España.
A varied diet of mainstream releases and art-house productions. Comfortable environment and pleasant café.

California
C/Andrés Mellado 53 ✆91 544 00 58. Metro Moncloa.
Giant single-screen cinema in the midst of studenty Moncloa. After a brief experiment showing dubbed foreign films it has reverted once again to *v.o.* only.

Cines Ideal
Map 6, B6. C/Doctor Cortezo 6 ✆91 369 25 18. Metro Sol/Tirso de Molina.

A massive nine-screen complex south of Sol with something for everyone – a mixture of mainstream, art-house, independent and Spanish films.

Filmoteca/Cine Doré

Map 5, F2. C/Santa Isabel 3 ☏91 549 60 11. Metro Antón Martín. Beautiful old cinema, now home to an art-film centre, with imaginative programmes of classic and contemporary films. In summer, there are open-air screenings on a little *terraza* – they're very popular, so buy tickets in advance. See p.45 for more on the Cine Doré.

Festivals

t's always worth checking out which **festivals** (*fiestas*) your visit to Madrid coincides with. There are dozens throughout the year, some involving the whole city, others just an individual *barrio*. The more important dates are listed below.

Religious fiestas aside, the city council organizes cultural festivals, in particular the **Veranos de la Villa** (July–Sept) and **Festival de Otoño** (Sept–Nov) concerts (classical, rock, flamenco), theatre and cinema events. Many events are free and they're often open-air, taking place in the city's parks and squares. Full programmes are published in the monthly *En Madrid* tourist hand-out, free from any of the tourist offices (see p.7 for addresses).

JANUARY

Cabalgata de los Reyes (Cavalcade of the Three Kings)

January 5. An evening procession through the city centre to celebrate the arrival of the Three Kings, in which children are showered with sweets. Most Spanish children receive their Christmas presents the next day.

Carnaval

Taking place the week before Lent, the *Carnaval* is an excuse for a lot of partying and fancy-dress parades, especially in the gay zone around Chueca. The end of *Carnaval* is marked by the bizarre and entertaining parade, *El Entierro de la Sardina* (The Burial of the Sardine), on the Paseo de la Florida. The parade reputedly originates from the time of Carlos III, when a delivery of rotting sardines arrived in the city, prompting the king to order their immediate burial. The burial thus signifies the end of the *Carnaval* celebrations and the arrival of the abstinence of Lent.

Semana Santa

Easter Week is celebrated with processions of penitents in Madrid – the most traditional of which is in La Latina – although they're not as impressive as those in Toledo.

Fiesta del Dos de Mayo

May 2. Celebrated especially in Malasaña, where there are bands and partying around the Plaza Dos de Mayo. It was the funkiest festival in the city during the 1980s, but has been a bit low-key in recent years.

Fiestas de San Isidro

May 15. The festival of Madrid's patron saint extends a week either side of May 15, and is one of the biggest festivals in Spain. There's a non-stop round of carnival events: bands, parades and loads of free entertainment. Bands play every night in the Jardines de las Vistillas (south of the

Palacio Real), and the evenings are full of *chotis* music and dancing (music and dance typical of Madrid). The festival also heralds the start of the bullfighting season.

La Feria del Libro
At the end of May, Madrid's great book fair takes place, with hundreds of stands set up in El Retiro.

JUNE

Fiesta de la Ermita de San Antonio de la Florida
June 13. Events based around the church (see p.119).

Fiestas de San Juan
June 17–24. Bonfires and fireworks in El Retiro, marking the traditional start of summer.

JULY

La Virgen del Carmen
July 9–16. Local fiesta in Chamberí.

AUGUST

Castizo fiestas
August 6–15. Traditional fiestas of *San Cayetano*, *San Lorenzo* and *La Virgen de la Paloma* in La Latina and Lavapiés *barrios*. Much of the activity takes place around the Plaza de la Paja and Las Vistillas.

DECEMBER

Navidad
During the Christmas period, Plaza Mayor is filled with stalls selling all manner of decorations and displaying a large

model of a crib, a traditional feature of many Spanish homes. El Corte Inglés, at the bottom of c/Preciados, has a vast all-singing-all-dancing clockwork Christmas scene over the entrance facing c/Maestro Vitoria, which is set to work at certain times of the day and is very popular with the children.

Nochevieja

December 31. New Year's Eve is celebrated in bars, restaurants and parties all over the city, with bands in some of the squares. Puerta del Sol is the traditional place to gather, waiting for the strokes of the clock – it is traditional to swallow a grape on each strike for luck.

Sport and bullfighting

S paniards, and *Madrileños* in particular, are **sport** crazy. Basketball, cycling, handball, tennis and motorcycling all generate plenty of interest, but without a doubt, the great national obsession is **fútbol** (*el deporte rey*, the king of sports). The biggest-selling daily paper in Spain is the sports tabloid *Marca*, and ninety percent of its pages are taken up with football (mainly coverage of Real Madrid). Fierce rivalry between Madrid and Barcelona dominates the two major sports of football and basketball, but there is also stiff competition within the city between football clubs **Real Madrid** and **Atlético Madrid** and basketball's Real Madrid and Estudiantes.

Sports facilities in Madrid are good, although very heavily used. You shouldn't have too much difficulty finding somewhere to swim (in summer), play tennis or go running – there are plenty of *polideportivos* (sports centres) run by the council and scattered across the city and its suburbs – and even the most obscure sports can be tracked down through the Consejo Superior de Deportes (☏91 589 67 00; fax 91 589 66 14).

While many Spaniards regard **bullfighting** as more of a refined art form than a sport, it does have much in common with professional sport with its multimillion dollar turnover, highly paid preening stars and massive exposure on television. It's a phenomenon linked very closely to the history, culture and character of Spain.

FOOTBALL

Madrid has three football clubs in the *Primera División* (First Division), **Atlético Madrid**, **Real Madrid** and the recently promoted **Rayo Vallecano**. In addition, in the Second Division (*Segunda A*) it has Getafe and Leganés, local stalwarts from the tough industrial suburbs whose name they bear, and Atlético Madrid B, Atlético's second team. The **season** runs from September to June, and league matches are usually played on Sunday afternoon at either 5pm or 7pm, depending on the time of year. Many of the bigger matches are now shown live on pay-per-view TV, while one match, which is played on a Saturday evening, is shown on regular TV.

In the post-Bosman era there has been a massive influx of expensive foreign imports, many from South America and Eastern Europe; recent, past and present players have included Anelka, Roberto Carlos, Seedorf, McManaman and Suker for Real, and Juninho, Vieri and Hasselbaink for Atlético. However, there are also plenty of classy **Spanish players** on the scene, notably Atlético's José Mari and Kiko and Real's Raul and Hierro. Entertainment on the pitch is matched by the antics off it, with larger-than-life club chairmen such as Atlético's Jesús Gil and Real's Lorenzo Sanz continually embroiled in disputes with each other or with the Spanish football federation – Gil even managed to floor Compostela's chairman with a punch in 1996 and is presently entangled in a long-running legal battle with the state over his alleged misuse of funds from his mayoral fiefdom of Marbella to bail out Atlético.

Tickets usually only go on sale a couple of days before matches, with massive queues building up outside the stadium box offices. Real Madrid have recently introduced a telephone booking system through the bank Caja Madrid (©902 324 324), but you still have to queue at the special bus parked at one of the corners of the stadium to collect the tickets before the match. For big matches you may have to resort to the touts, who can be knocked down quite substantially if you're prepared to bargain. For the smaller games, however (those that are not Madrid derbies or don't involve Barcelona), tickets can be obtained quite easily.

Fans tend to congregate in the bars that ring the stadiums well before kick-off, as **alcohol** is banned inside the ground, although it's a common sight to see a *bota* (hide pouch full of cheap red wine) being passed around the crowd. At half-time there's a general rustle of tin foil as almost everyone settles down to enjoy their homemade *jamón* or *tortilla bocadillo* – the food inside the grounds is pretty poor.

Atlético Madrid

Estadio Vicente Calderón, Paseo de la Virgen del Puerto 67 ©91 366 47 07. Metro Pirámides.
Ticket office Mon–Fri 5–8pm; two days before each match also 11am–2pm. Tickets from 3000ptas.

Atlético Madrid, given the not-so-glamorous nickname of *Los Colchoneros* (The Mattress Makers) because of the colours of their shirts, which resemble the formerly ubiquitous red and white Spanish mattresses, have always been the rather poor relations of Real Madrid. Originally set up by young Basques and *Madrileños* as a branch of Athletic de Bilbao, the club soon became independent (although its strip is still the same colour as the Basque club) and has enjoyed considerable success during its 94-year history. They have won nine league titles and nine cups, as well as the Cup Winners' Cup in 1962, the high point being the *doblete* (league and cup double) in the 1995–96 season, when their loyal and long-suffering fans at last had an excuse to celebrate in the Neptuno fountain just down the road from Cibeles. Although not as impressive as Real Madrid's Bernabéu stadium, the newly equipped all-seater **Vicente Calderón Stadium** has a not insubstantial 57,000 seating capacity and usually enjoys a far better atmosphere than its more glamorous neighbour.

Real Madrid

Estadio Santiago Bernabéu, c/Concha Espina ℗91 344 00 52. Metro Santiago Bernabéu.
Ticket office Mon–Fri 5–8pm; match days 11am–1.30pm. Tickets from 2000ptas go on sale three days before each match.

Of the three main Madrid football clubs, the one with the best record and richest heritage is **Real Madrid**, seven times winners of the European Cup and 27 times winners of the Spanish League. *El Equipo Merengue* (The Meringues), after their traditional all-white strip have, in recent times, been eclipsed by the successes of their arch-rivals, Barcelona. However, in their heyday they dominated not just Spanish, but also European and world football, with players of the quality of Puskás, Di Stefano and Gento. Real also participated in arguably the greatest football match on British soil, the 7–3 humbling of Eintracht Frankfurt in the final of the European Cup at Hampden Park in 1960. Under Franco's regime they became the showpiece of Spanish sport and have always enjoyed a privileged financial position compared to their local rivals, despite recent financial crises. They have a small but repellent neo-fascist group of hooligan followers known as the *Ultra Sur*, but they are heavily outnumbered by vast numbers of decent fans at the

FOOTBALL

frequently packed ground. Their magnificent **Santiago Bernabéu Stadium**, venue of the 1982 World Cup Final, is one of the greatest grounds in the world, even with its recently reduced capacity of 87,000. Whenever they have something to celebrate, Real fans throng to the fountain of Cibeles at the top of Paseo del Prado, more than 300,000 choosing to do so when they beat Juventus in the 1998 Champions League.

Rayo Vallecano

Estadio de María Teresa Rivero, Avda Payaso Fofó ©91 478 22 53. Metro Portazgo.
Ticket office Mon–Sat 5.30–8.30pm & two hours before each match. Tickets from 2000ptas.

After relegation to the Second Division, **Rayo Vallecano** bounced back to top-league status in the 1998–99 season. Their modest stadium in the working-class suburb of Vallecas holds a mere 15,500, but there is still plenty of atmosphere. They openly admit they cannot compete financially with big brothers Real and Atlético and frequently reschedule games for Sunday mornings so as not to clash with their neighbours' fixtures. The best position they have managed in the league was tenth in 1977–78. The fact that the club has the only female football president in Spain, María Teresa Rivero, wife of the controversial entrepreneur, José María Ruiz Mateos, adds a little extra colour to this friendly local club.

BASKETBALL

Basketball is the second most popular spectator sport in Spain, and Madrid has two top-class teams, **Estudiantes** and **Real Madrid** (part of the football club), who play at the Palacio de Deportes, Avda Felipe II 19 (Metro Goya; ticket office daily 11am–2pm & 5–8pm; ©91 401 91 00;

tickets from 1000ptas) and the Pabellón de Deportes del Real Madrid, Paseo de la Castellana 259 (Metro Begoña; tickets available in advance through Caja Madrid ticket line ℂ902 488 488; tickets from 700ptas) respectively. The **season** runs from September to May, the high points being the playoffs from April onwards and the Torneo de Navidad in the last week in December.

Scattered throughout the city, several *polideportivos* **(sports centres) cater for most sports: Polideportivo de la Chopera, Parque del Retiro (Metro Atocha; daily 8.30am–9.30pm; ℂ91 420 11 54); Estadio de Vallehermoso, Avda Islas Filipinas s/n (Metro Cuatro Caminos/Ríos Rosas; daily 8am–10pm; ℂ91 534 77 23); Parque Deportivo La Ermita, c/Sepúlveda 3–5 (Metro Puerta del Angel; Mon–Fri 9am–11pm, Sat 10am–8pm, Sun 10am–3pm; ℂ91 470 01 11).**

BOWLING

You'll find plenty of ten-pin **bowling alleys** in Madrid. Two of the largest are Bowling Azca, Paseo de la Castellana 77 (Metro Nuevos Ministerios; daily 11am–midnight, Fri & Sat till 2am; ℂ91 555 76 26; 350–600ptas) and AMF Bowling Centre, La Vaguada (Metro Herrera Oria/Barrio del Pilar; daily 10pm–1am, Fri & Sat till 4am; ℂ91 549 23 76; 400–650ptas).

GOLF

Golf is prohibitively expensive at the private clubs in Madrid. The most accessible public facilities are the two courses (18 and 9 holes) at Olivar de la Hinojosa on the eastern outskirts of the city – Avda de Dublin s/n, Campo de las Naciones (Metro Campo de las Naciones; daily 8.30am–8pm; ✆91 721 18 89). It costs 5800ptas for eighteen holes. There is also a driving range in the Parque Empresarial de la Moraleja (✆91 661 44 44), just outside the city on the NI road to Burgos.

GYMS AND FITNESS CENTRES

Some private **gyms** provide short-term membership: try Club Abascal, c/José Abascal 46 (✆91 442 07 49); Palestra, c/Bravo Murillo 5 (✆91 448 98 22); Holiday Gym Castellana, Plaza Carlos Trías Bertrán 4 (✆91 555 96 24); or Holiday Gym Princesa c/Serrano Jover 3 (✆91 547 40 33).

RUNNING

There are plenty of places to **run** in the major parks, Parque del Oeste, Casa de Campo and the Retiro; the last two have specially marked-out routes for *footing*, the one in the Casa de Campo is by the lake, and the one in the Retiro is on the north side of the park. There is a popular marathon held in the city in late April.

SWIMMING

Madrid is well supplied with **open-air pools** (*piscinas*), which is just as well given that summer temperatures can soar above 40°C. Most have shade and pleasant sunbathing areas, and some offer other activities such as volleyball. Most open-air pools are open from mid-May to mid-September daily 10.30am–8pm and admission is usually 500ptas. The most central open-air pools include: Barrio del Pilar, c/Monforte de Lemos (Metro Barrio del Pilar/Begoña; ✆91 314 79 43); Canal de Isabel II, Avda de las Islas Filipinas 54 (Metro Ríos Rosas; ©91 533 96 42); Casa de Campo, Avda del Angel (Metro Lago; ©91 463 00 50); Chamartín, Plaza del Perú (Metro Pío XII; ©91 350 12 23); Concepción, c/José del Hierro (Metro Concepción/Quintana; ©91 403 90 20); La Elipa, Parque de la Elipa, c/O'Donnell (Metro Estrella; ©91 430 35 11); José María Cacigal, c/Santa Pola (Metro Príncipe Pío; ©91 541 37 16).

Another option is the rooftop pool at the *Hotel Emperador*, Gran Vía 53 (Metro Gran Vía; ©91 547 28 00). It'll cost you 1500ptas, but you get spectacular views of the city as you swim. In addition, there are **indoor pools** at Moratalaz, c/Valdebernardo (Metro Pavones; closed Aug; ©91 772 71 21) and **La Latina**, Plaza de la Cebada 1 (Metro La Latina; ©91 365 80 31). For **aquaparks**, see "Kids' Madrid", p.247.

TENNIS

Most of the *polideportivos* and the Casa de Campo (Metro Lago, near the lake) have a variety of courts for rent at around 600ptas an hour, but you'll need your own equipment.

BULLFIGHTING

Bullfighting (*los toros*) is a multibillion-peseta business and it is estimated that around half a million Spaniards are employed either directly or indirectly in the bullfighting world. Nevertheless, there are many Spaniards who have never been to a bullfight and may only have seen one on TV; there is even some opposition to the activity from animal welfare groups, but it is not widespread. Despite claims that bullfighting was beginning to die out, the last few years have seen it become even more fashionable – audiences include a full cross-section of society from farmers and villagers to show-business stars and politicians. *Los toros* is culture and ritual rolled into one, where the emphasis is on the way man and bull "perform" together – the art is at issue rather than the cruelty. *Aficionados* argue that the life of a bull destined for the ring is infinitely preferable and more honourable than that of the majority which end ignominiously in the slaughterhouse.

Regular **corridas** are held in the smaller bullrings of a number of towns surrounding Madrid during their fiestas. Many also feature **encierros**, where young bulls pursue often rather drunken runners making a mad dash along a set route into the *plaza de toros*. The more famous of these *ferias* (all late Aug) include: **Chinchón**, a picturesque setting in the ancient plaza; **Colmenar Viejo**, a prestigious *feria* in the heart of bull-breeding country; **Manzanares el Real**; and **San Sebastián de los Reyes**, which features highly rated *encierros*. Towns to the north and west of Madrid, such as Pozuelo and Las Rozas, hold their *ferias* in September.

All manner of taurine-related memorabilia, including the *traje de luces* worn by Manolete in his last and fatal corrida, photos, paintings and statues, are displayed in the Museo Taurino, Plaza de las Ventas (Tues–Fri 9.30am–2.30pm, Sun & hols 10am–1pm; free; Metro Ventas). It's a little unimaginative and old-fashioned, but there is just about enough to keep budding Hemingways satisfied.

Alongside the established and popular **matadores** – Enrique Ponce, César Rincón, Curro Romero, Joselito, Litri, Jesulín de Ubrique, Ortega Cano, José María Manzanares and Finito de Córdoba – are two newer stars, El Cordobés, a young pretender of spectacular technique, who claims to be his legendary namesake's illegitimate son, and the even more precocious sixteen-year old El Juli, who hails from Madrid.

Plaza de Toros de Las Ventas

C/Alcalá 237 ©91 726 48 00 or 91 356 22 00. Metro Ventas.
Box office March–Oct Thurs–Sun 10am–2pm & 5–8pm; tickets
2000–12,000ptas.

Madrid's neo-*Mudéjar* bullring, **Las Ventas**, with its 23,000 capacity, is probably the most illustrious in the world. The season lasts from March to October and *corridas* are held every Sunday at 7pm and every day during the three main *ferias*: *La Comunidad* (early May), *San Isidro* (mid-May to June) and *Otoño* (late Sept to Oct). **Tickets** go on sale at the ring only a couple of days in advance, with many already allocated to season-ticket holders. The cheapest seats are *gradas*, the highest rows at the back, from where you can see everything that happens without too much of the detail; the front rows are known as the *barreras*. Seats are also divided into *sol* (sun), *sombra* (shade), and *sol y sombra* (shaded after a while). The *sombra* seats are more expensive, not so much for the spectators' personal comfort as the fact that most of the action takes place in the shade. On the way in, you can rent cushions – two hours sitting on concrete is not much fun. Beer and soft drinks are sold inside.

Shopping

Shopping districts in Madrid are pretty defined. The biggest range of shops is along Gran Vía and around Puerta del Sol, and this is where you'll find the **department stores** such as El Corte Inglés. In addition, Marks & Spencer has a branch at c/Serrano 52 in Salamanca and one in the La Vaguada shopping centre (Metro Barrio del Pilar), as does C&A. Although Madrid has its fair share of stylish designer shops it has also managed to retain many of its **traditional establishments**, and it is these eccentric little shops, still serving the local community, that provide the greatest interest value for casual browsers and shopaholics alike.

For **fashion** (*moda*) and designer labels, the smartest addresses are c/Serrano, c/Goya, c/Ortega y Gasset and c/Velázquez in Salamanca, north of the Retiro, while more alternative designers are to be found in Malasaña and Chueca (on c/Almirante, especially). For shoes the road to head for is c/Augusto Figueroa in Chueca where there are a number of factory outlets selling a wide range at very good prices. Anything **electrical**, particularly sound systems, can be found in nearby c/Barquillo. The **antiques** trade is concentrated on and around c/Ribera de Curtidores, near the Rastro, and in the Puerta de Toledo shopping centre, while for truly idiosyncratic items, it's hard to beat the shops just

Opening hours

Usual **opening hours** are Monday–Friday 9.30am–2pm & 5–8pm, Saturday 10am–2pm, but the big department and chain stores do not tend to close for lunch. There are also two chains of late-night shops – VIPS and 7 Eleven – that stay open into the early hours and on Sundays. Each branch sells newspapers, cigarettes, groceries, books, CDs – all the things you need to pop in for at 3am. Larger branches also have café/restaurants, one-hour photo developing and other services. Nearly all shops are closed on Sunday, but the larger stores do open on the first Sunday of each month (not in Aug). All the larger stores take credit cards, but many require photographic identification, for example a passport, as well.

off Plaza Mayor, where luminous saints rub shoulders with surgical supports and fascist memorabilia. The cheapest, trashiest **souvenirs** can be collected at the Todo a Cien Pesetas (Everything 100ptas) shops scattered all over the city.

Most areas of the city have their own *mercados del barrio* (indoor **markets**), devoted mainly to food. Among the best are those in Plaza San Miguel (just west of Plaza Mayor); La Cebada in Plaza de la Cebada (Metro La Latina); Antón Martín in c/Santa Isabel (Metro Antón Martín); and Maravillas, c/Bravo Murillo 122 (Metro Cuatro Caminos). The city's biggest market is, of course, the **Rastro** – the flea market – which takes place on Sunday in the area south of Plaza Mayor. Other specialized markets include a secondhand **book market** on the Cuesta de Moyano, at the southwest corner of El Retiro (see p.95), and the stamp and coin market in Plaza Mayor every Sunday (Metro Sol; 9am–2pm), where collectors gather to buy, sell and inspect.

SHOPPING

For more on the Rastro see box, p.41.

BOOKS, MAPS AND POSTERS

In addition to specialist bookstores, the museum and art gallery shops, especially in the Centro Arte de Reina Sofía, all have a good range of posters, prints and books.

Casa del Libro

Gran Vía 29 (**Map 7, F7**) and c/Maestro Victoria 3 (**Map 7, E8**). Both Metro Callao.

Mon–Sat 9.30am–9.30pm.

The Casa del Libro's Gran Vía branch is the city's biggest bookstore, with four floors covering just about everything, including a wide range of fiction in English and translations of classic Spanish works from Lope de Vega to Benito Pérez Galdós. The branch at Maestro Victoria has a good section on maps, guides and books about Madrid.

Crisol

Map 2, K3. C/Serrano 24 (Metro Serrano) and C/Juan Bravo 38 (Metro Diego de León).

Mon–Sat 10am–10pm, Sun & public holidays 11am–3pm & 5–9pm.

Good selection of English-language books. Records and foreign newspapers too.

The International Bookshop

Map 3, E3. C/Campomanes 13. Metro Ópera/Santo Domingo.

Mon–Fri 10.30am–2.30pm & 4.30–8.30pm, Sat 10.30am–3pm. Aug Mon–Sat 11am–3pm.

Wide range of secondhand books in most European languages.

La Librería

Map 3, D6. C/Mayor 78. Metro Sol.
Mon–Fri 10am–2pm & 4.30–7.30pm, Sat 11am–2pm.
Tiny bookshop full of books just about Madrid. Also a good place to pick up old postcards, historic maps and photos of the city.

Pasajes

Map 7, J3. C/Genova 3. Metro Colón.
Mon–Fri 10am–2pm & 5–8pm, Sat 10am–2pm.
Specializes in English and foreign-language books. Also has a useful noticeboard where people advertise flats for rent, Spanish classes, etc.

La Tienda Verde

C/Maudes 23 & 38. Metro Cuatro Caminos.
Mon–Sat 9.30am–2pm & 4.30–8pm.
A small shop crammed with trekking and mountain books, guides and survey (*topográfico*) maps. The helpful staff will point you in the right direction.

CLOTHES AND SHOES

Chain stores selling good-value **clothes** can be found all over the city; look out for Massimo Dutti, Springfield, Milano Trajes for men, and Zara and Mango for women, while Cortefiel caters for both sexes.

Adolfo Domínguez

Map 9, D6 and E3. C/José Ortega y Gasset 4 and c/Serrano 96.
Both Metro Serrano.
Mon–Sat 10am–2pm & 5–8.30pm. The c/Serrano branch doesn't close for lunch.
The classic modern Spanish look – sober colours, little extra decoration and free lines. Domínguez's designs are quite pricey,

but he has a cheaper *Básico* range. Men's clothes only at the Ortega y Gasset branch. Expect to pay in the region of 10,000ptas for a shirt.

Agatha Ruiz de la Prada
Map 9, B5. C/Marqués de Riscal 8. Metro Rubén Darío.
Mon–Fri 10am–2pm & 5–8pm, Sat 10am–2pm.
Movida designer who shows and sells her striking clothes and accessories at this outlet.

Ararat
Map 7, K6 and J6. C/Conde Xiquena 13; c/Almirante 10 & 11. Both Metro Chueca.
Mon–Sat 11am–2pm & 5–8.30pm.
A trio of shops with clubby Spanish and foreign designs at reasonably modest prices. Men's clothes are at c/Conde Xiquena 13, women's in c/Almirante. No. 10 specializes in more formal wear, while no. 11 goes for a younger, more modern look.

Berlín
Map 7, J6. C/Almirante 10. Metro Chueca.
Mon–Sat 11am–2pm & 5–8.30pm.
Next door to Ararat. Women's clothes from a selection of vanguard European and American designers, as well as Spaniard Roberto Torretta. Trousers start at around 15,000ptas, dresses at 35,000ptas.

Camper
Map 7, D6. C/Gran Vía 54. Metro Callao.
Mon–Sat 10am–2pm & 5–8.30pm.
Spain's best shoe-shop chain for men and women, selling practical and comfortable designs at modest prices, with the odd quirky fabric and unusual heel thrown in. There are lots of other branches around the city.

CLOTHES AND SHOES

Ekseptión

Map 2, L3. C/Velázquez 28. Metro Velázquez.

Mon–Sat 10.30am–2.30pm & 5–8.30pm.

A dramatic walkway bathed in spotlights gives on to some of the most *moderno* women's clothes in Madrid, from Sybilla and Antoni Miró, among others. Versace, Jean-Paul Gaultier *et al* are also represented.

Excrupulus Net

Map 7, J6. C/Almirante 7. Metro Chueca.

Mon–Sat 11am–2pm & 5–8.30pm.

Groovy shoes from Spanish designers, Muxart and Looky, starting at 15,000ptas. Also sells some original and stylish accessories. Men and women.

Glam

Map 7, G6 and H6. C/Fuencarral 35 (Metro Gran Vía/Chueca); c/Hortaleza 62 (Metro Chueca).

Mon–Sat 10am–2pm & 5–9pm.

Club, street-style clothes. The clientele and the clothes wouldn't look out of place in an Almodóvar film. Good value, with shirts and tops around 5000ptas.

Hernanz

Map 4, G3. C/Toledo 30. Metro Tirso de Molina.

Mon–Fri 9.30am–1.30pm & 5–8.30pm, Sat 9.30am–1.30pm; no cards.

Established more than a hundred and fifty years ago, this shoe shop stocks over one hundred different types of *alpargata* (espadrille) in just about every imaginable colour and style, including ones with shiny silver trimming for evening wear. The king reputedly buys his here, so they must be good. Prices range from 900 to 3000ptas.

CLOTHES AND SHOES

Sybilla
Map 2, K3. C/Jorge Juan 12. Metro Retiro.
Mon–Sat 10am–2pm & 4.30–8.30pm.
Sybilla was Spain's top designer of the 1980s – a Vivienne
Westwood of Madrid. She remains at the forefront of the
scene, and her prices show it. The shop is a comfortable place
to while away the time, with its armchairs and sofas, clashing
with Sybilla's trademark vivid colours. Women's clothes only.

CHILDREN

Bazar Mila
Map 7, F7. Gran Vía 33. Metro Gran Vía/Callao.
Mon–Sat 9.30am–8.30pm.
Standard toy shop that is just the place to get your Spanish set of
Monopoly or your plastic models of Real or Atlético players.

Caramelos Paco
Map 4, F5. C/Toledo 55. Metro La Latina.
Mon–Sat 9.30am–2pm & 5–8pm, Sun 11am–3pm.
A child's dream and a dentist's nightmare, with a window
crammed full of every imaginable sugary sweet. Giant lollipops,
sugar-coated figures and almond-flavoured sticks of rock are
among the delights.

Prénatal
Map 7, G7. C/Fuencarral 17. Metro Quevedo.
Mon–Sat 10am–1.45pm & 4.30–8pm.
The Spanish version of Mothercare; if you need something in
an emergency this is probably your best bet.

Puck
C/Duque de Sesto 30. Metro Goya.
Mon 4.30–8pm, Tues–Sat 10am–1.30pm & 4.30–8pm.

An old-fashioned toy shop now celebrating 25 years in business. The fabulous dolls' houses are complete down to the very smallest detail, and customers can select their own decor. Thankfully, not a Nintendo or Playstation in sight.

CRAFTS AND SOUVENIRS

Alvarez Gómez
Map 2, J4. C/Serrano 14. Metro Serrano.
Mon–Sat 9.30am–2pm & 4.45–8.15pm.
Gómez has been making the same perfumes in the same bottles for the last century. The fragrances – carnation, rose and violet – are as simple and straight as they come. The elegant shop, complete with its chandeliers, also sells stylish toilet bags, hats and umbrellas.

El Arco de los Cuchilleros
Map 4, G2. Plaza Mayor 9. Metro Sol.
Mon–Sat 11am–8pm, Sun 11am–2.30pm.
El Arco houses thirty or so workshops and artesans, who reflect Spanish *artesanía* at its most innovative and contemporary. Crafts include ceramics, leather, wood, jewellery and textiles, and there's a gallery space used for five or six exhibitions each year. Prices are very reasonable and staff helpful.

Casa Jiménez
Map 3, G2. C/Preciados 42. Metro Callao.
Mon–Sat 10am–1.30pm & 5–8pm. Closed Sat afternoon in July and all day Sat in Aug.
One of the oldest established shops in Spain. Here you can buy elaborately embroidered *mantones* (shawls) made in Seville, with prices ranging from 17,000 to 100,000ptas, as well as gorgeous fans from around 6000ptas.

Casa Yustas

Map 4, G1. Plaza Mayor 30. Metro Sol.
Mon–Fri 9.45am–1.30pm & 4.30–8pm, Sat 9.45am–1.30pm; no cards.
Madrid's oldest hat shop, established in 1894. Every conceivable model and price, from pith helmets and commando berets to panamas and bowlers.

Fútbol Total

C/Cardenal Cisneros 80. Metro Quevedo.
Mon–Sat: July–Sept 10.30am–2pm & 5.30–8.30pm; Oct–June 10.30am–2pm & 5–9pm.
Just the place to get your Real, Atlético or even Rayo shirt. In fact the strip of practically every Spanish team is available, for around 7000ptas.

José Ramírez

Map 4, H3. C/Concepción Jerónima. Metro Sol/Tirso de Molina.
Mon–Fri 9.30am–2pm & 5–8pm, Sat 10am–2pm.
One of the most renowned guitar workshops in Spain; it even has a museum of antique instruments. Prices start at around 15,000ptas and head skywards for the quality models and fancy woods. Famous clients include Segovia.

Mercado de Artesanos

Map 7, D3. Plaza de las Comendadoras. Metro San Bernardo.
Every Sat afternoon.
The weekly market in this pleasant plaza is a good place to pick up handicrafts and original souvenirs. There are also performances and workshops to add to the interest.

Palomeque

Map 3, G4. C/Hileras 12. Metro Ópera.
Mon–Fri 10am–2pm & 5–8pm, Sat 10am–2pm.
A religious department store stocking everything from rosary

beads and habits down to your very own plastic baby Jesus. If
you want to complete your postcard collection of Spanish saints
and virgins, this is for you.

Seseña

Map 6, B4. C/de la Cruz 23. Metro Sol.
Mon–Sat 10am–1.30pm & 4.30–8pm.
Tailor specializing in traditional *Madrileño* capes for royalty and
celebrities. Clients have included Luis Buñuel and Gary Cooper.

DEPARTMENT STORES

El Corte Inglés

Map 3, I4. C/Preciados 1–4. Metro Sol. Branches at c/Princesa 42
(Metro Argüelles); c/Goya 76 & 87 (Metro Goya); Paseo de la
Castellana 71 & 85 (Metro Nuevos Ministerios).
Mon–Sat 10am–9.30pm.
The Spanish department store *par excellence*. It's not cheap, but
the quality is very good and the advantage is that you can get
practically anything you want under one roof. Highly profes-
sional staff (the majority of whom speak English) and a classy
food department. Good for sports equipment and not bad for
CDs.

Fnac

Map 3, H2. C/Preciados 28. Metro Callao.
Mon–Sat 10am–9.30pm, Sun noon–9.30pm.
Not really a true department store, but it does have excellent
sections for books, videos, CDs and electrical equipment. Also
sells concert tickets. The book department is good for English-
language fiction and has a decent section for English-language
teachers/learners. The store has a price promise that it will
return your money if you find any article cheaper anywhere else.

FOOD AND DRINK

Baco – La Boutique del Vino
C/San Bernardo 117. Metro Quevedo.
Mon–Fri 11am–2pm & 5–8pm, Sat 10am–2pm; no cards.
Supermarket-type wine store with a good-value range of quality Spanish wines, *cavas*, brandies and also Asturian cider (*sidra*). It's certainly worth splashing out on one of the *reservas* from Ribera del Duero or Rioja. Look out too for good reds from Navarra and Valdepeñas and whites from Rueda and Galicia.

Bruin
Map 2, A1. Paseo del Pintor Rosales 48. Metro Argüelles.
Daily 10am–midnight.
Great ice-cream parlour with a nice *terraza* next to Parque del Oeste. Over twenty different flavours, plus the full range of chilled drinks.

Casa Mira
Map 6, D4. Carrera de San Jerónimo 30. Metro Sevilla.
Mon–Sat 10am–2pm & 5–9pm.
The place to go for *turrón* (flavoured nougat) – eaten by nearly all Spaniards at Christmas – and marzipan. The family business has been open for nearly a hundred and fifty years since the founder, Luis Mira, arrived from Asturias and set up a stall in Puerta del Sol.

Mallorca
Map 2, J4. C/Serrano 6. Metro Serrano.
Daily 9.30am–9pm.
The main branch of Madrid's best deli chain – a pricey but fabulous treasure trove for picnics, cakes and chocolates. All branches have small bars serving drinks and canapés.

La Mallorquina

Map 3, I5. Puerta del Sol 2. Metro Sol.
Mon–Sat 9am–9.45pm.

Wonderful-smelling pastry shop and café selling everything you've always been told not to eat. Try the small ball-shaped *buñuelos* filled with cream or the tray of assorted *pasteles*. Upstairs there's a salon which overlooks Puerta del Sol – a great place for people-watching while sampling a milky coffee and a slice of truffle cake.

Mariano Aguado

Map 6, D5. C/Echegaray 19. Metro Sevilla.
Mon–Fri 9.30am–2pm & 5.30–8.30pm, Sat 9.30am–2pm.

Atmospheric wine seller's with an assuringly musty atmosphere. Fine selection of Spanish wines and, especially, sherries (*vinos de Jerez*) at prices to suit any pocket.

Mariano Madrueño

Map 3, H3. C/Postigo San Martín 3. Metro Callao.
Mon–Fri 9.30am–2pm & 5–8pm, Sat 9.30am–2pm.

Great traditional wine seller's established back in 1895. There's an overpowering smell of grapes as you peruse its vintage-crammed shelves. Intriguing tipples include powerful Licor de Hierbas from Galicia and homemade Pacharán sloe gin.

Museo del Jamón

Map 6, B3. Carrera de San Jerónimo 6. Metro Sol.
Mon–Sat 9am–midnight, Sun & public holidays 10am–midnight.

A fantastic range of hams hanging from the ceiling, but it'll set you back a bit – a quality *Jamón de Jabugo* from pigs fed exclusively on acorns weighs in at 8000ptas a kilo, while the more industrially manufactured *Jamón de Serrano* is a mere 2500ptas. At the very least stay for a glass of red wine and sample one of the selection plates available. Staff are always willing to provide advice. Branches all over town.

FOOD AND DRINK

241

Patrimonio Comunal Olivarero

Map 7, I4. C/Mejía Lequérica 1. Metro Alonso Martinez.
Mon–Sat 9.30am–2.30pm & 5.30–7.30pm.

Outlet for an olive growers' co-operative, with information sheets to guide you towards purchasing the best olive oils. A vast range of grades and quantities are available from all over the peninsula.

RECORDS AND CDS

Madrid Rock

Map 7, G7. Gran Vía 25. Metro Callao.
Daily 10am–10pm.

By Spanish standards this is a huge record store, selling a good range of rock, jazz, Pop Español and flamenco CDs. Tickets for most concerts are available here.

La Metralleta

Map 3, G3. Plaza de San Martín. Metro Ópera.
Mon–Sat 10am–2.30pm & 4.30–8.30pm.

Down the steps on the edge of the plaza, La Metralleta buys and sells CDs, records, film posters, calendars and anything connected with the entertainment industry. Lots of bargains, with CDs at around 900ptas – a good place to find more obscure stuff.

Kids' Madrid

Although many of the main sights and museums in Madrid lack child-specific services or activities, there is plenty in the city to keep **children** occupied and interested for a short stay. Most of the parks have playgrounds, and, in addition to the city's swimming pools (see p.226), there are a couple of aquaparks situated out of town. The colourful parades and events during fiestas are also worth investigating, particularly during *Carnaval* (Feb) and at Christmas.

Children are, in general, doted on in Spain and are welcome in nearly all cafés and restaurants. Most are more than willing to provide special child portions, while the VIPS chain of café/restaurants and all the burger bars provide children's menus. Spanish children stay up later than in many other countries and frequently accompany parents for a late evening stroll or drinks at a *terraza*.

Acuarium de Madrid
Map 3, H4. C/Maestro Vitoria 8 ✆91 531 81 72. Metro Callao/Sol. Daily 11am–2pm & 5–9pm; 375ptas.
A small-scale, but quite intriguing exhibition of fish, reptiles and spiders located in the heart of the shopping zone of Madrid. Instant distraction for bored children.

Imax Madrid

Parque Tierno Galván Meneses ©91 467 48 00. Metro Méndez
Álvaro.

Continuous shows: Mon–Fri 11.20am–1pm & 3.45pm–1am, Sat &
Sun 11.20am–2.15pm & 3.45pm–1am; 900–1400ptas.

Three different types of screen at this futuristic cinema – a
giant flat one, a dome-shaped one for all-round viewing and
one for 3D projections. Natural-history style documentaries
dominate the schedules.

Mirador del Faro

Avda del Arco de la Victoria. Metro Moncloa.

Tues–Sun: Sept–May 10.30am–2pm & 5.30–7.30pm; June–Aug
11am–1.45pm & 5.30–8.45pm; 200ptas, 100ptas for 3–10-yr olds.

The futuristic *mirador* (viewing gallery) provides fantastic views
over the city and is very popular with children.

Museo de Cera (Wax Museum)

Map 7, L4. Paseo de Recoletos 41 ©91 308 08 25. Metro Colón.

Mon–Fri 10.00am–2.30pm & 4.30–8.30pm, Sat, Sun & holidays
10am–8.30pm; 900ptas, under-12s & over-65s 600ptas, under-4s
free.

Over 450 different personalities and a chamber of horrors feature in this expensive and tacky museum, which is nevertheless
popular with children.

Museo de Ciencias Naturales

C/José Gutiérrez Abascal 2 ©91 411 13 28. Metro Nuevos
Ministerios.

Tues–Fri 10am–6pm, Sat 10am–8pm, Sun 10am–2.30pm; 400ptas,
under-14s 300ptas.

The Natural History Museum is the most interactive of the
traditional musems in the city centre, with audiovisual displays
on the evolution of life on earth and plenty of dinosaur
exhibits.

Museo Thyssen-Bornemisza

Map 6, F4. Palacio de Villahermosa, Paseo del Prado 8 ©91 369 01 51. Metro Banco de España.

Tues–Sun 10am–7pm; permanent collection: 700ptas, concessions 400ptas, under-12s free.

The gallery offers children's workshops for accompanied 5–10-year-olds on Saturdays and Sundays at 11.30am and 4.30pm. Ring to confirm. For more on the Museo Thyssen-Bornemisza see p.72.

Parque de Atracciones

Casa de Campo ©91 526 80 30 or 91 463 29 00. Metro Batán/bus #33 & #65.

July & Aug daily noon–1am, Fri & Sat till 2am; Sept–June daily noon–11pm, Sat till 1am. Entry without rides 600ptas; entry with unlimited access to rides (*Calco Supertrasto*) 2675ptas, under-7s (*Calco Infantil*) 1500ptas.

A theme park full of rides, whose attractions include the vertical drop (*la lanzadera*), the stomach-churning *la máquina*, the whitewater raft ride, *los rápidos*, and the haunted mansion, *el viejo caserón*. Spanish singers and groups perform in the open-air auditorium during the summer months and there are frequent parades. Plenty of places to eat and drink of the burger/pizza variety.

Planetario

Avda del Planetario 16, Parque Tierno Galván ©91 467 34 61. Metro Méndez Álvaro.

Tues–Sun 11am–1.45pm & 5–7.45pm; shows at 11.30am, 12.45pm, 5.30pm & 6.45pm; 475ptas, under-14s 200ptas.

Exhibition halls, audiovisual displays and projections on a variety of astronomical themes (all in Spanish).

Teleférico

Map 2, A2. Paseo del Pintor Rosales ©91 541 74 50. Metro Argüelles.

April–Sept daily 11am–2.30pm & 4.30pm–dusk; Oct–March Sat, Sun & public holidays only; 360ptas single, 515ptas return.

A popular cable-car ride over to the restaurant-bar on the far side of Casa de Campo, with great views of the city. You can't use it to get to the zoo or Parque de Atracciones, however, as they're on the other side of the park.

Zoo–Aquarium

Casa de Campo ©91 711 99 50. Metro Batán/bus #33.

Daily 10am–dusk; 1615ptas, under-7s 1300ptas, under-3s free.

The zoo, situated on the southwestern edge of Casa de Campo, is laid out in sections corresponding to the five continents. Most animals are kept in by moats and they have plenty of space to move around. There are over 2000 different species, a dolphinarium with regular shows, an aquarium which includes sharks, pavilions dedicated to venomous snakes and the "mysteries of nature", as well as a children's zoo and parrot show. Boats are available for rent and there are train tours of the site, as well as self-service restaurants and hamburger stalls.

PARKS AND GARDENS

Casa de Campo

Metro Lago/Batán.

The Zoo, Parque de Atracciones and boating lake are all here. However, be aware that the park has become increasingly populated by prostitutes and their clients (see p.120).

Parque Juan Carlos I

Metro Campo de las Naciones.

With the new metro connection, this is now a feasible trip from the city centre. There's plenty to do here, including boat and train rides, playgrounds and kite flying. From mid-June to mid-September a spectacular *son et lumière* show takes place at the fountains (10.30pm Thurs–Sun; 400ptas, 200ptas children).

Parque del Oeste

Map 2, A2. Metro Moncloa/Príncipe Pío.
Very pleasant shady parkland with a small river, the Egyptian Templo de Debod and the starting point of the Teleférico cable car (see p.245).

Parque del Retiro

Map 8. Metro Retiro/Ibiza/Atocha.
Plenty of activities for children, including a boating lake, puppet shows (all year round Sat & Sun 1pm; also July–Sept Mon, Wed, Fri, Sat & Sun 7.30pm & 10.30pm) and playgrounds. Room for roller skating and cycling too (see p.89).

AQUAPARKS

Aquamadrid

Carretera de Barcelona (N-II) km 15.5 ©91 673 10 13. Bus Continental Auto #281, #282, #284, or #385 from Avda de América. Train *cercanías* C-2 or C-7 to San Fernando.
June–Sept Mon–Fri noon–8pm, Sat & Sun 11am–8pm; Mon–Fri 1500ptas, under-11s 1000ptas; Sat & Sun 1800ptas, under-11s 1400ptas; half-day entry (after 4pm) Mon–Fri 1200ptas, Sat & Sun 1500ptas.
Busy waterpark with the usual monster slides and large lake, plus toddlers' pool and nighttime disco.

Aquópolis

Villanueva de la Cañada, Carretera de la Coruña (N-VI) km 25 ©91 815 69 11. Free bus from Plaza de España weekdays 11am & noon, Sat & holidays 11am, noon, 1pm.
June–Sept daily noon–8pm; Mon–Fri 1600ptas, under-10s

1250ptas; Sat & Sun 1800ptas, under-10s 1200ptas.

The largest of the waterparks, with a variety of giant slides, a wave machine, a water-based assault course and plenty of grass for a picnic. Smaller rides for younger kids too.

FOOD

Hard Rock Café
Map 9, C9. Paseo de la Castellana 2 ✆91 436 43 40. Metro Colón.
Daily 12.30pm–2am. Moderate.
A children's favourite, with its tried-and-tested formula of burgers, merchandising and rock memorabilia.

Planet Hollywood
Map 6, F5. Plaza de las Cortes 7 ✆91 360 14 00. Metro Banco de España.
Daily 12.30pm–12.30am. Moderate.
Similar to the *Hard Rock Café* – just substitute film for the rock memorabilia.

Directory

AIRLINES Most airlines have their offices on the Gran Vía or on its continuation beyond the Plaza de España, c/Princesa. American Airlines, c/Pedro Teixeira 8, 5° (Metro Lima; ✆ 91 597 20 68 or 90 010 05 56); Avianca, Gran Vía 88 (Metro Plaza de España; ✆ 91 205 43 20); British Airways, c/Serrano 60 5° (Metro Serrano; ✆ 91 376 96 66 or 902 11 113 33); Iberia, c/Goya 29 (Metro Serrano; ✆ 91 587 47 47 or 91 587 75 92); KLM, Gran Vía 59 (Metro Santo Domingo; ✆ 91 247 81 00); TWA, Plaza de Colón 2 (Metro Colón; ✆ 91 310 30 94). The Iberojet counter at the airport sells discounted standby seats on scheduled flights.

AIRPORT INFORMATION Flights ✆ 91 305 83 43, 91 305 83 44 or 91 305 83 45. General enquiries ✆ 91 393 60 00.

AMERICAN EXPRESS Plaza de las Cortes 2, entrance on Marqués de Cubas (Metro Sevilla; ✆ 91 572 03 03). Open Monday–Friday 9am–5.30pm, Saturday 9am–noon for mail, transactions and exchange.

BANKS AND EXCHANGE The main Spanish banks are concentrated on c/Alcalá and Gran Vía. Opening hours are normally Monday–Friday 9am–2pm, but they're also often open on Saturday 9am–1pm from October to May. International banks include: Bank of

America, c/Capitán Haya 1 (Metro Lima); Barclays, Plaza de Colón 1 (Metro Colón); Citibank, c/José Ortega y Gasset 29 (Metro Núñez de Balboa); Lloyds, c/Serrano 90 (Metro Núñez de Balboa). In addition to the banks, branches of El Corte Inglés department store all have exchange offices with long hours and highly competitive rates; the most central is on Puerta del Sol. Barajas airport has a 24-hour currency exchange office. Although they don't usually charge commission, the rates at the exchange bureaux scattered around the city are often very poor.

BICYCLES For rental and repairs try Bicicletas Chapinal, c/Alcalá 242 (Metro El Carmen; Mon–Fri 10am–1.30pm & 4.30–8pm, Sat 10am–2pm; ☏ 91 404 18 53); Calmera, c/Atocha 98 (Metro Antón Martín; Mon–Sat 9.30am–1.30pm & 4.30–8pm; ☏ 91 527 75 74); Karacol, c/Montera 32 (Metro Gran Vía/Sol; Mon–Fri 10am–2pm & 5.30–8.30pm, Sat 10.30am–2pm; ☏ 91 532 90 73).

BUSES Long-distance buses terminate at the Estación Sur de Autobuses on c/Méndez Álvaro (Metro Méndez Álvaro; ☏91 468 42 00). Companies and services change with great frequency and it's always worth checking schedules with the Turismo or the information line (☏91 435 22 66). Two of the largest companies are Auto–Res (☏91 551 66 44) and La Sepulvedana (☏91 530 48 00).

CAR RENTAL Major operators have branches at Barajas airport and around the city centre: Atesa, c/Infanta Mercedes 90 (Metro Estrecho; ☏91 571 19 31); Avis, Gran Vía 60 (Metro Plaza de España; ☏91 547 20 48); Europcar, c/San Leonardo 8 (Metro Plaza de España; ☏91 541 88 92); Hertz, Estación de Atocha (Metro Atocha; ☏91 468 13 18); Rent Me, Plaza de Herradores 6, just off Plaza Mayor (Metro Sol; ☏91 559 08 22).

DISABILITY Madrid is not particularly well geared up for the disabled (*minusválidos*), although the situation is gradually improving. The Organizacíon Nacional de Ciegos de España (ONCE) at c/Prado 24 (©91 589 46 00 or 91 577 37 56) provides the best specialist advice. Major museums and some of the larger, more expensive hotels have adapted facilities, some buses have been altered for wheelchairs and all metro trains and buses have designated seats. However, there are no lifts in the metro and train stations. Wheelchair-adapted taxis can be ordered from Radio Taxi (©91 547 82 00).

DOCTORS English-speaking doctors are available at the Anglo-American Medical Unit, c/Conde de Aranda 1 (Metro Retiro; Mon–Fri 9am–8pm, Sat 10am–3pm; ©91 435 18 23).

ELECTRICITY 220 volts AC. Most European appliances should work as long as you have an adaptor for European-style two-pin plugs. North Americans will need this plus a transformer.

EMBASSIES Australia, Paseo de la Castellana 143 (Metro Cuzco; ©91 441 93 00); Canada, c/Núñez de Balboa 35 (Metro Núñez de Balboa; ©91 431 43 00); France, c/Salustiano Olozaga 9 (Metro Banco de España; ©91 435 55 60); Germany, c/Fortuny 8 (Metro Rubén Darío; ©91 319 91 00); Ireland, Paseo de la Castellana 46 (Metro Rubén Darío; ©91 436 40 93); Italy, C/Lagasca, 98 (Metro Núñez de Balboa; ©91 577 65 29); Netherlands, Paseo de la Castellana 178 (Metro Cuzco; ©91 359 09 14); New Zealand, Plaza Lealtad 2 (Metro Banco de España; ©91 523 02 26); Norway, Paseo de la Castellana 31 (Metro Rubén Darío; ©91 310 31 16); South Africa, c/Claudio Coello 91 (Metro Núñez Balboa; ©91 435 66 88); Sweden, c/Caracas 25 (Metro Sevilla; ©91 308 15 35); UK, c/Fernando el Santo 16 (Metro Alonso Martínez; ©91 319 02 00); USA, c/Serrano 51 (Metro Serrano; ©91 577 40 00).

EMERGENCIES Madrid has recently introduced an all-purpose emergency number ©112 for police, medical services and the fire brigade. You can still, however use the old numbers if you prefer. For an ambulance dial ©061, ©91 588 45 00 or 91 522 22 22 – or get a taxi, which will be quicker, if no paramedics are necessary. For the police dial ✆091 or 092.

HEALTH Residents of European Union countries are entitled to free medical treatment and prescribed medicines under the EU Reciprocal Medical Treatment arrangement, provided you have a completed E111 form (available from post offices in Britain and Social Security offices elsewhere). Citizens of non-EU countries will be charged at private hospital rates, so it is essential to take out medical insurance before travelling.

HOSPITALS The most central are: El Clínico, Plaza de Cristo Rey (Metro Moncloa; ✆91 330 37 47); Hospital Gregorio Marañón, c/Dr Esquerdo 46 (Metro O'Donnell; ✆91 586 80 00); and Ciudad Sanitaria La Paz, Paseo de la Castellana 261 (Metro Begoña; ✆91 358 28 31).

INTERNET ACCESS To log on to the Internet or check your email try the following Internet cafés: *Aroba 25*, Gran Vía 80 (Metro Gran Vía); *La Casa de Internet*, c/Luchana 20, 1° (Metro Bilbao); *Cybermad*, c/Laurel 6 (Metro Embajadores/Acacias); *Net Café*, c/San Bernardo 7 (Metro San Bernardo). Prices range from 450–600ptas per hour, often with a drink included.

LANGUAGE COURSES Madrid has numerous language schools, offering intensive courses in Spanish language and culture. One of the most established is International House, c/Zurbano 8 (Metro Alonso Martínez; ✆91 310 13 14).

LAUNDRY Central *lavanderías* include: c/Barco 26 (Metro Gran Vía); c/Cervantes 1–3 (Metro Sol); c/Donoso Cortés 17 (Metro Quevedo); c/Hermosilla 121 (Metro Goya); c/Palma 2 (Metro Tribunal).

LEFT LUGGAGE There are *consignas* at the Airport (between Terminals One and Two), Estación Sur (daily 6.35am–11.45pm),

Auto–Res and Continental Auto bus stations; at the airport bus terminal beneath Plaza de Colón; as well as lockers at Atocha and Chamartín train stations.

PARKING Parking is difficult in the city centre, and, although the law appears to be flouted all the time, parking is banned on the main streets. If you have a car, your best bet is to leave it at your hotel or in one of the many underground car parks, especially if it has foreign plates, as these are often targeted by car thieves. Illegally parked cars are towed away by the *grúa* (tow truck) and you have to ring ✆91 345 00 50, quoting your number plate, and pay in the region of 20,000ptas to recover your vehicle.

PHARMACIES *Farmacias* are distinguished by a green cross; each district has a rota with one staying open through the night. For details call ✆098 (Spanish only) or check the notice on the door of your nearest pharmacy or the listings magazines. Madrid also has quite a number of traditional herbalists, best known of which is Maurice Mességue, c/Goya 64 (Metro Goya; Mon–Fri 10am–2pm & 5–8pm, Sat 10am–2pm).

POLICE The headquarters of the Policía Nacional are near to Plaza de España at c/Fomento 24 (✆91 541 71 60). If you report a crime you will have to make an official statement or *denuncia* – often a time-consuming and laborious business, especially as few policemen speak English, but a necessary procedure for any insurance claim. Other centrally located police stations (*comisarías*) are to be found at c/Luna 29 (Metro Callao; ✆91 521 12 36), and c/Huertas 76 (Metro Antón Martín; ✆91 249 09 94). In an emergency call ✆091 or 112.

POST OFFICE The main one is the Palacio de Comunicaciones in the Plaza de las Cibeles (Metro Banco de España; Mon–Sat 8.30am–9.30pm, Sun 8.30am–2.30pm for stamps and telegrams; Mon–Fri 9am–8pm, Sat 9am–2pm for poste restante (*lista de* *correos*). Branch offices throughout the city are open Monday–Saturday 9am–2pm, but the easiest places to buy stamps are the *estancos*, small shops selling stamps and tobacco, recognizable by their brown and yellow signs bearing the word *Tabacos*.

PUBLIC HOLIDAYS The main national holidays when shops and banks will be closed are: Jan 1 (*Año Nuevo*); Jan 6 (*Reyes*); Easter Thursday (*Jueves Santo*); Good Friday (*Viernes Santo*); May 1 (*Fiesta del Trabajo*); May 2 (*Día de la Comunidad*); May 15 (*San Isidro*); Aug 15 (*Virgen de la Paloma*); Oct 12 (*Día de la Hispanidad*); Nov 1 (*Todos los Santos*); Nov 9 (*Virgen de la Almudena*); Dec 6 (*Día de la Constitución*); Dec 8 (*La Inmaculada*); Dec 25 (*Navidad*).

PUBLIC TOILETS There are very few public toilets in Madrid, so your best bet is to pop into a local bar, café or department store.

TELEPHONES International calls can be made from any phone box or from any *telefónica*. The main *telefónica* at Gran Vía 30 (Metro Gran Vía) is open until midnight. To make a local call the minimum charge is 15ptas, but you won't usually get any change from a 25ptas coin. Phones that will accept coins, phonecards and credit cards are increasingly common and many have instructions in English as well as other languages. Phonecards cost 1000ptas or 2000ptas and can be bought at post offices or *estancos*. To make an international call, dial ✆00 and then dial the country code followed by the area code – omitting initial zero – and then the number. For international directory enquiries ring ✆025; for national directory enquiries ring ✆1003. To make a reverse charge call ask the operator for *cobro revertido*.

TICKETS For theatre and concert tickets, plus some sports events, credit-card booking services are run by Caixa Catalunya (✆902 10 12 12), Caja Madrid (✆902 488 488), Servicaixa (✆902 33 22 11) or Caja de Catlunya (✆91 538 33 33). Tickets are also available from El

Corte Inglés (☎91 432 93 00, 902 400 222 or 902 262 27 67). Localidades Galicia, Plaza del Carmen 1 (Metro Sol; credit-card lines ☎91 531 27 32 or 91 531 91 31) sells tickets for football games, bullfights, theatres and concerts.

TOURIST INFORMATION PHONELINE Mon–Fri 8am–9pm. For enquiries about events in Madrid dial ☎010 if you're phoning from within the city or ☎901 300 600 if you're ringing from outside Madrid. For general enquiries about the whole Comunidad de Madrid dial ☎012.

TRAINS information ☎91 563 02 02 or 91 328 90 20; reservations ☎91 562 33 33. Tickets can be bought at the individual stations, or at Barajas airport arrivals and at the city-centre RENFE office, c/Alcalá 44 (Metro Banco de España; Mon–Fri 9am–7pm, Sat 9am–1.30pm; ☎91 562 33 33).

TRAVEL AGENCIES Viajes Zeppelin, Plaza Santo Domingo 2 (Metro Santo Domingo; ☎91 542 51 54), is an English-speaking and very efficient company, offering excellent deals on flights and holidays. Nuevas Fronteras, c/Luisa Fernanda 2 (Metro Ventura Rodríguez; ☎91 542 39 90) and in the Torre de Madrid, Plaza de España (Metro Plaza de España; ☎91 247 42 00) can be good for flights, or try Top Tours, c/Capitán Haya 20 (Metro Cuzco; ☎91 555 06 04). Many other travel agents are concentrated on and around the Gran Vía. For student travel go to TIVE, c/Fernando el Católico 88 (Metro Moncloa; ☎91 543 02 08).

OUT OF THE CITY

El Escorial and El Valle de los Caídos

Fifty kilometres northwest of Madrid, in the foothills of the Sierra de Guadarrama, lies one of Spain's best-known and most visited sights – Felipe II's vast monastery-palace complex of **El Escorial**. An exceptional building in itself, it also provides an unprecedented insight into the mindset of Spain's greatest king. The town around the monastery, **San Lorenzo del Escorial**, is an easy day-trip from Madrid and you can also take in **El Valle de los Caídos** (The Valley of the Fallen), 9km further north. This is an equally megalomaniacal, yet far more chilling monument: an underground basilica hewn under Franco's orders, allegedly as a monument to the Civil War dead of both sides, though in reality as a memorial to the Generalísimo and his regime.

Regular **trains** run from Estación de Atocha on the *cercanías* line C-8a (daily 5.45am–11.30pm; 50min; 760ptas return), calling at Charmartín on the way out of the city. From the station at El Escorial take the local bus up the hill to the monastery. **Buses** (run by Autocares Herranz) leave every thirty minutes on weekdays and hourly at weekends

(Mon–Fri 7.15am–10pm, Sat 9am–9.30pm, Sun & public holidays 9am–11pm) from Moncloa bus station (55min; 740ptas). The **Turismo** in San Lorenzo del Escorial is at c/Floridablanca 10 (summer: Mon–Sat 11am–6pm & Sun 10am–3pm; winter: Mon–Fri 10am–2pm & 3–5pm, Sat & Sun 10am–3pm; ✆91 890 15 54).

A direct local bus departs from El Escorial to El Valle de los Caídos at 3.15pm and returns at 5.30pm (Tues–Sun). Tickets are sold at the *Bar Manises*, opposite the post office, just up from the monastery.

EL ESCORIAL

Tues–Sun: April–Sept 10am–6pm; Oct–March 10am–5pm; 850ptas, 350ptas concessions, free Wed for EU citizens. Separate admission charge of 325ptas for the outlying lodges and formal gardens.

El Escorial was the largest Spanish building of the Renaissance. Rectangular, overbearing and severe, from the outside it resembles more a prison than a palace. Built between 1563 and 1584 by Juan Bautista de Toledo and Juan de Herrera, **Felipe II** planned the enormous complex as part monastery, part mausoleum and part palace, where he would live the life of a monk and "rule the world with two inches of paper". Seven kilometres out of town, on the Ávila road, there are great views of the monastery from the Silla de Felipe (Philip's Seat), a chair carved into a rocky outcrop from where Felipe II is supposed to have watched the construction of the complex.

The monastery itself commemorates the victory over the French at St Quentin on San Lorenzo's feast day (August 10, 1557), and above the **west gateway** is a gargantuan statue of the patron saint holding the gridiron on which he was burned to death. The gridiron emblem is also present on the builders' trowels displayed in the basement exhibi-

MONASTERIO DE
SAN LORENZO
DEL ESCORIAL

La Casa del Rey

Felipe II's
apartments

Panteón
Real

Panteón de
Infantes

Museos Nuevos

Sacristía

Palacio de
los Borbones

Claustro Grande

Sala de las Batallas

Salas capitulares

Basílica

Vestíbulo

Visitor's entrance

Monasterio

Colegio

Colegio

Patio de
los Reyes

Monasterio

Biblioteca

Colegio entrance

Main entrance

tion, and the whole complex is said to have been designed around this pattern. Within is the **Patio de los Reyes**, named after the six statues of the kings of Israel which adorn the facade of the basilica, on one side of the Patio. Linking the secular and religious zones of the monastery complex is the **Biblioteca**, a splendid hall with multi-coloured vivid frescoes by Tibaldi, showing the seven Liberal Arts. The Biblioteca's collections include Santa Teresa's personal diary, some gorgeously executed Arabic manuscripts and a Florentine planetarium of 1572 demonstrating the movement of the planets according to the Ptolemaic and Copernican systems.

EL ESCORIAL

261

The enormous, cold, dark interior of the **Basílica** contains over forty altars, designed to allow simultaneous Masses to be held. Behind the main altar lies some of Felipe's mammoth collection of saintly relics, including six whole bodies, over sixty heads and hundreds of bone fragments set in fabulously expensive caskets. The two bronze sculptural groups at the east end, depicting Carlos V with his family and Felipe II with three of his wives, were carved by the father-and-son team of Leone and Pompeo Leoni.

Many of the monastery's religious treasures are contained in the **Sacristía** and **Salas Capitulares** (Chapter Houses) around the Basílica and include paintings by Titian, Velázquez and José Ribera. Below these rooms is the **Panteón Real**, where deceased Spanish monarchs lie in their gilded marble tombs, while just above the entrance you pass the doorway to the **Pudrería**, a separate room in which the bodies rot for twenty years or so before the cleaned-up skeletons are moved downstairs. The royal children are laid in the **Panteón de los Infantes** and there is also a wedding-cake babies' tomb with room for sixty infants.

What remains of the Escorial's **art collection** – works by Bosch, Gerard David, Dürer, Titian, Zurbarán and many others, which escaped transfer to the Prado – is kept in the elegant suite of rooms known as the **Museos Nuevos**. Finally, there are the treasure-crammed **Salones Reales** (Royal Apartments), containing the austere quarters of Felipe II, with the chair that supported his gouty leg and the deathbed from which he was able to contemplate the high altar of the basilica.

....

To escape the worst of the crowds, especially in the Royal Apartments, avoid Wednesdays and try visiting just before lunch.

....

Eating and drinking

For **refreshments** you'll need to head away from the monastery, up c/Reina Victoria into town. *La Genara*, at Plaza San Lorenzo 2, is a good-value restaurant filled with theatrical mementos, while the more expensive *Charolés*, c/Floridablanca 24, is renowned for its fish and stews. The best bar is the friendly *Cervecería Los Pescaítos*, c/Joaquín Costa 8, which also serves fish dishes.

EL VALLE DE LOS CAÍDOS

Tues–Sun: April–Sept 9.30am–7pm; Oct–March 10am–6pm; 650ptas, free Wed for EU citizens.

The **basilica complex** denies its claims of being a memorial "to the Civil War dead of both sides" almost at a glance. The dour, grandiose architectural forms employed, the constant inscriptions "Fallen for God and for Spain", and the proximity to El Escorial clue you in to its true function – the glorification of **General Franco** and his regime. The dictator himself lies buried behind the high altar, while the only other named tomb is that of his guru, the Falangist leader José Antonio Primo de Rivera, who was shot dead by Republicans at the beginning of the war. The "other side" is present only in the fact that the complex was built by the Republican army's survivors – political prisoners on quarrying duty.

Above the complex is a vast **cross**, reputedly the largest in the world, and visible for miles around. From the entrance to the basilica a shaky **funicular** (Tues–Sun: April–Sept 11am–1.30pm & 4–6.30pm; Oct–March 11am–1.30pm & 3–5.30pm; 350ptas) ascends to the base of the cross, offering superlative views over the Sierra de Guadarrama and of the giant, grotesque figures propping up the cross.

Aranjuez and Chinchón

little oasis on the way to Toledo, the town of **Aranjuez** was used by the eighteenth-century Bourbon rulers as a spring and autumn retreat, and you can still see their legacy of palaces with their luxuriant gardens, most notably the Palacio Real. A visit in summer is enhanced by stalls dotted along the roads selling strawberries and cream - *fresas con nata*. If you're travelling by train you can break your journey here and then continue on to Toledo. The nearby picturesque town of **Chinchón** is also worth a visit, and it's home to Spain's best-known *anís* (aniseed liqueur) – a mainstay of breakfast drinkers across Spain.

Aranjuez is served by **trains** from Estación de Atocha (*cercanías* line C-3 daily every 15–30min, 5am–11.55pm; 45min; 970ptas return) and by hourly **buses** from Estación Sur (40min; 810ptas return). An old wooden **steam train**, *El Tren de la Fresa*, also makes weekend runs between Madrid and Aranjuez (mid-April to July & mid-Sept to Oct; 1hr). It leaves Atocha at 10am and returns from Aranjuez at 6.30pm (Sat & Sun). The 3100ptas fare includes a guided bus tour in Aranjuez, entry to the monuments, plus strawberries on the train. The **Turismo** in Aranjuez is in the Casa de Infantes, facing the Plaza de San Antonio (Tues–Sun 10am–2pm & 4–6pm; ©91 891 04 27).

Chinchón is connected to Aranjuez by sporadic buses from c/Almíbar 138, Aranjuez (Mon–Fri 4 daily; Sat 2 daily), and to Madrid by hourly services on the La Veloz bus from Avda del Mediterraneo 49 (Metro Conde de Casal; 1hr; 800ptas return).

ARANJUEZ

The beauty of **Aranjuez**, 50km from the capital, is its greenery, studded with opulent palaces and luxuriant gardens. In summer, Aranjuez functions principally as a weekend escape from Madrid, and most people come out for the day, as there's no accommodation.

The centre-piece of the town and its main attraction is the eighteenth-century **Palacio Real** (Tues–Sun: April–Sept 10am–6.15pm; Oct–March 10am–5.15pm; 650ptas, 250ptas concessions, free Wed for EU citizens) with its **gardens** (daily: April–Sept 8am–8.30pm; Oct–March 8am–6.30pm; free). Although there has been a summer residence for the royals on this site since the late sixteenth century, the present building dates from the eighteenth century and was an attempt by the Spanish Bourbon monarchs to create a Versailles in Spain. Aranjuez clearly isn't in the same league, but it's a pleasant place to while away a few hours. The palace is more remarkable for its interior ornamental fantasies than for any architectural virtues. The **Porcelain Room**, for example, is entirely covered in decorative ware from the factory which used to stand in Madrid's Retiro park, while the **Smoking Room** is a copy of one of the finest halls of the Alhambra in Granada, though executed with less subtlety. Most of the palace dates from the reign of the "nymphomaniac" Queen Isabel II,

ARANJUEZ

and many of the scandals and intrigues which led to her eventual abdication were played out here.

Outside, on a small island, are the fountains of the **Jardín de la Isla**. The **Jardín del Príncipe**, on the other side of the main road, is more attractive, however, with shaded walks along the river and plenty of spots for a siesta. At its far end stands the **Casa del Labrador** (Peasant's House; same hours as Palacio Real; visits by appointment only – ©91 891 03 05 – phone at least a week in advance; 500ptas, Wed free for EU citizens), which is anything but what the name implies, for the house is crammed with silk, marble, crystal and gold, as well as a huge collection of fancy clocks. The guided tour goes into great detail about the weight and value of every item. Also in the gardens, by the river, is the small Casa de los Marinos (Sailors' House), containing the **Museo de Faluas** (same hours as Palacio Real; 325ptas, Wed free for EU citizens), a museum displaying the brightly coloured launches in which royalty would take to the river. A bus service occasionally connects the various sites, but all are within easy walking distance of each other, and it's a lovely place to stroll around.

Eating and drinking

Casa José
C/Asbastos 32. Tasty and expensive *nouvelle cuisine*.

Casa Pablete
C/Stuart. An offshoot of *Casa Pablo* and one of the best places in town for tapas. Closed Aug.

Casa Pablo
C/Almíbar 42. A traditional place, the walls of which are covered with pictures of local dignitaries and bullfighters. Closed Aug.

Mercado de San Antonio
C/Stuart near the Jardines Isabel II. Just the place to buy your

own food for a picnic.

El Rana Verde

C/Reina 1. Probably the best-known restaurant in Aranjuez, this pleasant riverside establishment dates back to the late nineteenth century and serves a wide-ranging *menú* at 1600ptas.

CHINCHÓN

Chinchón, 45km southeast of Madrid, is a highly picturesque little town, with a fifteenth-century castle and a medieval Plaza Mayor, encircled by wooden balconied houses. Next to the plaza stands the **Iglesia de la Asunción**, containing a panel by Goya of *The Assumption of the Virgin*. Most visitors, however, come to visit the three **anís distilleries**, a couple of which are housed in the castle. After a few tastings, the modestly priced *Mesón del Duende* and *Mesón del Comendador*, both on the Plaza Mayor are good places for a **meal**; alternatively, there's the more expensive *Mesón Cuevas del Vino*, once an olive-oil mill and today with its own *bodega*.

The best bet for **accommodation**, though it's not cheap, is the *parador* at c/Generalísimo 1 (©91 894 08 36; ⑦–⑧), housed in a sixteenth-century convent, with wonderful Moorish-style gardens and a magnificent seventeenth-century dining room.

If you're visiting over **Easter**, you'll be treated to the townsfolk's own enactment of the *Passion of Christ*, when participants and audience process through the town. In April 1995, Chinchón launched its **Fiesta del Anís y del Vino**, an orgy of anis- and wine-tasting; understandably, it was an immediate success and is now held every year in mid-April. An older annual tradition takes place on July 25, when the feast of St James (Santiago) is celebrated with a bullfight in the Plaza Mayor.

Toledo

Toledo epitomizes the soul of Spain and shares many of its contradictions. From imperial greatness it declined into isolation, and from religious toleration it came to be dominated by a stark vision of Catholicism. Home to many artists, most notably **El Greco**, and a setting for Cervantes' writing, the city is also famous for its majestic **cathedral**, its Toledan swords and the towering **Alcázar**.

Surrounded on three sides by the Río Tajo, slowly meandering its way towards Lisbon, every available inch of this rugged outcrop has been built on. Churches, synagogues, mosques and houses are heaped upon one another in a haphazard spiral which the cobbled lanes infiltrate as best they can. Certainly, it's a city redolent of past glories, and is packed with sights, although the extraordinary number of day-trippers has taken the edge off what was once the most extravagant of Spanish experiences. Still, the setting is breathtaking, and if you're an El Greco fan, you'd be mad to miss this city. Toledo also hosts one of the best celebrations of **Corpus Christi** (late May/early June) in the country, with street processions and the full works. Other local festivals take place on May 25 and August 15 and 20, and the **Easter processions** here are much more impressive than those in Madrid.

To see Toledo at its best, you'll need to stay at least a night. A day-trip will leave you hard-pressed to see everything and, more importantly, in the evening, when the crowds have gone, Toledo is a completely different city, lit up by floodlights, so that it resembles one of El Greco's moonlit paintings. However, as it's such a tourist honeypot, booking a **room** in advance is important, especially at weekends and during the summer.

Getting to Toledo, some 70km south of Madrid, is straightforward, with nine **trains** a day (fewer on Sat & Sun) from Estación de Atocha (7am–8.30pm; 1hr 15min; 1290ptas return). Toledo's train station is some way out, so either make the beautiful twenty-minute walk into town or take bus #5 or #6. **Buses** from Madrid operate every thirty minutes from Estación Sur de Autobuses (6.30am–10pm; 1hr; 1140ptas return), dropping you just outside the old city, with regular buses into the heart of town. If you're driving, you'll need to park outside the old city, as the streets are far too narrow inside and there are no public places to park. Toledo's main **Turismo** is also outside the city walls at Puerta de Bisagra (July & Aug Mon–Sat 9am–7pm, Sun 9am–3pm; Sept–June Mon–Fri 9am–6pm; ☏925 22 08 43).

ALCÁZAR AND HOSPITAL Y MUSEO DE SANTA CRUZ

Dominating the **Plaza de Zocódover**, indeed all of Toledo, is the bluff, imposing **Alcázar** (Tues–Sun 9.30am–2.30pm; 200ptas), entered off Cuesta del Alcázar. It was founded by Carlos V, but has been burned and bombarded so often that almost nothing of the original building remains. The most recent destruction occurred in 1936 during one of the most symbolic and extraordinary episodes of the Civil War, involving a two-month siege of the Nationalist-occupied Alcázar by the Republican town. The besieged Nationalists under Colonel José Moscardo were

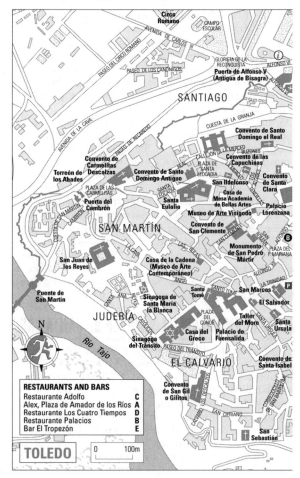

Circo Romano

CAMPO ESCOLAR

AVENIDA DE CARLOS III

PASEO DEL CIRCO ROMANO

PASEO DE LOS CANONIGOS

GLORIETA DE LA RECONQUISTA

ALFONSO VI

Puerta de Alfonso V (Antigua de Bisagra)

SANTIAGO

CUESTA DE LA GRANJA

AVENIDA DE LA CAVA

Convento de Santo Domingo el Real

PASEO DE RECAREDO

CALLEJÓN DE LA MERCED

BUZONES

Convento de las Capuchinas

PLAZA DE SANTA LEOCADIA

Convento de Carmelitas Descalzas

Convento de Santo Domingo Antiguo

San Ildefonso

Convento de Santa Clara

Torreón de los Abades

PLAZA DE LAS CARMELITAS

SANTA LEOCADIA

Casa de Mesa Academia de Bellas Artes

Palacio Lorenzana

Puerta del Cambrón

Santa Eulalia

Museo de Arte Visigodo

Convento de San Clemente

SAN MARTÍN

LA CAVA

SAN CLEMENTE

Monumento de San Pedro Mártir

PLAZA DE P. MARIANA

B

DE SAN MARTÍN

DE SAN MARTÍN

CAMBRÓN

LAS BULAS

Casa de la Cadena (Museo de Arte Contemporáneo)

ALFONSO XII

LA TRINIDAD

San Juan de los Reyes

ÁNGEL

SANTO TOMÉ

Santo Tomé

San Marcos

P

Puente de San Martín

SANTA ANA

REYES

CATÓLICOS

Sinagoga de Santa María la Blanca

PLAZA DEL CONDE

El Salvador

Taller del Moro

Santa Ursula

Río Tajo

JUDERÍA

Casa del Greco

Palacio de Fuensalida

N

Sinagoga del Tránsito

PASEO DEL TRÁNSITO

Convento de Santa Isabel

EL CALVARIO

Convento de San Gil o Gilitos

LOS DESCALZOS

SAN CIPRIANO

CADAVAL

CORREDOR DE SAN SEBASTIÁN

San Sebastián

RESTAURANTS AND BARS

Restaurante Adolfo	C
Alex, Plaza de Amador de los Ríos	A
Restaurante Los Cuatro Tiempos	D
Restaurante Palacios	B
Bar El Tropezón	E

TOLEDO

0   100m

TOLEDO

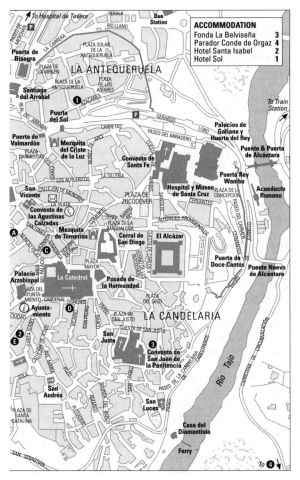

eventually relieved by a Nationalist army heading for Madrid, which then took severe retribution on the town – not one prisoner was taken. After the war, Franco's regime completely rebuilt the fortress as a monument to the glorification of its defenders, and their propaganda models and photos are still displayed.

Just north of Plaza de Zocódover is the **Hospital y Museo de Santa Cruz** (Mon 10am–2pm & 4–6.30pm, Tues–Sat 10am–6.30pm, Sun 10am–2pm; 200ptas), a superlative Renaissance building in itself, housing some of the greatest El Grecos in Toledo, including *The Coronation of the Virgin* and *The Assumption of the Virgin*. As well as outstanding works by Goya and Ribera, the museum also contains a huge collection of ancient carpets and faded tapestries, a military display, sculpture and a small archeological collection.

THE CATHEDRAL

Daily 10.30am–noon & 4–6pm; Treasury, Sacristy, Chapter House and the New Museums (Mon–Sat 10.30am–6.30pm, Sun 2–6.30pm); 500ptas. The *Coro* is closed on Sun morning, and the New Museums on Mon.

Toledo's **cathedral**, situated to the south of Plaza de Zocódover down the c/Comercio, really is something special, reflecting the importance of the city that for so long outshone its near neighbour, Madrid. A robust Gothic construction, which took over two hundred and fifty years (1227–1493) to complete, it is richly decorated in almost every conceivable style, with masterpieces of the Gothic, Renaissance and Baroque periods. The exterior is best appreciated from outside the city, where the hundred-metre spire and the weighty buttressing can be seen to advantage. The cavernous interior is home to some magnificent stained glass, an outstanding **Coro** (Choir) and a wonderfully Gothic **Capilla Mayor**, depicting a synopsis of the entire New Testament. Directly behind the main altar is an extraordinary piece of fantasy – the **Transparente**, a Baroque chapel, wonderfully and wildly extravagant, with its marble cherubs sitting on fluffy marble clouds. It's especially magnificent when the sun reaches through the hole punched in the roof for that purpose.

There are well over twenty **chapels** embedded in the walls, all of which are of some interest, many housing fine tombs. The **Tesoro** (Treasury), the **Sacristía** (Sacristy), the **Sala Capitular** (Chapter House) and the **Nuevos Museos** (New Museums) house hugely impressive accumulations of wealth and artistic riches, including paintings by El Greco, Goya and Velázquez, as well as one of El Greco's few surviving pieces of sculpture.

SANTO TOMÉ AND THE CASA DEL GRECO

Domenico Theotocopoulos, or **El Greco** (the Greek), settled in Toledo in about 1577 and it is mainly through the portrayal of the city in his extraordinary mystical paintings that the skyline of Toledo has become so famous. A tour of Toledo's El Grecos is a must and an ideal complement to viewing his other work in the Prado. El Greco's masterpiece, *The Burial of the Count of Orgaz* is housed, alone, in a small annexe to the church of **Santo Tomé** (daily 10am–6.45pm, winter till 5.45pm; 200ptas) to the west of the cathedral, and depicts the count's funeral, at which Saint Stephen and Saint Augustine appeared and lowered him into the tomb. It combines El Greco's genius for the mystic, exemplified in the upper half of the picture, where the count's soul is being received into heaven, with his great powers as a portrait painter and master of colour. El Greco himself, his son and Felipe II are said to be amongst the onlookers portrayed in the lower half.

The misleadingly named **Casa del Greco**, just to the south of Santo Tomé in Plaza del Conde (Tues–Sat 10am–2pm & 4–6pm, Sun 10am–2pm; 400ptas, free Sat pm and Sun), was never actually the artist's home, but is a reconstruction of a typical Toledan home of the period. It does, however, display a number of El Greco's classic works, including his famous *View and Map of Toledo*.

For thrilling, uncluttered **views** of Toledo – the skyline so familiar from various El Greco paintings – head for the ring road Carretera de Circunvalación which runs along the south bank of the Tajo, the opposite bank from the city. It takes about an hour to walk from one of the medieval fortified bridges to the other.

THE JEWISH QUARTER

The area to the west of the Casa del Greco was once the *Judería*, the Jewish quarter of medieval Toledo. The synagogues, **El Tránsito** and **Santa María de la Blanca** (daily: 10am–2pm & 3.30–6pm; 200ptas), both built by *Mudéjar* craftsmen, are stunning reminders of Toledo's cosmopolitan past, while the superb church of **San Juan de los Reyes** (daily: May–Sept 10am–1.45pm & 3.30–6.45pm; Oct–April 10am–1.30pm & 3.30–5.45pm; 200ptas), whose exterior is bizarrely festooned with the chains worn by Christian prisoners from Granada released on the reconquest of their city, is a legacy of more intolerant times under the *Reyes Católicos*.

As you wind your way back towards Plaza de Zocódover, the **Museo de Arte Visigodo** (Tues–Sat 10am–2pm & 4–6.30pm, Sun 10am–2pm; 100ptas, free Sat pm and Sun) stands on Calle de San Clemente in a very different, though equally impressive building – the church of San Román. Moorish and Christian elements (horseshoe arches, early murals and a splendid Renaissance dome) combine to make this the most interesting church in Toledo. Visigothic jewellery, documents and archeological fragments make up the bulk of the collection.

Northwest of Plaza de Zocódover, a short distance from Calle de la Sillería, up Cuesta del Cristo de la Luz, is the tiny mosque of **Mezquita del Cristo de la Luz**. Although this is one of the oldest Moorish monuments in Spain (it was built in the tenth century on the foundations of a Visigothic church), only the nave, with its nine different cupolas, is the original Arab construction. The apse was added when the building was converted into a church, and is claimed to be the first product of the *Mudéjar* style.

HOSPITAL DE TAVERA

Situated outside the city walls to the north of the Puerta de Bisagra, the private collection of the Duchess of Lerma is housed in the **Hospital de Tavera** (daily 10.30am–1.30pm & 3.30–6pm; 500ptas), a Renaissance palace, with beautiful twin patios. The gloomy interior is a reconstruction of a sixteenth-century mansion and is scattered with fine paintings by Bassano, El Greco and Ribera, while the church contains the ornate marble tomb of Cardinal Tavera, the hospital's founder.

ACCOMMODATION

Fonda La Belviseña
Cuesta del Can 7 ©925 22 00 67. South of the Alcázar, a fairly basic, cheap, good-value *hostal* and hence very popular. ①.

Parador Conde de Orgaz
Cerro del Emperador ©925 22 18 50; fax 925 22 51 66. A couple of kilometres' walk uphill in the south of the city is Toledo's top hotel offering superb views from its terrace. ⑥.

Hotel Santa Isabel
C/Santa Isabel 24 ⓒ925 25 31 20; fax 925 25 25 31/36. The best of the mid-range hotels, right in the centre and with safe parking. ④.

Hotel Sol
C/Azacanes 15 ⓒ925 21 36 50; fax 925 25 21 61/59. A good-value place on a quiet side street just off the main road up to the Plaza de Zocódover, before the Puerta del Sol. The owners also run the cheaper hostal across the street – ask at reception. ③–④.

EATING AND DRINKING

Alex, Plaza de Amador de los Ríos
At the top end of c/Nuncio Viejo. Reasonable-value restaurant in a lovely location, with a much cheaper café at the side.

Bar El Tropezón
Travesía de Santa Isabel 2. A stone's throw from the cathedral, this outdoor bar offers generous meals for under 1000ptas. The fish is particularly good.

Restaurante Adolfo
C/Granada 6. One of the best restaurants in town, tucked behind a marzipan café, in an old Jewish town house (ask to see the painted ceiling downstairs). Expect to pay 5000ptas a head. Closed Sun eve.

Restaurante Los Cuatro Tiempos
c/Puerta Llana, at the southeast corner of the cathedral. Excellent mid-price restaurant with local specialities and good tapas.

Restaurante Palacios
C/Alfonso X El Sabio 3. Friendly and popular local restaurant, with two *menús* – the cheaper one costs just 900ptas.

Segovia

After Toledo, **Segovia** is the second best trip from Madrid. A relatively small city, strategically sited on a rocky ridge, it is deeply and haughtily Castilian, with a panoply of squares and mansions from its days of golden-age grandeur. For a city of its size, Segovia has an amazing number of architectural monuments. Most celebrated are the **Roman aqueduct**, the **cathedral** and the fairy-tale **Alcázar**, but the less obvious attractions – the cluster of ancient churches and the many mansions in the lanes of the old town, all in a warm, honey-coloured stone – are what really make Segovia worth visiting. Also, just a few kilometres outside the city, is the Bourbon palace of **La Granja**.

Well connected by road and rail, Segovia is an easy trip from Madrid. Eight **trains** leave daily from Atocha (6am–8pm; 2hr; 1550ptas return) and up to fifteen **buses** operated by La Sepulvedana make the run from their terminal at Paseo de la Florida 11 (Metro Príncipe Pío; Mon–Sat 6.30am–10.15pm, Sun 8am–10.15pm; 1hr 45min; 1230ptas return). It's worth noting that buses also operate between Ávila and Segovia (2–4 daily; 1hr), so you could consider combining the two in a day-trip. Segovia's own **train station** is some distance out of town and you'll need to take bus #3 to the Plaza Mayor. If you are **driving** it's best to park outside the old city below the aqueduct. The **Turismo**

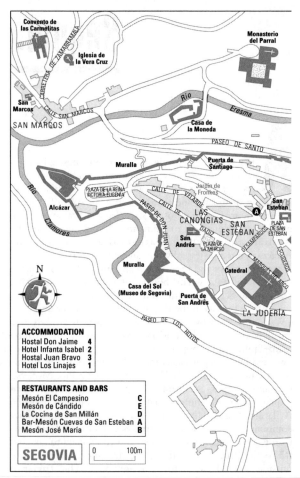

ACCOMMODATION
Hostal Don Jaime 4
Hotel Infanta Isabel 2
Hostal Juan Bravo 3
Hotel Los Linajes 1

RESTAURANTS AND BARS
Mesón El Campesino C
Mesón de Cándido E
La Cocina de San Millán D
Bar-Mesón Cuevas de San Esteban A
Mesón José María B

SEGOVIA 0 100m

SEGOVIA

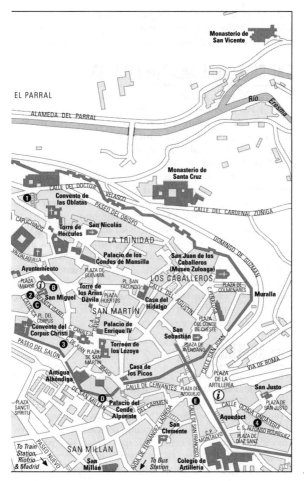

Monasterio de
San Vicente

EL PARRAL

Río Eresma

ALAMEDA DEL PARRAL

Monasterio de
Santa Cruz

CALLE DEL DOCTOR VELASCO

1 Convento de
las Oblatas

PASEO DEL OBISPO

CALLE DEL CARDENAL ZÚÑIGA

CAPUCHINOS

Torre de
Hércules

San Nicolás

LA TRINIDAD

DOMINGO DE GUZMÁN

VALDELAGUILA

Palacio de los
Condes de Mansilla

San Juan de los
Caballeros
(Museo Zuloaga)

Ayuntamiento

PLAZA DE
GUEVARA

LOS CABALLEROS

PLAZA DE
COLMENARES

PLAZA
MAYOR

i **B**

2 San Miguel

C

Torre de
los Arias
Dávila

PL. SAN
FACUNDO

CALLE DEL AGUSTÍN

Muralla

SANTA ISABEL

PLAZA
HUERTOS

Casa del
Hidalgo

SAN MARTÍN

PL. DEL
CORPUS

PLAZA
DEL CONDE
DE CHESTE

Convento del
Corpus Christi

C. CANALEJA

Palacio de
Enrique IV

San
Sebastián

C. DE JUAN

3

PLAZA
DE SAN
MARTÍN

Torreón de
los Lózoya

PLAZA DE
AVENDAÑO

CALLE SAN JUAN

VÍA DE ROMA

PASEO DEL SALÓN

BRAVO

Casa de
los Picos

PLAZA
DE LA
ARTILLERÍA

San Justo

Antigua
Alhóndiga

DE SAN MILLÁN

CALLE DE CERVANTES

PLAZA DE
AZOGUEJO

i

PLAZA DE
SAN JUSTO

PLAZA
SANCTI
SPIRITU

D

Palacio del
Conde
Alpuente

DEL CARMEN

E

CALLE OCHOA ONDÁTEGUI

To Train
Station,
Ríofrío
& Madrid

PASEO NUEVO

SAN MILLÁN

AVDA. DE FERNÁNDEZ LADREDA

San
Clemente

CALLE DE SAN FRANCISCO

C.P.
MONTALVO

Aqueduct

C. S. ALFONSO RODRÍGUEZ

4

PLAZA DE
DÍAZ SANZ

San
Millán

To Bus
Station

Colegio de
Artillería

(May–Sept Mon–Sat 10am–2pm & 5–8pm, Sun 10am–2pm; Oct–April Mon–Fri 10am–2pm & 5–8pm, Sat 10am–2pm; ©921 46 03 34) is centrally located in the Plaza Mayor.

THE CATHEDRAL AND THE ALCÁZAR

Segovia's **cathedral** (daily: April–Oct 9am–7pm; Nov–March 9am–6pm; museums 300ptas) was the last major Gothic building constructed in Spain, and arguably the last in Europe. Pinnacles and flying buttresses are tacked on at every conceivable point, although the interior is surprisingly bare and its space is cramped by a great green marble choir in the very centre. The treasures are almost all confined to the museum which opens off the cloisters.

From the cathedral c/de Daoiz leads to the **Alcázar** (daily: May–Sept 10am–7pm; Oct–Apr 10am–6pm; 400ptas), an extraordinary fantasy of a castle, with its narrow towers and flurry of turrets. It will seem eerily familiar to just about every visitor, having served as the model for the original Disneyland castle in California. Although it dates from the fourteenth and fifteenth centuries, it was almost completely destroyed by a fire in 1862 and rebuilt as a deliberately exaggerated version of the original. It's worth visiting if only for the magnificent panoramas from the tower.

THE AQUEDUCT

The most photographed site in Segovia is its stunning **aqueduct**. Over 800m long and at its highest point towering some 30m above the Plaza de Azoguejo, it stands up without a drop of mortar or cement. No one knows exactly when it was built, but it was probably around the end of the first century AD under the Emperor Trajan. It no longer carries water from the Río Frío to the city and in recent years traffic vibration and pollution have been threatening to undermine the entire structure. Stairs beside the aqueduct lead up on to a surviving fragment of the city walls, giving an excellent view. For the best **view** of all, however, take the main road north for 2km or so towards Cuéllar, and a panorama of the whole city, including the aqueduct, gradually unfolds.

VERA CRUZ

The best of Segovia's ancient churches is undoubtedly **Vera Cruz** (Tues–Sun 10.30am–1.30pm & 3.30–6pm; closed Nov; 200ptas), a remarkable twelve-sided building in the valley facing the Alcázar, reached by taking one of the paths that descend from the north side of the city walls. The church was built by the Knights Templar in the early thirteenth century on the pattern of the church of the Holy Sepulchre in Jerusalem, and once housed part of the supposed True Cross (hence its name). You can climb the tower for a highly photogenic view of the city.

Nearby is the prodigiously walled **Convento de las Carmelitas** (daily: summer 10am–1pm & 4–8pm; winter 10am–1.30pm & 4–6pm; closed Tues 10am–1.30pm; free), also referred to as the monastery of San Juan de la Cruz, which contains the gaudy mausoleum of its founder-saint.

LA GRANJA

Just 10km southeast of Segovia on the N601 Madrid road, and connected by regular bus services, lies the Bourbon summer palace of **La Granja**, built by the first Bourbon king of Spain, Felipe V, no doubt homesick for the luxuries of Versailles. Its glories are the mountain setting, and the extravagant wooded grounds and gardens, but it's worth casting a quick eye over the **palace** (April & May Tues–Sat 10am–1.30pm & 3–5pm, Sun 10am–2pm; June–Sept Tues–Sun 10am–6pm; Oct–March Tues–Sat

10am–1.30pm & 3–5pm, Sun 10am–6pm; compulsory guided tour 650ptas, Wed free for EU citizens). The highlight of the **gardens** (daily 10am–7pm; 325ptas) is its series of fountains, which culminate in the fifteen-metre-high jet of La Fama. They're a fantastic spectacle, but usually only operate at 5.30pm at weekends and on Wednesdays, with special displays on May 30, July 25 and August 25 (check at the Turismo first).

ACCOMMODATION

Rooms can be hard to come by, even out of season, it's worth booking ahead when considering more than a day-trip.

Hostal Don Jaime
C/Ochoa Ondategui 8 ©921 44 47 87. Excellent *hostal* near Plaza de Azoguejo. All doubles have their own bathroom. ③.

Hotel Infanta Isabel
C/Isabel la Católica 1 ©921 46 13 00; fax 921 46 22 17. Comfortable hotel – and better value than the *parador* outside town – ideally positioned on Plaza Mayor. ⑤.

Hostal Juan Bravo
C/Juan Bravo 12 ©921 46 34 13. Lots of big, comfortable rooms and plant-festooned bathrooms. ②–③.

Hotel Los Linajes
C/Dr Velasco 9 ©921 46 04 75; fax 921 46 04 79. Good-value, atmospheric hotel located in a quiet corner of the walled city, with a fine garden overlooking the river valley. ⑤.

EATING AND DRINKING

Segovia takes its cooking seriously, and culinary specialities include **roast suckling pig** (*cochinillo asado*) and **lamb** (*cordero*). There's a concentration of cheaper **bar–restaurants** on c/Infanta Isabel, off the Plaza Mayor, and **late-night bars** on c/Escuderos and c/Judería Vieja, and along Avenida Fernández Ladreda.

Mesón El Campesino

C/Infanta Isabel 14. One of the best budget restaurants in town, serving decent-value *menús* and *combinados* to a young crowd. Closed Aug.

Mesón de Cándido

Plaza Azoguejo 5 ℗921 42 81 03. The city's most famous restaurant, reopened in 1992 by the founder's son and still the place for *cochinillo* and the like. The *menú* is 3000ptas, although with the *cochinillo* you are more likely to top 4000ptas.

La Cocina de San Millán

C/San Millán 3 ℗921 43 62 26. A little out of the way, but the cooking is imaginative and prices are reasonable. Closed Sun eve & Jan 7–31.

Bar-Mesón Cuevas de San Esteban

C/Valdeláguila 15, off the top end of Plaza San Esteban. A cavern-restaurant and bar (serving draught beer), popular with locals. Excellent value.

Mesón José María

C/Cronista Lecea 11, just off Plaza Mayor ℗921 46 11 11. Currently reckoned to be the city's best and most interesting restaurant, with modern variations on Castilian classics. The *menú* is a hefty 4000ptas, but there are dishes costing around 2000ptas.

Ávila

Two things distinguish **Ávila** – its eleventh-century **walls**, two perfectly preserved kilometres of which surround the old town, and the mystic writer **Santa Teresa**, who was born here and whose shrines are a major focus of religious pilgrimage. Set on a high plain, with the peaks of the Sierra de Gredos behind, the town is an impressive sight, especially if you time it right and approach with the evening sun highlighting the golden tone of the walls and the details of the 88 towers. There are also a number of fine **Romanesque churches** dotted in and about the old town.

From **Madrid** (Chamartín and Atocha) there are up to seventeen **trains** a day to Ávila (daily 6.40am–8.30pm; 1hr 30min; 1700ptas return). **Buses** (operated by Larrea from Estación Sur de Autobuses; Metro Méndez Alvaro) are less frequent (daily; 2hr; 1290ptas return). Buses also operate between Ávila and Segovia (2–4 daily; 1hr), so you could consider combining the two in one day. The main **Turismo** (daily: July–Sept 9am–2pm & 5–7pm; Oct–June 10am–2pm & 4–7pm; ©920 21 13 87) is in the Plaza de la Catedral.

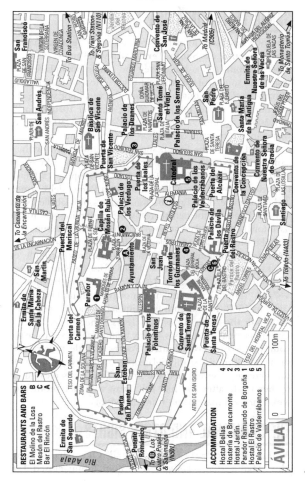

RESTAURANTS AND BARS
El Molino de la Losa   B
Mesón del Rastro   C
Bar El Rincón   A

ACCOMMODATION
Hostal Bellas   4
Hostería de Bracamonte   3
Hostal Jardín   2
Parador Raimundo de Borgoña   1
Hostal El Rastro   6
Palacio de Valderrábanos   5

ÁVILA   0   100m

SANTA TERESA IN ÁVILA

The obvious place to start a tour of Santa Teresa's Ávila is the **Convento de Santa Teresa** (daily 8.30am–1.30pm & 3.30–7.30pm; free), built over the saint's birthplace, just inside the south gate of the old town. Most of the convent remains *in clausura*, but you can see the very spot where she was born. In a small reliquary (daily: summer 10am–1pm & 4–7.30pm; winter 9.30am–1.30pm & 3.30–7.30pm; free) there are memorials of Teresa's life, including her rosary beads and one of the fingers she used to count them with.

In the **Convento de la Encarnación** (daily: May–Sept 9.30am–1pm & 4–7pm; Oct–April 3.30–6pm; 150ptas), reached by leaving the old town through Puerta del Carmen and following c/de la Encarnación, each room is labelled with the act Teresa performed there, while everything she might have touched or looked at is on display. A small museum section also provides a reasonable introduction to the saint's life.

A third sight connected with the saint lies a couple of blocks east (away from the walls) of Plaza de Santa Teresa. The **Convento de San José** (daily 10am–1.30pm & 4–7pm; 150ptas) was the first monastery founded by the saint, in 1562. Its museum contains relics and memorabilia, including the coffin in which Teresa once slept, and assorted personal possessions. Lastly, you might want to make your way up to **Los Cuatro Postes**, a little four-posted shrine, 1500m along the Salamanca road west of town. It was here, aged seven, that the infant Teresa was recaptured by her uncle after she had run away with her brother to seek Christian martyrdom from the Moors.

THE CATHEDRAL AND OTHER SIGHTS

Ávila's **cathedral** (daily: April–Oct 10am–7pm; Nov–March 10am–1.30pm & 3.30–5.30pm; closed 1–6

Jan, 15 Oct & 25 Dec; 250ptas) was started in the twelfth century, but has never been finished, as evidenced by the missing tower above the main entrance. The earliest Romanesque parts were as much fortress as church, and the apse actually forms an integral part of the city walls. Inside, the succeeding changes of style are immediately apparent; the Romanesque parts are made of a strange red-and-white mottled stone, then there's an abrupt break and the rest of the main structure is pure white stone and Gothic forms.

Although the proportions are exactly the same, this newer half of the cathedral seems infinitely more spacious. Here you can admire the carved stalls in the *Coro* and the treasury-museum with its monstrous silver *custodia* (monstrance) and ancient religious images, and the tomb of a fifteenth-century bishop known as *El Tostado* (the "toasted" or "swarthy").

Just outside the city walls, on the northeast corner, is the basilica of **San Vicente** (daily 10am–1.30pm & 4–6.30pm; 200ptas), which, like the cathedral, is a mixture of architectural styles. Its twelfth-century doorways and the portico which protects them are magnificent examples of Romanesque art, while the church itself shows the influence of later trends. San Vicente and his sisters were martyred on this site, and their tomb narrates the gruesome story of their torture and execution by the Romans. Legend has it that following their martyrdom a rich Jew who had been poking fun at them was enveloped and suffocated by a great serpent that miraculously emerged from the rocks. On the verge of asphyxiation, he repented and converted to Christianity, later building the church on the very same site; he, too, is said to be buried here. In the crypt you can see part of the rocky crag where San Vicente and his sisters were executed and from which the serpent later supposedly appeared. The warm pink glow of the sandstone of the church is a characteristic feature of Ávila, also notable in the church of **San Pedro**, on Plaza de Santa Teresa.

THE CATHEDRAL AND OTHER SIGHTS

Just over half a kilometre to the southeast stands the **Monasterio de Santo Tomás** (daily 10am–1pm & 4–8pm; *Coro* and cloisters 50ptas; museum 11am–1pm & 4–7pm; 100ptas), a Dominican monastery founded in 1482, but greatly expanded over the following decade by Fernando and Isabel, whose summer palace it became. Inside are three exceptional cloisters, the largest of which contains an **oriental collection**, a strangely incongruous display built up by the monks over centuries of missionary work in the Orient. Notice also the elaborate tombs and the thrones occupied by the king and queen during services. The notorious inquisitor **Torquemada** is buried in the sacristy here.

Just outside the city walls, through the Puerta de los Leales, is Ávila's small **Museo Provincial**, housed in the sixteenth-century Palacio de los Deanes (Tues–Sat 10.30am–2pm & 4.30–7.30pm, Sun 10am–2pm; 200ptas, free Sat & Sun), where the cathedral's deans used to live. Today, its exhibits include collections of archeological remains, ceramics, carpets and furnishings from around the Ávila province.

One of the best things to do in Ávila is to walk along the **city walls** from Puerta del Alcázar to Puerta del Rastro; the view of the city is stunning. Tickets (Tues–Sun 10am–8pm; 200ptas) are available from the kiosk by the Puerta del Alcázar.

ACCOMMODATION

Hostal Bellas
C/Caballeros 19 ✆920 21 29 10. Friendly and fairly central. Most rooms have showers and there are discounts out of season. ②.

Hostería de Bracamonte
C/Bracamonte 6 ✆920 25 12 80. Atmospheric and elegant hotel, between the city walls and the Plaza de la Victoria, created from a number of converted Renaissance mansions. ⑤.

Hostal Jardín

C/San Segundo 38 ✆920 21 10 74. Large *hostal* near Puerta de los Leales, which often has rooms when others are full. ②–③.

Parador Raimundo de Borgoña

C/Marqués de Canales y Chozas 2 ✆920 21 13 40; fax 92 022 61 66. A converted fifteenth-century mansion, set right next to the city walls. The rooms in the tower are a little cramped, but it's the cheapest of Ávila's top hotels. ⑥.

Hostal El Rastro

Plazuela del Rastro 1 ✆920 21 12 18; fax 920 25 16 26. A good mid-range option, this characterful old inn is set right against the walls, with a pleasant garden and popular restaurant. ③.

Palacio de Valderrábanos

Plaza de la Catedral 9 ✆920 21 10 23; fax 920 25 16 91. This former bishop's palace beats the *Parador* for ambiance and the rooms are equally luxurious. ⑥.

EATING AND DRINKING

El Molino de la Losa

Bajada de la Losa 12 ✆920 21 11 01. Converted fifteenth-century mill, with a deserved reputation, and handy if you're with kids, as there's a play area in the garden. The *menú* is 3000ptas. Closed Mon & mid-Oct to mid-March.

Mesón del Rastro

Plazuela del Rastro 1. Excellent bar, attached to the *hostal* of the same name, with a range of tapas. Behind it is a modest-priced restaurant, an old-fashioned place with solid, traditional food.

Bar El Rincón

Plaza Zurraquín 4. To the north of Plaza de la Victoria, this bar serves a generous three-course *menú* for 1500ptas.

CONTEXTS

CONTEXTS

A brief history of Madrid

Although there is some evidence of small-scale prehistoric settlements on the banks of the Manzanares, of Roman villas around Carabanchel and a minor Visigoth settlement on the banks of a stream running down what is now Calle de Segovia, the city of Madrid was effectively founded by the **Muslims** in the ninth century. Even then it was more of a defensive outpost than a settlement in its own right. Arabic engineers soon saw the military potential of the escarpment, with its commanding views of the main routes stretching south from the Sierra Guadarrama, and used it as a way of shoring up the communications to the more prestigious city of **Toledo**. The area's other key attribute was its ready supply of water, hence its early name "mayrit" – place of many springs – successively modified to Magerit and then Madrid. Fragments of the old Arabic wall still remain on the Cuesta de la Vega beside the Catedral de la Almudena.

In the late eleventh century, the city was taken by the Christians under **Alfonso VI**, although the Muslims did try to recapture it in an unsuccessful siege, launched from below the Alcázar in the Campo del Moro in 1109. Nevertheless, many Muslims remained in the tangled web of streets and alleyways of **La Morería**, making the most of their skills as builders and masons to help construct churches and residences; the distinctive *Mudéjar* towers of San Nicolás and San Pedro el Viejo still remain from this era. Despite being used as a royal stopover for the itinerant Castilian monarchy and the establishment in the city of several powerful religious centres, such as the friary of San Francisco and the church of San Andrés, Madrid still remained a relatively insignificant backwater. The city was even given to Leo V of Armenia as a consolation prize for losing his kingdom to the Turks, although it later reverted to Castilian control.

Capital of the Empire

What changed Madrid's destiny from obscure provincial town into **capital** of the glittering Spanish empire was the caprice of one man, **Felipe II** (1556–98), who decided in 1561 to permanently locate the court here. His decision was prompted by the city's position in the centre of the recently unified Spain and his fear of giving undue influence to one of its overmighty regions. The population of Madrid immediately surged with the arrival of the royal entourage and there was a boom in the building industry. Much of this building was highly provisional, as few thought Madrid would last very long as the capital. However, they had underestimated the determination of Felipe II, who had also begun to construct the huge monastery complex-cum-mausoleum of **El Escorial** in the nearby mountains. Greater solidity and a touch of grandeur was added to the city with the appointment of **Juan Gómez de Mora** as city architect during the reign of Felipe III (1598–1621). He left his mark on the old city centre and his characteristic buildings of red brick, slate roofs and needle spires can still be seen in the Plaza Mayor and the Plaza de la Villa.

Between the mid-sixteenth and mid-seventeenth centuries, Madrid's population grew from 20,000 to over 150,000. Building continued, with the foundation of a large number of **convents and monasteries** inside the city, including the Encarnación, Carboneras and Comendadoras, which survive today. It was during this period also that the palace **El Buen Retiro** was built on the east side of the city to house and provide entertainment for the court. The only parts of this royal village that remain today are the Casón del Buen Retiro (see p.71) and the Museo del Ejército (see p.92).

However, the city was still very much one of outsiders and immigrants, a city of consumption rather than production. All was not well with the overstretched and beleaguered Spanish empire, and the increasingly inbred Habsburg dynastic line dried up with the chronically ill and malformed Carlos II. He died in 1700, his demise hastened no doubt by the succession of cures doled out to him by his doctors.

With the emergence of the **Bourbon dynasty**, a touch of French style was introduced into the capital. Used to the luxuries of Versailles, **Felipe V** was somewhat disappointed with the capital that he'd inherited, and proceeded to construct a grand country villa at **La Granja**. In the wake of the 1734 fire at the Alcázar, he took the opportunity to build an altogether more sumptuous affair in the shape of the **Palacio Real**. Baroque flourishes were added to the city with the buildings of **Pedro de Ribera**, including the Hospice (now the Museo Municipal) and the Cuartel del Conde Duque, while under **Carlos III** (1759–88), the "Rey-Alcalde" (King-Mayor), more thoroughgoing plans were made to make the city into a home worthy of the monarchy. The notoriously filthy streets were cleaned up, sewers and street lighting installed and work began on the creation of an intellectual showcase of museums and research centres along the **Paseo del Prado**. Madrid undoubtedly became a more pleasant place to live in, but Carlos's foreign tastes didn't always meet with the approval of the *Madrileño* population. **Riots** broke out in 1766 over increased food prices and the introduction of a ban on long capes and wide-brimmed hats, which the Italian minister Squillache claimed were used by thieves to conceal their weapons.

Invasion and occupation

The improvements in Madrid lost momentum under the slothful **Carlos IV**, and the rise of the corrupt **Manuel**

Godoy in the early years of the nineteenth century increasingly placed Spain under the influence of Napoleonic France. In March 1808, **French troops** entered the capital, and many suspected that the royal family was preparing to flee. Tension mounted until it culminated in a rising against the French troops on **May 2, 1808**, with the heavily outgunned *Madrileños* eventually having to admit defeat. The rising and the subsequent reprisals by the French entered Spanish folklore and were immortalized by Goya in his two magnificent canvases now hanging in the Prado. **Napoleon** installed his brother Joseph (nicknamed "*Pepe Botella*" because of his alleged susceptibility to a drink or two) on the throne, and although highly unpopular, he did begin a whole series of projects designed to create more open spaces in the cramped city; his legacy can be seen in the plazas Santa Ana and Oriente. Nevertheless, there was also much **destruction**, with the plundering of the Prado and the virtual destruction of El Buen Retiro.

Division and instability

Once the French were removed by a combined Spanish and English army, the monarchy made a return under the myopic reactionary figure of **Fernando VII** in 1814, who soon annulled Spain's first – and decidedly liberal – constitution, drawn up by the Cortes (parliament) in Cádiz in 1812. The lines were now drawn that were to scar Spanish society and politics for the next one hundred and fifty years. One Spain lined up against another: progressive, anti-clerical and constitutional against conservative, Catholic and authoritarian forces. At first, these divisions confined themselves to the emerging café society and *tertulias*, but with the disputed succession after Fernando's death, they soon exploded into a series of conflicts known as the **Carlist wars** and led to constant political instability, including a brief period as a republic until the monarchy under

Alfonso XII was restored in 1875.

At the same time, Madrid was experiencing significant **social changes**, with a rapid growth in population from 200,000 at the end of the eighteenth century to 300,000 by the 1860s and with the emergence of a genuine **working class** less tied to the established state institutions. The socialist party, the **PSOE**, was founded in 1879 in *Casa Labra* in the city. Madrid began to expand north, with the construction of the working-class district of **Chamberí** and the development of **Salamanca** by the flamboyant speculator, the Marqués de Salamanca. The railway, improved water supply via the Canal Isabel II, the metro, electricity, trams and the construction of the Gran Vía all came to Madrid within the next 35 years. Despite these improvements, many of the underlying divisions in Spanish society remained. Confidence was further undermined and the monarchy further discredited by the loss of Cuba and the Philippines in 1898. This prompted a period of serious reflection by intellectuals and politicians, sparking off the great work of writers such as Baroja and Antonio Machado known as the "**Generation of '98**".

The Second Republic and the rise of Franco

Despite Spanish neutrality in **World War I**, the economy ran into problems in the 1920s, and a hard-line military regime under the Captain-General of Barcelona, **Miguel Primo de Rivera**, took control from 1923 to 1930, with King Alfonso XIII relegated to the background. When Republican candidates unexpectedly swept the board in the 1931 municipal elections, the king decided to quit. The **Second Republic** was ushered in amid a host of unrealistic expectations, and had to cope not only with the divided Spanish society, but also with the impact of the Great Depression. Political polarization continued, and when the Popular Front won the 1936 elections the Right grew increasingly restless and called for the army to save the country. The ensuing **rising by the generals** in July 1936 was only partially successful and in Madrid the troops that barricaded themselves inside the Montaña barracks in Parque del Oeste were massacred by defenders of the Republic. Thus Madrid became a **Republican stronghold**. A revolutionary atmosphere prevailed and many of the city's churches and religious institutions were torched by Anarchists. By late October, the city was under attack by **Franco's Nationalists**, with some of the fiercest fighting of the war occurring along the Carretera de la Coruña and in the Ciudad Universitaria. However, the arrival of the International Brigades, the firm resistance of the *Madrileño* population and the discovery of the Nationalist plans to attack the city, thwarted Franco's efforts and a long drawn-out **siege** began. The city was regularly shelled by the Nationalists camped out in Casa de Campo, where traces of trenches and bunkers can still be found. There were severe food shortages, and meat and vegetables were hardly ever available. By 1939, divisions began to emerge between Republican groups prepared to negotiate with Franco and those who, together with the Communists, saw this as tantamount to political suicide. **Franco** and his victorious Nationalists eventually entered the city in March 1939. There was little sign of graciousness in victory from the general – mass reprisals took place and Republicans were executed, imprisoned, forced into hiding or had to flee the country. While *El Caudillo* installed himself in the country residence of **El Pardo**, just to the north of the city, Republican prisoners were put to work on the monstrous war memorial – later to house *El Caudillo's* tomb – **El Valle de los Caídos**.

Spain had to endure yet more suffering during the postwar years – *los años de hambre* (the years of hunger) until the turnaround in **American policy**, which rehabilitated

Franco in a desperate search for anti-Communist Cold War allies. Madrid again experienced massive growth, with the population trebling between 1930 and 1970 to reach three million. The **monumentalist architecture** of this period can be seen in the buildings of the Ministerio del Aire, Nuevos Ministerios and the Edificio de España. Waves of **immigrants** set up home on the outskirts of town, many in shanty-town developments (*chabolas*). As the Spanish economy took off with mass tourism and the assistance of the IMF and World Bank, Madrid became more industrial with significant enterprises developing in the south and east of the city.

The return to democracy

By the early 1970s, Franco was clearly ailing, and the assassination by the Basque terrorist organization, ETA, of the man he was grooming to be his successor, **Admiral Carrero Blanco**, shook the regime to its foundations. The admiral was killed in a spectacular car bomb in c/Claudio Coello, that catapulted his car over a nearby five-storey building. Franco himself died in November 1975 and was succeeded by his appointee **King Juan Carlos**. The king eventually appointed **Adolfo Suárez** to take over the reins of government and presided over the transition to democracy, with the holding of the first democratic elections since 1936 and the drawing up of a new constitution. Much greater power was given to Spain's regions and Madrid became a *Comunidad Autónoma*, with its own elected regional government. The military, however, hadn't quite given up and in its last-gasp attempt to re-establish itself, the Civil Guard commander, **Colonel Tejero**, stormed the Cortes in Madrid, firing his revolver and demanding everyone hit the floor. For a moment it looked as if the days of dictatorship were about to return, but lack of support from Juan Carlos in his TV broadcast and lack of commitment from a number of the army brigades saw it collapse. It was the Socialists under **Felipe González** who profited from the bungled coup attempt and proceeded to win the 1982 elections.

The new spirit: la movida and beyond

In Madrid, the freedom from the shackles of military dictatorship and the release of long pent-up creative forces helped to create **la movida**, an outpouring of hedonistic, highly innovative and creative forces that was embodied by the rise of **Pedro Almodóvar** and his internationally acclaimed films. The work of the city's Socialist mayor, **Enrique Tierno Galván**, also helped make Madrid the place to be in the late 1970s and early 1980s. He rejuvenated Madrid's old fiestas of San Isidro, poured money into cultural events and helped oversee the **modernization** of the city. The concentration on international-prestige projects like the Olympics, Expo and the more downbeat nomination of Madrid as European Cultural Capital in 1992 placed Spain firmly on the international map once again.

However, the transition to democracy hasn't been quite as smooth as it may appear. The Socialists became increasingly discredited as they moved to the Right and were engulfed in a web of ever-more incredible **scandals and corruption** until they lost control of Madrid in 1991 and the country in 1996 to the conservative Partido Popular (PP) under **José María Aznar**, the former tax collector and antithesis of charisma. Cuts in spending replaced generous funding and the days of *la movida* were certainly over. The 1999 local elections saw the PP retain power in both the city and *comunidad* (region) of Madrid. The present authorities are committed to rehabilitating some of the more run-down areas in the centre of Madrid and to improving the transport network throughout the city –

although it is unlikely that this will do much to solve the city's acute traffic problem. The PP has more restrictive attitudes towards bar and club licensing, but this has done little to dent the city's appetite for enjoying itself. Madrid has made the transition from provincial backwater to major European capital, yet at the same time preserves its own stylish and quirky identity.

Books

The **book** reviews below represent a highly selective reading list on Spain in general and on Madrid itself. In the reviews, publishers follow each title: first the UK publisher, then the US. Only one publisher is listed if the UK and US publishers are the same. Where books are published in only one of these countries, UK or US comes after the publisher's name. Out-of-print books are indicated by o/p. If you have difficulty finding any titles, an excellent source for books about Spain – new, used and out of print – is Books on Spain, PO Box 207, Twickenham TW2 5BQ, UK ⓒ020/8898 7789.

The best introductions

Ian Gibson, *Fire in the Blood: The New Spain* (Faber/BBC, UK). This is a splendid commentary on the Spanish people which accompanied the author's television series on Spain in 1992. Gibson is a passionate writer who wears his heart on his sleeve, but he makes a valiant attempt to describe and explain the complexity and contradictions of modern Spain and Spanish society.

John Hooper, *The New Spaniards* (Penguin). Revised, expanded and updated edition of Hooper's guide to contemporary Spain which first appeared as *The Spaniards*. It provides excellent and comprehensive coverage of all aspects of life in modern

301

Spain, including the monarchy, the Church, the role of women, education, corruption, the regions and bullfighting. A perfect book for anyone wanting to scratch deeper.

History

J.H. Elliott, *Imperial Spain 1469–1716* (Penguin). The standard work on the Spanish golden age. It is elegantly written, highly readable and characterized by thorough research throughout.

Ronald Fraser, *Blood of Spain* (Pantheon, US). Subtitled "The Experience of Civil War, 1936–39", this is an impressive piece of research, constructed entirely of vivid oral accounts of these turbulent years.

Geoffrey Parker, *Philip II* (Hutchinson, UK o/p). Entertaining, accurate and revealing portrait of the most powerful man of his age, based upon Philip's personal papers and memoranda. Philip is brought to life in this compelling biography.

Paul Preston, *Franco* (HarperCollins). On a par with Thomas's epic account of the Civil War, this monumental biography of *El Caudillo* is a truly enthralling read, tracing the genesis of Franco's dictatorship right through to his final few hours. There are perceptive insights into Franco's background and upbringing and the evolution of his icy character.

Francisco Romero Salvadó, *Twentieth-Century Spain* (Macmillan/St. Martin's Press). A good introduction to modern Spain, tracing its political, social and economic development throughout the twentieth century.

Hugh Thomas, *Madrid, A Traveller's Companion* (Constable, UK); *The Spanish Civil War* (Penguin). The first is a varied anthology of travel writings on Madrid with a fine introduction to the city's history, while the latter gives a masterful account of the causes and course of the tragic history of the Spanish Civil War. An immense work of scholarship, this is the definitive account of the war. It's initially difficult to wade through the complexities of the prewar era, but this is ultimately an extremely rewarding book.

Recent Travels

David Gilmour, *Cities of Spain* (Pimlico/Ivan R. Dee). Contains a
well-written and evocative chapter on Madrid.

Michael Jacobs, *Madrid Observed* (Pallas Athene, UK).
Opinionated, witty and well observed, containing thoroughly
researched thematic walks around Madrid.

Art and Architecture

Jonathan Brown, *Velázquez: Painter and Courtier* (Yale, US). A
detailed study of the great painter.

J.H. Elliott and Jonathan Brown, *A Palace for a King: The Buen
Retiro and the Court of Philip IV* (Yale, US). Closely researched
account of the grandeur of the Habsburg Court.

Pierre Gassier, *Goya, A Witness of His Times* (Alpine, UK). A
comprehensive biography of the painter and the period in
which he lived.

Fiction

Miguel de Cervantes, *Don Quixote* (Penguin/Signet). No
apologies for including a classic sixteenth-century novel in a
reading list for contemporary Spain. The highly amusing
account of the adventures of the eccentric knight is a must if
you are to understand the Spanish character and outlook on
life, at least from the perspective of Castile La Mancha.

Benito Pérez Galdós, *Fortunata y Jacinta* (Penguin). Late
nineteenth-century classic piece of detailed social observation
set against the backdrop of the political turmoil of 1860s
Madrid.

Camilo José Cela, *The Family of Pascual Duarte* (Little Brown).
The Nobel Prize-winner's portrayal of a family in the aftermath
of the Spanish Civil War. Another masterpiece, *The Hive*,
focuses on the comings and goings of a group of characters in
a Madrid café in the postwar years.

Glossary of Spanish terms

Alcázar Moorish fortified palace.

Ayuntamiento Town hall or council.

Azulejo Glazed ceramic tilework.

Barrio Suburb or quarter.

Bodega Cellar, wine bar or warehouse.

Calle Street.

Capilla Mayor Chapel containing the high altar.

Capilla Real Royal chapel.

Castizo Authentic *Madrileño*.

Chotis Madrid's traditional dance.

Convento Monastery or convent.

Coro Central part of church built for the choir.

Correos Post office.

Corrida de toros Bullfight.

Cortes Parliament.

Custodia Monstrance.

Ermita Hermitage.

Iglesia Church.

Madrileño Inhabitant of Madrid, or used to describe something pertaining to the city.

Mercado Market.

Mirador Viewing point.

Monasterio Monastery or convent.

La Movida a term used to describe the "happening Madrid" of the 1980s, but also signifying areas where there is plenty of nightlife.

Mudéjar Muslim Spaniard subject to medieval Christian rule, but retaining Islamic worship. Most commonly a term applied to architecture which includes buildings built by Moorish craftsmen for the Christian rulers, and later designs influenced by the Moors.

Palacio Palace.

Parador State-run luxury hotel.

Paseo Promenade; also the evening stroll.

Patio Inner courtyard.

Plateresque Elaborately decorative Renaissance style. Named for its resemblance to silversmiths' work.

Plaza Square.

Plaza de toros Bullring.

Posada Old name for an inn.

Puerta Gateway.

Sacristía Sacristy or sanctuary of a church.

Terraza Outdoor bar or café annexe, often summer only.

Tertulia Semi-formalized discussion group.

Turismo Tourist office.

Verbena Traditional street fair.

Zarzuela Madrid's own form of light opera.

GLOSSARY OF SPANISH TERMS

INDEX

around the world

Alaska ★ Algarve ★ Amsterdam ★ Andalucía ★ Antigua & Barbuda ★
Argentina ★ Auckland Restaurants ★ Australia ★ Austria ★ Bahamas ★
Bali & Lombok ★ Bangkok ★ Barbados ★ Barcelona ★ Beijing ★ Belgium &
Luxembourg ★ Belize ★ Berlin ★ Big Island of Hawaii ★ Bolivia ★ Boston
★ Brazil ★ Britain ★ Brittany & Normandy ★ Bruges & Ghent ★ Brussels ★
Budapest ★ Bulgaria ★ California ★ Cambodia ★ Canada ★ Cape Town ★
The Caribbean ★ Central America ★ Chile ★ China ★ Copenhagen ★
Corsica ★ Costa Brava ★ Costa Rica ★ Crete ★ Croatia ★ Cuba ★ Cyprus ★
Czech & Slovak Republics ★ Devon & Cornwall ★ Dodecanese & East
Aegean ★ Dominican Republic ★ The Dordogne & the Lot ★ Dublin ★
Ecuador ★ Edinburgh ★ Egypt ★ England ★ Europe ★ First-time Asia ★
First-time Europe ★ Florence ★ Florida ★ France ★ French Hotels &
Restaurants ★ Gay & Lesbian Australia ★ Germany ★ Goa ★ Greece ★
Greek Islands ★ Guatemala ★ Hawaii ★ Holland ★ Hong Kong & Macau ★
Honolulu ★ Hungary ★ Ibiza & Formentera ★ Iceland ★ India ★ Indonesia
★ Ionian Islands ★ Ireland ★ Israel & the Palestinian Territories ★ Italy ★
Jamaica ★ Japan ★ Jerusalem ★ Jordan ★ Kenya ★ The Lake District ★
Languedoc & Roussillon ★ Laos ★ Las Vegas ★ Lisbon ★ London ★

in twenty years

London Mini Guide ★ London Restaurants ★ Los Angeles ★ Madeira ★ Madrid ★ Malaysia, Singapore & Brunei ★ Mallorca ★ Malta & Gozo ★ Maui ★ Maya World ★ Melbourne ★ Menorca ★ Mexico ★ Miami & the Florida Keys ★ Montréal ★ Morocco ★ Moscow ★ Nepal ★ New England ★ New Orleans ★ New York City ★ New York Mini Guide ★ New York Restaurants ★ New Zealand ★ Norway ★ Pacific Northwest ★ Paris ★ Paris Mini Guide ★ Peru ★ Poland ★ Portugal ★ Prague ★ Provence & the Côte d'Azur ★ Pyrenees ★ The Rocky Mountains ★ Romania ★ Rome ★ San Francisco ★ San Francisco Restaurants ★ Sardinia ★ Scandinavia ★ Scotland ★ Scottish Highlands & Islands ★ Seattle ★ Sicily ★ Singapore ★ South Africa, Lesotho & Swaziland ★ South India ★ Southeast Asia ★ Southwest USA ★ Spain ★ St Lucia ★ St Petersburg ★ Sweden ★ Switzerland ★ Sydney ★ Syria ★ Tanzania ★ Tenerife and La Gomera ★ Thailand ★ Thailand's Beaches & Islands ★ Tokyo ★ Toronto ★ Travel Health ★ Trinidad & Tobago ★ Tunisia ★ Turkey ★ Tuscany & Umbria ★ USA ★ Vancouver ★ Venice & the Veneto ★ Vienna ★ Vietnam ★ Wales ★ Washington DC ★ West Africa ★ Women Travel ★ Yosemite ★ Zanzibar ★ Zimbabwe

also look out for our maps, phrasebooks, music guides and reference books

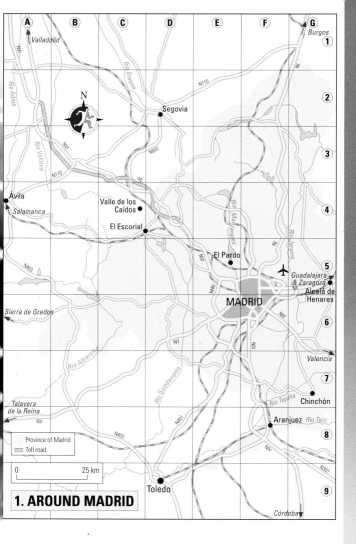

1. AROUND MADRID

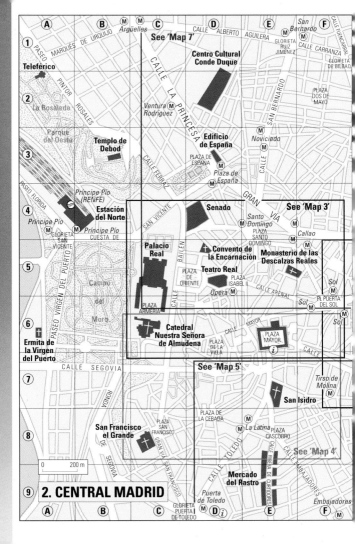

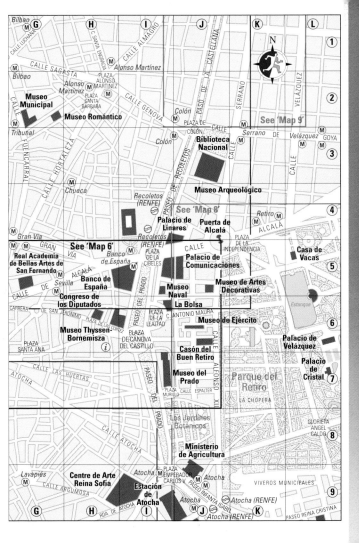

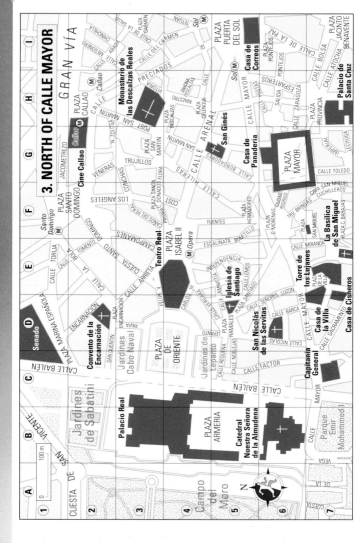

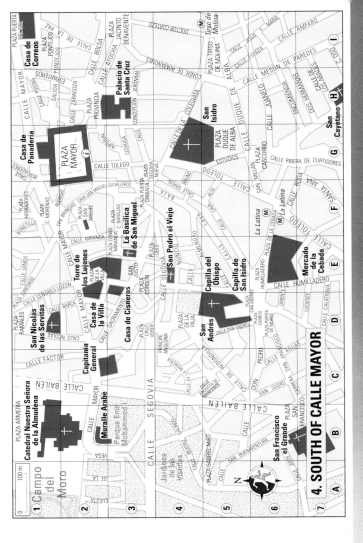

4. SOUTH OF CALLE MAYOR

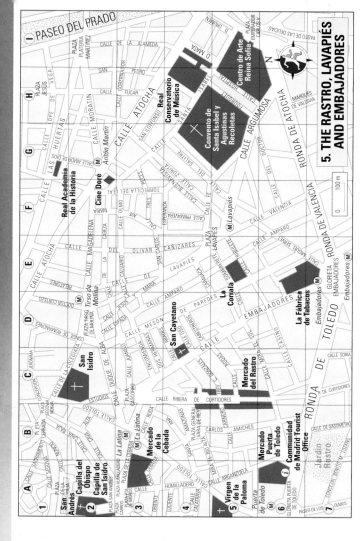

5. THE RASTRO, LAVAPIÉS AND EMBAJADORES

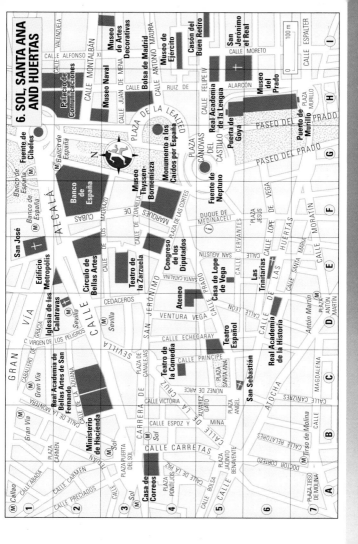

6. SOL, SANTA ANA AND HUERTAS

Museo de Artes Decorativas

Museo Naval

Palacio de Comunicaciones

Bolsa de Madrid

Museo del Ejército

Casón del Buen Retiro

San Jerónimo el Real

CALLE MORETO

100 m

CALLE ESPALTER

VALENZUELA

CALLE ALFONSO XI

CALLE MONTALBÁN

CALLE JUAN DE MENA

CALLE ANTONIO MAURA

RUIZ DE

ALARCÓN

CALLE FELIPE IV

Museo del Prado

PLAZA MURILLO

Real Academia de la Lengua

Puerta de Goya

PASEO DEL PRADO

Puerto de Murillo

PASEO DEL PRADO

PLAZA DE LA LEALTED

Fuente de Cibeles

Banco de España

Museo Thyssen-Bornemisza

Monumento a los Caídos por España

PLAZA CÁNOVAS DEL CASTILLO

Fuente de Neptuno

DUQUE DE MEDINACELI

PLAZA JESÚS

CALLE LOPE DE VEGA

Banco de España

ALCALÁ

CUBAS

CALLE MADRAZO

MARQUÉS DE

CALLE DE ZORRILLA

PLAZA DE LAS CORTES

CALLE LOS

San José

Edificio Metrópolis

Círculo de Bellas Artes

Teatro de la Zarzuela

Congreso de los Diputados

Ateneo

Casa de Lope de Vega

Las Trinitarias

CALLE HUERTAS

CALLE MORATÍN

CALLE SANTA MARÍA

CALLE CERVANTES

CALLE SAN AGUSTÍN

Antón Martín

VEGA

GRAN VIA

Iglesia de las Calatravas

C. VIRGEN DE LOS PELIGROS

Real Academia de Bellas Artes de San Fernando

CALLE DE LA ABADA

CEDACEROS

CALLE

SEVILLA

SAN JERÓNIMO

VENTURA VEGA

Teatro de la Comedia

CALLE PRÍNCIPE

Teatro Español

CALLE LEÓN

CALLE DE LAS

Real Academia de la Historia

CALLE PRADO

SANTA CATALINA

CABALLERO DE GRACIA

Gran Via

CALLE DE LA MONTERA

Ministerio de Hacienda

CALLE DE LA ADUANA

CARRERA DE SAN JERÓNIMO

PLAZA DE CANALEJAS

NÚÑEZ DE ARCE

CALLE VICTORIA

CALLE ESPOZ Y MINA

CALLE

CRUZ

PLAZA SANTA ANA

PLAZA DEL ÁNGEL

ÁLVAREZ GATO

San Sebastián

ATOCHA

MAGDALENA

CALLE CAÑIZARES

Callao

PLAZA CARMEN

CALLE CARMEN

CALLE PRECIADOS

Sol

Sol

PLAZA PUERTA DEL SOL

Casa de Correos

CALLE PONTEJOS

CALLE CARRETAS

CALLE DE LA CRUZ

PLAZA JACINTO BENAVENTE

CALLE BOLSA

DOCTOR CORTEZO

PLAZA TIRSO DE MOLINA

Tirso de Molina

CALLE RELATORES

CALLE DE MOLINA

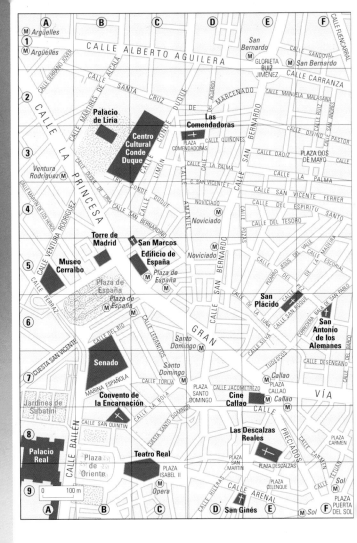

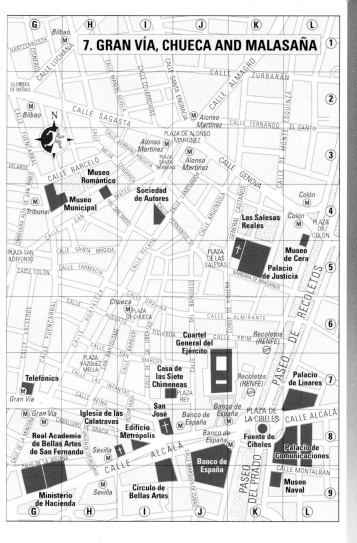

7. GRAN VÍA, CHUECA AND MALASAÑA

Museo Romántico
Museo Municipal
Sociedad de Autores
Las Salesas Reales
Museo de Cera
Palacio de Justicia
Chueca
Cuartel General del Ejército
Recoletos (RENFE)
Recoletos (RENFE)
Palacio de Linares
Telefónica
Casa de las Siete Chimeneas
Palacio de Comunicaciones
Iglesia de las Calatravas
San José
Banco de España
Fuente de Cibeles
Real Academia de Bellas Artes de San Fernando
Edificio Metrópolis
Banco de España
Museo Naval
Ministerio de Hacienda
Círculo de Bellas Artes
Banco de España

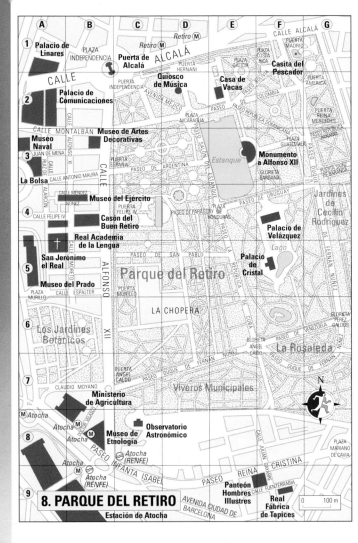

A   **B**   **C**   **D**   **E**   **F**   **G**

CALLE ALCALÁ

1 Palacio de Linares
PLAZA INDEPENDENCIA
Retiro Ⓜ   Retiro Ⓜ
Puerta de Alcalá
ALCALÁ
PUERTA HERNANI
PUERTA MADRID
PLAZA COSTA RICA
PUERTA MADRID
Casita del Pescador

CALLE
PUERTA INDEPENDENCIA
Quiosco de Música
PLAZA GALICIA
PUERTA AMÉRICA

2 Palacio de Comunicaciones
AVENIDA MÉJICO
Casa de Vacas
PASEO REPÚBLICA DE COLOMBIA
PUERTA REINA MERCEDES

CALLE MONTALBÁN
Museo de Artes Decorativas
PLAZA NICARAGUA
PASEO REPÚBLICA DOMINICANA

3 Museo Naval
CALLE JUAN DE MENA
CALLE RUIZ DE ALARCÓN
PUERTA ESPAÑA
PASEO DE ARGENTINA
Estanque
PLAZA GUATEMALA
Monumento a Alfonso XII
PUERTA SAINZ DE BARANDA

La Bolsa
CALLE ANTONIO MAURA
GLORIETA SARDANA

CALLE MÉNDEZ NÚÑEZ
Museo del Ejército
PUERTA FELIPE IV
PASEO DE PARAGUAY
PLAZA URUGUAY
Jardines de Cecilio Rodríguez

4 CALLE FELIPE IV
Casón del Buen Retiro
PASEO DE PARAGUAY DE HONDURAS
Palacio de Velázquez
CALLE FERNAN NÚÑEZ

Real Academia de la Lengua
PASEO DE SAN PABLO

5 San Jerónimo el Real
CALLE MORETO
CALLE ALFONSO
Parque del Retiro
PUERTA MURILLO
Palacio de Cristal
Lago

Museo del Prado
PLAZA MURILLO
CALLE ESPALTER
PASEO DE CUBA

6 Los Jardines Botánicos
XII
LA CHOPERA
GLORIETA PÉREZ GALDÓS
La Rosaleda
PASEO DE VENEZUELA
PASEO DE FERNAN

7 CLAUDIO MOYANO
PUERTA ÁNGEL CAÍDO
PASEO DUQUE DE FERNAN NÚÑEZ
Viveros Municipales
GLORIETA ÁNGEL CAÍDO
N

Ministerio de Agricultura

8 Ⓜ Atocha
Ⓜ Atocha
Atocha
Observatorio Astronómico
Museo de Etnología
Ⓜ Atocha (RENFE)
CALLE JULIÁN GAYARRE
PLAZA MARIANO DE CAVIA

9 Atocha
Ⓜ Atocha (RENFE)
PASEO INFANTA ISABEL
PASEO REINA CRISTINA
CALLE FUENTERRABÍA
Panteón Hombres Illustres
Real Fábrica de Tapices

8. PARQUE DEL RETIRO
AVENIDA CIUDAD DE BARCELONA
Estación de Atocha
0   100 m

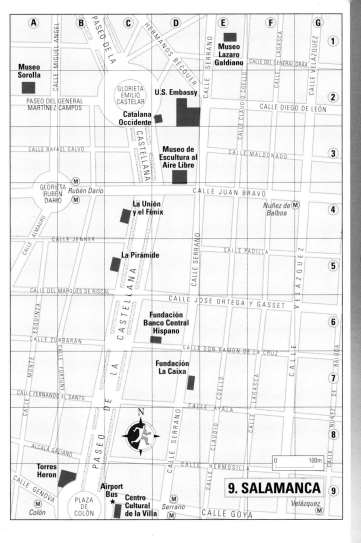

9. SALAMANCA

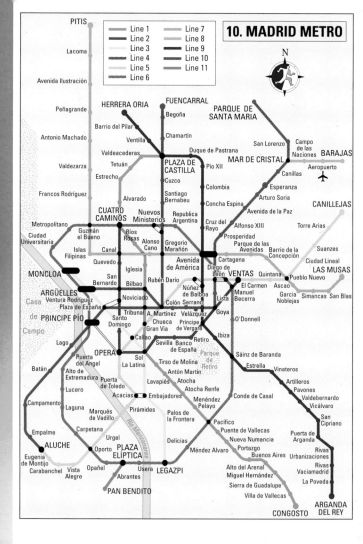